PILATE'S PRISONER

The coin is a Roman denarius bearing the image of the
Emperor Julius Caesar Tiberius.

PILATE'S PRISONER

A PASSION PLAY

———◆———

Edward Hays

This is a work of historical fiction, based on actual persons and events. The author has taken creative liberty with many details to enhance the reader's experience.

Published in the United States by BookLocker.com, Inc., Port Charlotte, Florida.

Map illustrations by Edward Hays

Cover design by Thomas Turkle

Cover art: *Quod Est Veritas? Christ and Pilate* by Nikolai Ge (1831-1894)

Printed in the United States of America on acid-free paper.

BookLocker.com, Inc.
2012

First Edition

www.edwardhays.com

INTRODUCTION

The passion and death of Jesus of Nazareth were first recorded in the four gospels written seventy to eighty years after his crucifixion. Mark wrote the first account based on oral stories, and his gospel was the basis for the other three.

This novel is based on these gospel passion accounts, contemporary scriptural research, and the recent discoveries of Palestinian archeology. In the second half of the first century and early in the second century, the four gospel writers wrote and creatively tailored their passion stories to address the needs of Christians in different places. Following that apostolic practice, this story of the passion of Jesus has been written for 21st-century Christians. It strives to give them insights into how they can take up their crosses and, as Jesus requested, follow him.

The secondary purpose of this novel is to paint a picture of the person of Pontius Pilate, the Roman procurator-governor at the trial of Jesus of Nazareth, and the historical and cultural setting of that time. Pilate is a neglected historical personage, even though he had the distinctive honor being named in the Christian Apostles' Creed.

This novel also is intended to be invite contemplation. Mystics, saints, and ordinary Christians throughout the ages have used the passion and death of Jesus of Galilee to meditate on their own sufferings. It is my hope that those who read this new passion play will likewise gain spiritual insights into their own sufferings, cross, and death.

IMPORTANT HISTORICAL NOTE

Pontius Pilate became procurator-governor of Judea in 26 C.E. (Christian or Common Era). In the year 35 C.E., Pilate encountered Jesus, who at the time was close to 37 years of age, not 33 years, which has long been accepted as the age at which he was crucified. This difference reflects the correction of an error made by a sixth-century-C.E. monk, who determined Jesus' birth to be four years later than it actually was. Today scholars place the birth of Jesus at around 4 B.C.E., the year King Herod the Great died, because two of the gospels speak of King Herod being alive at the time of the birth of Jesus.

Pontius Pilate's residence was in Caesarea at the former palace of King Herod on the coast of the Mediterranean Sea. As procurator he came to Jerusalem with additional troops to ensure public order during the great festivals such as Passover when the city was crowded with pilgrims. While in Jerusalem during these temporary visits, Pilate resided at King Herod's great palace located along the western wall of the city.

This novel begins in spring on the eve of the Passover in the year 35 C.E. when Joseph Caiaphas was high priest and Julius Caesar Tiberius was emperor of the Roman Empire.

This stone from the Israel Antiquities Museum in Jerusalem was discovered in Caesarea Maritima in 1962.

Carved into it is a Latin inscription:

"...this Tiberium, Pontius Pilate, prefect of Judea, did erect."

It is archeological proof of the existence of Pilate as prefect-procurator of Judea.

A PASSION PLAY
IN FIVE ACTS

◆━━━━━━━━━━━━━━━━━━━━◆

CAST OF CHARACTERS

Pontius Pilate~ *procurator-governor*

Jesus of Galilee~ *the prisoner*

Centurion Petronius~ *Pilate's military aide*

Claudia Procula ~ *wife of Pilate*

Lucius ~ *Pilate's slave, secretary, and mentor*

Quintus ~ *Pilate's personal slave*

Marcus ~ *Pilate's personal slave and bodyguard*

Aristocles ~ *Pilate's slave and assistant scribe*

Joseph Caiaphas ~ *high priest*

Abarim Jacob ~ *Pilate's spy in Caiaphas' household*

Zechariah ~ *Caiaphas' priest messenger*

Lucius Vitellius ~ *Roman Legate of Syria*

ACT I

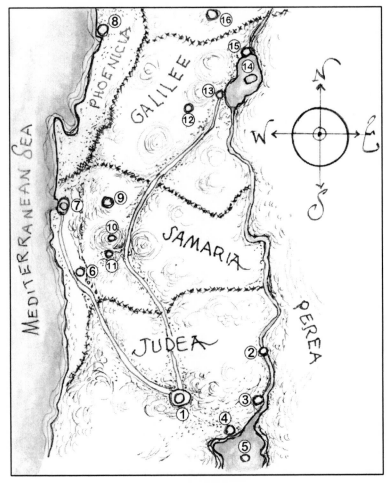

Map of Palestine

1. Jerusalem
2. Jordan River
3. Jericho
4. Qumran
5. Dead Sea
6. Lydda
7. Caesarea Maritima
8. Tyre

9. City of Samaria
10. Mount Gerizim
11. Tirathana
12. Nazareth
13. Tiberius
14. Sea of Galilee
15. Capernaum
16. Syria

SCENE I

THE FORMER PALACE OF
KING HEROD AGRIPPA

Jerusalem, Spring, 35 C.E.

"Ow — damn it!" swore Pilate. His hand flew to his right cheek, where he had just been nicked while being shaved by his body slave, Quintus. "The mirror...the mirror!" he barked, reaching out to Quintus, who quickly extended it to him.

"Excellency, forgive me," pleaded Quintus, drawing back at the sight of Pilate's frown and furled forehead, "I'm a clumsy ass!"

Looking into the metal mirror, Pilate used his index finger to touch the small bleeding cut on his right cheek. As he gazed in the mirror, his frown faded and was replaced with a thin smile. He was thinking to himself that he had a rather handsome Roman face and, although he was not a Roman aristocrat, he looked like one with his strong features and black hair trimmed short in the Imperial style. He was a head taller than the average Roman and, at age thirty-six, still had the broad chest and muscular body of a Roman Army officer.

"Your Excellency, pardon my clumsy mistake...I, uh...," Quintus' voice trailed off into a mumble as he reached for a swab of tallow and cobwebs to dab the bleeding cut. Quintus had been a slave in Pilate's family since birth, his parents being household slaves of the family. Now in his early forties, Quintus was bald headed, with a muscular body discernible beneath the white tunic reaching just above his knees.

With a nod of his head, Pilate wordlessly acknowledged Quintus' apology as he thought, *How could I be angry with Quintus? He's always been a trusted and dependable slave, and he's been in my household for years.* As he resumed looking at his image in the mirror, Pilate turned his shoulders slowly from the left to the right and said to himself, *I've still got a strong body, even though I've been living in comfort as a provincial governor. I must say I'm proud that I've maintained my military discipline and exercise regularly to preserve a soldier's physique.*

Pilate said aloud, "Quintus, it's so disgusting to see former army officers who have grown fat and soft, victims to the luxurious life. I've always tried to maintain the motto instilled in me as a young army officer — *Vir fortis ac stennus* — "A sturdy man in an iron-hard body.""

"Excellency, you've certainly done that! And your strong bearing serves you well as Governor of Judea and the representative of Imperial Rome." From the small, portable shaving table with its array of scissors, razors, and tweezers, Quintus picked up a white clay pot of salve and dipped his finger into it. As he gently dabbed some ointment on Pilate's cut, he was aware that if he were a slave of a Roman aristocrat he would have been severely beaten for his carelessness, and then he would have been expected to apply a small patch over the cut to conceal it. Pilate, however, being a military man, would deem that to be effeminate.

Pilate was distracted as his eye caught sight of the sun, which slowly crept up into the crimson sky over the purple hump of the Mount of Olives. He wondered if old King Herod watched the sunrise from this very window before he died and Rome requisitioned this royal palace to be the governor's residence.

Seated on a stool to Pilate's right was Lucius, Pilate's long-time slave and secretary, who had several scrolls in his lap. Prior to the shaving mishap, he had been summarizing for Pilate the various tasks awaiting him that day. Now Lucius sat patiently until he had Pilate's attention again. As Quintus prepared to continue shaving Pilate, elongated yellow bands of the rising sun flowed through the room's tall east windows, highlighting walls that were frozen rivers of colored marble. King Herod had adorned this palace and his palace in Caesarea with Italian marble imported by the shiploads to Judea. As Pilate watched the walls sparkle in the sunlight, he was thinking that, like any child, he had dreamt of impossible things, but never in his wildest fantasies had he ever pictured himself living in the magnificent palace of an Oriental king. Then, realizing he was daydreaming, he said in a crisp military voice, "Lucius, continue."

"Excellency, you need to respond to your centurion commander in Samaria who wrote to request your advice on how to deal with the disturbances around the Samaritan temple at Mt. Gerizim, and...."

"That's the temple built by Alexander the Great when he was here in Palestine?"

"Yes, Sir. Your centurion reported his grave concerns about a rabble-rousing Samaritan prophet whose followers are involved in hostile anti-Roman demonstrations at the temple of the Emperor Augustus built by King Herod."

"Governor Gratus, my predecessor, warned me about the Samaritans. He said the Judean Jews have intense hatred for the Samaritan Jews, who they see as violators of the true Jewish religion."

"Sir, another important issue for today is the annual tax report to Rome. Then, there is...."

"Enough, Lucius!" Pilate raised his hand up under his nose, indicating he was about to drown. "Those and my daily report to the Emperor are more than enough to occupy me today. Let's begin by reviewing the Emperor's daily report."

"Yes, Excellency," Lucius replied, picking up an unrolled scroll. Lucius was a Greek-born slave who had been given a Roman name when he became a slave of the household of Pilate's father, Marcus Pontius. His once-dark hair was now streaked gray and white, and with his fine facial features and slightly stooping shoulders he looked like an old scholar, which in fact he was. Educated in the Roman and Greek classics, he spoke fluent Latin, and having been Pilate's private childhood tutor, he possessed insights into Pilate's character and alternating moods.

"As your Imperial representative and Governor," Lucius began reading in his precise academic voice, "I customarily come to Jerusalem, the Temple City of the Jews, for their major religious pilgrimage feasts. I write to your Imperial Excellency on the eve of Passover, a most important Jewish religious festival. I have traveled from my official residence in Caesarea here to Jerusalem...."

"Stop, Lucius." Pilate interrupted him. "In that last sentence, right after 'traveled to Jerusalem,' insert the following: 'which is a journey of some sixty miles.' Emperor Tiberius enjoys those kinds of minor details in his reports."

After Lucius finished penning the inserted detail in the report, he continued, "...with a full detachment of our most capable troops to ensure the security of the city and to maintain crowd control...."

As Lucius continued reading the daily report, Quintus dipped his razor in the water bowl to rinse off the blood from Pilate's cut and began sharpening the razor by scraping it across a leather strap. Meanwhile, Pilate glanced down at the basin and saw in the water a small red droplet of his blood. As he watched, it began expanding outward in a crimson corkscrewing spiral, causing him to mutter under his breath, "*Absit omen,* 'an omen of the gods.'"

Although Pilate was a practical, unsentimental military man, he took omens seriously, seeing them as the way that the gods communicated with mortals. As he watched the growing bloody spiral expand, he wondered if the ominous sight of his own blood in his shaving bowl was an ill-fated omen. Was it a premonition of an approaching misfortune for him, or perhaps for a family member? As he stared intently at the expanding spiral of blood, he grew uneasy about what sort of misfortune might be awaiting him on this early spring Friday.

Previously, as a commander in the midst of battle, he had foreboding premonitions, intuitively feeling that his enemy was nearby and about to attack, but not knowing when or from where. Now once again he felt his old military sixth sense camped out in his heart.

The "scrape, scrape, scrape" of Quintus sharpening his razor on the leather strap caused Pilate to go deaf to the report Lucius was reading. This morning, for some reason, the rhythmic scraping of the razor reminded him of the time he heard that same sound at his very first ceremonial shave. Instantly, on the wings of memory he was transported from Jerusalem back to his childhood home in Rome on that morning of his seventeenth birthday. He saw himself vividly as a youth standing at his family's shrine encircled by his parents, brothers, sisters, and the family's household slaves. Among the slaves was his Greek tutor, the handsome, dark-haired Lucius. He remembered how proud he felt as the slave ceremonially shaved off his teenage growth of beard in the ritual of manhood. Then, bowing, the slave handed his youthful facial hair to his mother, who lovingly laid it in a small ornate ivory box that she then placed on the family altar.

As Quintus continued sharpening his razor, the rising sun was awakening ancient sleeping Jerusalem like some giant Leviathan being aroused from its slumber. A short distance north of Herod's palace was the western gateway of Jerusalem leading onto a broad street that ran eastward through the city's marketplace and onward to the great Temple of Herod. The morning air was full of loud noises coming from the nearby western gateway: the neighing of heavy-burdened donkeys, the bleating of sheep being herded to market, and the voices of boisterous, psalm-singing pilgrims entering the city for the Passover Festival. Pilate didn't hear the racket — since in his reverie he wasn't in Jerusalem but in Rome — and his face betrayed his absence.

"Excellency, is that last fact correct?" asked Lucius, inventing an excuse to call Pilate back to the present moment.

"Correct?" he snapped, scowling at Lucius. "If something isn't correct, then correct it. Now continue!"

Pilate reflected he shouldn't allow himself to become distracted while listening to the reading of these daily reports. Even if they were dull and repetitive, they were important for his political future. He also regretted snapping at Lucius, who had been indispensable to him all these years, and he reminded himself to watch his temper.

As Lucius artfully pretended to pen a correction in the report, Pilate, contrary to his best intentions, was kidnapped once again by the memory of the events of his seventeenth birthday. Submerged in a sea of realistic memories, he could actually feel himself lifting the cord of his *bulla* from around his neck. He had worn that small golden pouch with its lucky charm day and night since his parents had placed it around his neck as an infant when they presented him to the gods.

Discreetly, Lucius cleared his throat, causing Pilate to return to Jerusalem instantaneously. "I'm sorry, Lucius, once again it seems I was off in another place."

"Rome?" asked Lucius, softly.

"Yes, the Rome of my youth. For some reason, I'm having vivid memories of my seventeenth birthday this morning."

Smiling as he laid the report scroll in his lap, Lucius said, "A visit by a memory is a gift from the gods, or, as the Greeks call them, 'the immortal ones.' As Plato said, 'There exists in the mind...a wax tablet that is a gift of memory, the mother of the muses.' And Pilate, I too have a permanent imprint of that wonderful day in the wax of my memory. As you recall, I, along with the other household slaves, had the honor of attending your manhood ceremony. That was...what was it...nineteen years ago, yet even today I recall the surge of pride I felt when you placed your childhood bulla on the family altar. You were then a man who had no need of a child's good luck charm."

"It was such a joyous day, Lucius!"

Lucius silently nodded his head, even though it had actually been a time of mourning for him, for this act signified the death of their previous relationship. Because Pilate was now a man, he no longer needed a childhood charm, or even his tutor. Lucius grieved, because he had grown so fond of his pupil.

"Plato was right, Lucius. That day of days is deeply imprinted in my memory. Even this morning I can almost taste the intoxicating happiness I felt as my family triumphantly escorted me through the crowded streets of Rome to the Forum, where we prayed at the Temple of Jupiter."

"Although we household slaves weren't allowed to accompany the family to the Temple, I'll never forget what happened after you returned! Your father, Marcus Pontius, his eyes glistening with pride, robed you for the first time in the white toga of an adult man, and...."

"I know what you're going to say, as it was such an auspicious day when the gods smiled down on me. After my father vested me, he ordered you to come and stand in front of me, saying, 'Since your childhood, Lucius has been your tutor. Today, Pontius, as a gift, I present to you Lucius, who will now be your personal slave!'"

"Your Excellency, that truly was a gift, for it meant I could continue to be with you. Then you gifted me again when you made me your secretary! You and I have had such remarkable adventures together these past nineteen years, including the time the Emperor made you Governor of Judea."

"We have indeed, Lucius."

"Sir, with your permission, may I return to what happened after your father made me your personal slave?"

"You may."

"Word for word, Sir, I can repeat your very first order to me: 'I command you, Lucius, never again to address me as Pontius! From this day onward you will address me only as Pilate!' And your second order was that I instruct all the family household slaves to do likewise."

"Ah yes, Lucius, I had so yearned to be known not as Pontius, but as *Pilatus*, since it is such a strong, masculine name. True, it was also our family surname, meaning 'skilled with a javelin,' having been given long ago to my warrior ancestors. The throwing of a javelin requires great strength, and after that, expertise with a sword is the second skill required of a Roman soldier. I was only seventeen, young and inexperienced, but when people addressed me as *Pilatus* it declared that I was a man strong enough to use that warrior's weapon."

"It was fitting to address you as Pilate, for that was the kind of man you would become. Personally, I prefer 'Your Excellency,' as it fills me with pride to address you with such a distinguished title."

"Thank you, Lucius. As for you, Quintus, you have the patience of a marble statue that waits without grumbling while I reminisce with Lucius about my youth. What you are about to do for me, Quintus, is one of life's ironies. Every young boy eagerly yearns for the day when he must shave, yet when it actually arrives he finds it to be a daily, dreary chore that is a waste of time. Unless," gesturing toward Lucius, "he does what I am doing now and imitates the great Julius Caesar, who, while being shaved and having his hair trimmed, listened to reports being read. And now, Quintus, so you can safely shave me, I promise to stop talking. Lucius, continue with the report."

Lucius resumed reading the report, but Pilate listened with only one ear as he thought about Emperor Tiberius, to whom the report would be sent. He knew the emperor was notorious for being extraordinarily suspicious of omens. If this morning he saw as Pilate did an omen written in his own blood, he was sure old Tiberius would have judged it as being ominously dangerous. Then his thoughts changed to a silent prayer: *O Powerful Mars, god of war and patron of soldiers, protect me this day from all misfortune. Assist me so the report I send to Rome today will not contain anything implying that I acted in a politically incompetent manner. O Mars, prevent me from imprudent, reckless acts that could displease or anger the Emperor Tiberius.*

As Quintus resumed shaving him, Pilate thought about just having prayed to Mars. Even if he questioned the existence of the gods, he needed their help. More than ever before in his life, since coming to Judea, he had felt a craving for divine protection. He had done his best to govern these bearded, unwashed Jews, yet his destiny had been plagued again and again by unforeseen misfortunes. He felt defenseless here before the whims of the three fickle fates, especially the fate *Lachesis*, in this barren, god-infested Judean desert outpost. She of the three held the knife with which she could arbitrarily sever the thread of one's destiny. Was it her knife that stirred the blood in his shaving bowl into a frightening, swirling bloody omen? Oh, if only he had his childhood bulla once again!

Pilate blushed, reminding himself that he was no child in need of an infantile good luck charm. He was a man! Moreover, he was a former cavalry officer upon whom the goddess Fortuna had smiled, emptying her cornucopia horn of good luck and fortune. Nine years ago, when he was only two years older than the age required for Roman procurators, goddess Lady Luck gifted him when he was made the procurator of Judea. However, though Fortuna played her part, that promotion was more than luck. Rome must have thought he possessed the qualifications of a good administrator to send him here to Judea. True, it was a second-class Roman province, but it was also a strategic land bridge between Egypt and Syria.

SCENE II

THE SAME

Early That Morning

As the morning sun rose higher over Jerusalem, so did the noise of the Jewish pilgrims pouring through the western gate. Their zealous chanting enkindled smoldering embers in Pilate, who snorted, "Damn Jews! Quintus, they're worse than an infestation of desert fleas. My predecessor, Governor Gratus, warned me they wouldn't be easy to govern. I knew I'd face challenges in ruling an occupied people, but I didn't anticipate just how scheming and rebellious they'd be."

"Yes, Excellency," replied Quintus, who was trimming Pilate's hair, "when I'm walking among them here in Jerusalem I can actually feel their loathing and hatred for me because I'm a Roman."

"It's been ninety years, Quintus, since General Pompey conquered Judea, yet to this day these Jews remain defiant of the authority of Imperial Rome. Their intense resentment of our military occupation of their so-called 'holy' land makes Judea like a simmering pot about to boil over. They relentlessly scheme to find ways to avoid paying our taxes and to obstruct my every effort at civic progress with some obscure religious law that forbids it." Raising his eyes to the heavens, he cursed, "Oh gods of disaster, rain down a plague on the Jews!"

"Excellency, when we've finished the report," said Lucius, in an attempt to rescue Pilate from the quicksand of his Jewish prejudices, "would you like to dictate your reply to the legate Vitellius?"

Pilate ignored Lucius' question and continued his diatribe. "Quintus, you said you could feel their loathing, which is very true; the abhorrence these Jews have toward us is tangible. They've shown it by not allowing me to display the image of the Imperial Emperor Tiberius. Did you know that Judea is the only province in the entire Empire where it isn't displayed? And their priests justify this affront to the Emperor by saying that their god forbids images! No images, no statues, no art—doesn't this make these Jews the most barbaric of

11

all peoples? And when I complain to Rome about this imperial dishonor, I get no reply!"

Lucius, knowing that Pilate needed an audience to vent his resentments, sat with his hands folded in his lap, listening and occasionally nodding sympathetically.

"Lucius, the way Rome coddles these Jews is unfathomable, and being instructed by the Emperor and Senate to capitulate to their ridiculous religious beliefs is infuriating. As any good army commander knows, if you show the slightest weakness to an enemy, he will strike back at you like a serpent when you least expect it. It's my belief that Rome's political pampering of the Jews and their primitive religion only feeds their venom against us."

Pilate's voice grew louder. "By caving in to the ridiculous religious laws of the Jews, Rome sets a bad example for the rest of the Empire! Imagine the consequences if the Emperor gave the same liberties to the barbaric tribes of Gaul, or...."

Frowning, Lucius wordlessly shook his head at Pilate.

"Yes, yes, Lucius; your caution is wise. Tiberius has spies everywhere, and I know how dangerous it is to express any negative judgment of him or the Senate. But sometimes I just have to express my frustration or I'll burst!"

"Excellency, you can trust both Quintus and me to forget whatever we've heard the moment after you've said it. Now, shall I continue with the report?"

"I appreciate your discretion. Yes, Lucius, continue. We have much to do today, and soon it will be time for our morning prayers."

As Lucius resumed reading, Pilate again found himself snagged in the delicate spider web of his thoughts. He knew that even though his problems here in Judea were great, so too were his opportunities. He was glad that before departing from Rome to come to Judea he had gone to the ancient Temple of *Fortuna Pimiigenia*, the first-born daughter of Jupiter, and made an offering to her. With Fortuna's help he would be able to use his assignment as governor of this wretched, second-class province as a springboard to catapult himself to a more important position. He imagined himself as the Roman proconsul, legate of the province of Egypt! He thought, too, of the prestige and unlimited possibilities in Egypt for acquiring personal wealth. He knew he must never do anything to jeopardize his chances of becoming governor of Egypt or securing another advancement.

"Excellency," said Lucius, snapping Pilate's cobweb of ambitious thoughts, "is this report acceptable so far?"

"Yes, but I've heard that if the Emperor is having a bad day he can be picky about errors he finds in the reports, so when we're finished, check it again for any mistakes. Continue, Lucius."

Lucius nodded, and clearing his throat, read on: "...my personal accommodations here in Jerusalem in the former palace of King Herod Agrippa are excellent. The palace, being located on the city's western hill, provides excellent surveillance of the entire city of Jerusalem, all the way over to the massive Temple of Herod on the far eastern side of the city. Although Herod built this Temple many years ago, it continues to be enhanced by decorations, the completion of which is estimated to require another twenty or thirty years. Our Roman Fortress Antonio is located along the Temple's northern wall, and provides a good location to maintain control both of the Temple and the city. Control is essential because of the thousands of pilgrims who descend on the city at the time of the Passover, and because it commemorates their Exodus liberation...."

"Stop, Lucius! Change the word 'liberation' to...um...." A thin smile slowly formed on Pilate's lips. "Rather, say...'their rebellious uprising as mutinous slaves and subsequent escape from Egypt.'" With a grin and a wave of his hand, he proclaimed, "Continue."

After making the addition, Lucius went on. "While the Exodus is a potentially dangerous seditious memory, the Temple priesthood and the aristocratic elites have shrewdly castrated it. Now Passover is only a non-threatening spring religious festival, and memories of the rebellious Exodus are piously slumbering. However, as your Imperial Excellency knows, even sleeping memories of revolts must be cautiously monitored because, like melons, they contain seeds! A cousin to this Jewish memory of the Exodus is our Roman memory of the great slave rebellion of Spartacus. The sleeping seeds of both these slave uprisings must never ever be allowed to sprout!"

"Lucius," said Pilate, "repeat that last sentence where I coupled the Exodus insurrection with the revolt of Spartacus. I hope the Emperor likes that comparison as much as I do."

Having reread the sentence, Lucius continued, "A single spark in the dry historical memories of this Exodus celebration could ignite an incendiary incident in the crowds that would require quenching through the intervention of our soldiers. However, any show of armed force by us during this Passover festival is fraught with dangers. Your Imperial Excellency is aware that once aroused, the massive crowds easily become a monster that is notoriously difficult to control. As I write you, Jerusalem is swollen to over three times its normal size by the great influx of Passover pilgrims. On this Friday, my military advisers have estimated that within the walls of Jerusalem, the total population could be well over a hundred thousand."

A loud knock at the door interrupted Lucius. "Not now—I'm busy!" shouted Pilate, as Quintus rubbed his hair with aromatic oil. He nodded to Lucius to continue.

"From previous religious festivals we also know that hidden among these thousands of pious pilgrims are dangerous rebels and religious insurgents eager to foment rebellion against the Roman Empire. Naturally, I have taken the necessary precautions...."

Even louder knocking at the door ensued. An annoyed Pilate called out, "Enter!" Pilate's personal slave and bodyguard Marcus entered, bowed, and closed the door behind him. Marcus was a bronze-skinned Sicilian in his late twenties with short-cropped black hair. He had the muscular body of a gladiator and the strong legs of an athletic racer.

"Marcus, what is the reason for this interruption?"

"I apologize, Your Excellency," Marcus said, bowing again. "I know you gave orders that you were not to be interrupted, but a man just arrived who says he has an urgent message for you. I told him he'd have to wait, but I thought you would want to know of his arrival."

"Well done, Marcus. What is his name?"

"Abarim, Sir. He's a servant in the house of the High Priest Caiaphas."

Pilate groaned aloud at the idea of having to add something unexpected to his already busy day, but he relented. "Send him in!"

As Marcus departed, Quintus and Lucius withdrew discreetly to the far end of the room. Marcus returned moments later, ushered Abarim Jacob into the room, closed the door, and stood guard with his powerful arms folded across his chest.

Jacob Abarim was a short, wiry man with a narrow, pockmarked face, long hair, and a scraggly beard. He wore a threadbare gray cloak and worn-out sandals. Approaching Pilate with a series of profound bows, he hunched down like a frightened dog. He was preceded by the stench of his unwashed body as he approached Pilate's chair, leading Pilate to think to himself, *These dirty barbarians! Even their secret reports stink.*

"Most noble Excellency," began Abarim nervously, "I came quickly with news of a trial last night...I was able to squeeze inside the great chamber...I saw the Galilean troublemaker." So anxious was Abarim that his words spilled out in a jumble. "I heard witnesses accuse him of terrible offenses against God. The Galilean peasant contradicts them...the high priest himself questioned him...."

"Slow down and speak clearly!" demanded Pilate. "I can't understand what you're saying."

"In a hurry, yes...I can't be found here, Excellency. I couldn't hear what the Galilean said to the high priest, but whatever it was made him very angry. The high priest and Sanhedrin elders argued over what to do with the Galilean...then the high priest stood up and in a loud voice condemned the Galilean to death — today!"

"Today? That doesn't sound like Caiaphas; he's usually more politically astute than to order such a provocative act on the eve of the Passover Festival. You must have heard wrong; surely they'll wait until after the Passover to kill this man."

"No, no, Excellency, today! This morning the high priest, elders, and priests are coming here. I came to warn you...they're bringing this Galilean outlaw to you so you can sentence him to death."

"My day's already full with important matters! Whatever this affair is, I hope it doesn't take up too much of my time." Then Pilate realized he had no reason to be anxious—simply ordering some Galilean Jew to be executed shouldn't take long. There would be no need for a formal trial. He would simply pronounce the outlaw guilty and order his execution, as he had done in the past. But while the sentencing would be easily resolved, what was unclear to Pilate was why Caiaphas and his priests were involving him in the death of this Galilean.

"Abarim," Pilate said, "why they are bringing this Galilean to me to be condemned? If they have determined that he has violated one of your thousands of religious laws, why don't the elders simply have him stoned? They've never asked Rome's permission to carry out that sentence before."

"Only you can condemn someone to be crucified, Excellency!"

"Crucified? In the name of Jupiter and all the gods, why do they want to crucify this man, especially now that Passover is here? What crime has he committed to deserve such a punishment?"

"It's a bad time, Excellency, yes...the high priest says the same thing...there are too many pilgrims in the city, and some are from Galilee. I overheard servants in the house say the Galilean is called a healer, a holy man, a teacher sent by God, even...," Abarim rolled his eyes upward, "...even a prophet!"

"A prophet?" said Pilate sharply, instantly thinking of the other alleged prophet in Samaria. "Then his death will surely arouse the rabble."

"Yes, Excellency—so say some council elders. They argued that to crucify him now could create serious trouble among the Passover crowds. Others shouted loudly and overruled them."

"Others?"

"Powerful, rich Sanhedrin elders. They claim the death of this man is required to show Rome the unquestioned loyalty of the Jewish people. They say his death is a penalty for the crime of causing a riot earlier this week in God's Holy Temple."

"Riot?" snapped Pilate so loudly that Abarim jerked backward in fear. "What riot? It was reported to me as a minor fracas by an itinerant Galilean preacher visiting the city for the Passover. It didn't even happen inside the actual temple but in the courtyard of the Gentiles. It was a minor ruckus, so I'm told, over the exploitative exchanging of money and abuses of the selling of sacrificial animals — hardly a riot!"

Abarim replied, "Well, the High Court says it was a riot, and they're priests of God...."

"Abarim, you called this affair a 'crime.' In Roman law, overturning the tables of a few moneychangers and briefly interrupting the business of a handful of dove merchants' business isn't a crime. That's what we call a minor disturbance, and it certainly doesn't merit a sentence of death!"

"Yes, yes, as always, your Excellency is correct. However, I overheard a powerful group in the High Council demand that the Galilean be silenced...and the best way to seal his lips is by death! To ensure he dies, they've thrown a net over him like those used in the arena by gladiators — and this net is unbreakable."

"Unbreakable?"

"Excellency, it's a web woven with an allegation that neither the prisoner nor you can escape."

Pilate paused, pondering the situation. He thought, *How in the name of Jupiter can it trap me? These damn Jews — they're trying to ensnare me in an affair that can erupt into mob violence, which will have serious political consequences for my career.* He said to Abarim, "What do you mean I'm being trapped in an unbreakable net?"

"Excellency, they accuse this Galilean of claiming he's the King of the Jews, and thus a rival to Caesar!"

"What? That's impossible! Who in his sane mind would claim to be a rival to Caesar?"

"A Galilean named Jesus of Nazareth, Excellency. Now, I'm a simple man who knows nothing of these twisted issues, but I overheard some servants say that this Galilean peasant goes about Galilee telling people he brings a new kingdom that's greater than the Empire of Rome."

Silently, Pilate sat and pondered this now perilous situation. Even if this Galilean impostor was only a madman, he was guilty of high treason against Emperor Tiberius. As the Emperor's representative here in Judea, there was no way he could not hold a trial and judge him as being guilty or innocent. He wondered to himself, *Could this be a sham charge invented by the priests to trap or embarrass me?*

Meanwhile, Abarim fidgeted as he glanced out the window at the stone platform in front of the palace. "Excellency, I must go, I must go! I can't stay any longer; the High Priest Caiaphas and the elders will come soon with the Galilean. I beg of you, let me go quickly, for if I'm found here, I'm dead!"

With a wave of his hand Pilate dismissed Abarim, who quickly began walking backward, repeatedly bowing. Pilate dipped his index finger several times as a signal to Lucius that he should reward the spy with money. As Abarim departed, Pilate mused that just as he had a spy in Caiaphas' household, Caiaphas surely had his own spy in the palace. Pilate was confident it was not one of his household slaves, but perhaps a local Judean who performed menial tasks or one of his mercenary Syrian soldiers. Regardless, Pilate was certain that Caiaphas had hidden eyes and ears about the palace, as did old Tiberius!

Lucius returned and sat on his stool next to Pilate. "Lucius, spies — like flies — are everywhere! While they're despicable, they're also indispensable to the auspicious unfolding of one's destiny."

Lucius agreed with a nod as Pilate stood and walked over to one of the eastern windows. Pointing southward toward the palace of High Priest Caiaphas, he exclaimed, "I've been betrayed!" Yesterday Caiaphas had sent him a message informing him that some Galilean troublemaker was in Jerusalem, but Caiaphas assured Pilate that he would be taken care of and that Pilate would not need to become involved. Yet now, Abarim said that the High Council would demand that this Galilean be crucified! Pilate said, "They're devious, all right! They've been scheming behind my back to make me, Pontius Pilate, their Roman scapegoat to bear the guilt of this man's death!"

"Sir, I could overhear some of what the spy said, but not why they want him to be crucified," interrupted Lucius.

"Abarim said that this Galilean claims he is the King of the Jews. If that's true, Lucius, then his fate is the cross! Yet if the priests want to get rid of him, why do so with a public crucifixion when an assassin could easily stick a knife in his back in one of the city's crowded streets? Lucius, pray to the goddess Fortuna that the gods rule today on my behalf."

"Sir, as the poet Ovid said, 'The gods have their own rules.'"

"Ah, Lucius, ever my tutor. You're so right; the gods are fickle and have their own rules, as old Ovid himself found out when he was exiled by the Emperor Augustus." Returning from the window, Pilate leaned over and patted Lucius on his shoulder. "Your quote from Ovid makes me wonder what rules the gods have decreed for me this day."

"Sir, I know one rule for sure."

"Really? What is it?"

"That you must have today's report finished, signed, sealed, and aboard the mail ship if your report is to depart on today's tide."

"Oh," groaned Pilate, "the report! Let's finish it, so you can send it off to Rome."

A task required of all Roman governors was to send daily reports to the Emperor. The daily reports and important letters were always sent in duplicate to safeguard and ensure their delivery. A third copy was kept in the provincial archives. Pilate, like every governor, was the Emperor's eyes and ears, and those imperial ears were itchy for news of the Empire, for Tiberius believed that knowledge was power.

"Lucius, I hope this meeting with the high priest won't take too much time. It's important that I respond to my centurion delegate in Samaria about the unrest at Mt. Gerizim. It seems fate has given me not one but two thorns in my side—the Samaritan agitator Simon, and now a demented Galilean prophet who imagines he is Caesar."

"Sir, may the gods come to your aid," said Lucius, as he stood to leave.

"I pray the same," replied Pilate. "Once the report is on its way to the mail boat in the harbor, send a messenger to my military advisor Centurion Petronius asking him to see me. I need his advice about this situation in Samaria, and I'm hoping that as he spent several years in Galilee, he may have some knowledge of this Jesus. After that, go to our archives and search through the reports for anything about the Galilean, and...."

"Sir, with your permission: I'm not as young as I once was," Lucius said, grinning. "May I have Aristocles help me search through the archived reports?"

"Aristocles?"

"The young Greek slave who came with us from Rome; he's very trustworthy."

"Yes, have him help you, and when the two of you have completed the search, bring me whatever reports you find. I want to review them before this Jesus arrives here this morning. I know my predecessor, Governor Gratus, kept detailed spy reports on notorious public figures, like that locust-eating hermit John, called 'the Baptizer.' Abarim told me that the Galilean peasants call this Jesus a prophet, so I am hoping Governor Gratus kept some intelligence on his activities. While searching the archives, look especially for any accounts of him proclaiming some kind of kingdom."

Lucius departed. Pilate thought, *May the goddess Fortuna shower good luck on Governor Gratus for his excellent advice when I came here.* He reflected that having been governor here for eleven years, Gratus was adamant about what he called the first rule of a good governor—to keep detailed daily records of whatever happens in your jurisdiction. That especially included gathering information on any potential troublemakers and anyone who drew large crowds. Gratus also had coached Pilate in clever ways to profit from graft, such as the lucrative practice of annually awarding the office of high priest to the highest bidder. Finally, Gratus warned Pilate about the Samaritans.

The thought of the Samaritans recalled Pilate to the work awaiting him that day. Standing, he said to Quintus and Marcus, "Come—let us go to our morning prayers. It has been said that the wise always put ritual before business."

Quintus stepped up, adjusted Pilate's official white tunic with its broad purple stripe, and placed a fresh toga over his head. Then the two slaves escorted Pilate to his morning prayers.

SCENE III

THE PILATE FAMILY SHRINE

Later That Morning

The small room in the palace that Pilate used as his temporary family shrine while he was in Jerusalem was suffused with an orange-yellow glow from the flickering oil lamps on the small altar. As the priest of the family, Pilate stood in front of the altar. On his right was his wife, Claudia Procula, who had accompanied him from Caesarea. Claudia was an attractive Roman woman with cream-colored skin, oval brown eyes, and pitch-black hair, which this morning had been sculptured by her slaves into coiled rings around the top of her head. Since it was morning she wore little jewelry—only two gold bracelets on her right arm, and around her neck a slender necklace of emeralds. Being the wife of a Roman governor, she was dressed in an aristocratic Roman woman's floor-length white tunic, over which she wore a *stola,* a long sleeveless garment worn only by married women.

Behind Claudia and Pilate stood their trusted household slaves. Pilate began the morning ritual with an oblation to the household gods as he poured wine on the floor, asking them to bless this new day. The flickering oil lamps on the small family altar illuminated the statuettes of the gods that Pilate had brought with him from his home in Caesarea. These images accompanied him wherever he traveled. At the center of the altar, in the place of honor, was a small gold statue of the Emperor Caesar Tiberius.

"O great Caesar Tiberius, Father of the Empire, good health to you," prayed Pilate, raising his arms in the gesture of prayer. "May all the gods bless you with a long life, my Emperor and benefactor." Then he made a profound bow to the golden image of the Emperor and stood along with the others in adoration. In silence they watched as spiraling white threads of smoke ascended from the burning incense in a bronze bowl on the altar. In a final ritual gesture, Pilate reached out and touched the small gold statue of the god Apollo as he silently prayed, *Apollo the Divine, the information I've received from my spy and that strange omen I saw this morning have warned me that I'm in great need of your assistance. O Apollo, please protect me this day.*

The brief morning prayers concluded, Pilate turned and nodded to the household slaves, who gave greetings to both Pilate and Claudia as they departed. Among the slaves, Pilate noticed a striking young man with a swarthy completion and a head of thick ringlets of dark hair. He thought, *That must be the Greek slave Aristocles.*

After the last slave had departed, Pilate and Claudia stood outside the doorway of the family shrine, visiting about their two small children whom they had left behind in Caesarea. Pilate had thought it best not to bring them to Jerusalem during the Passover festival, as it was a potentially dangerous time.

"Claudia, I also miss the children, and I regret that being procurator here affects our time together as a family. However, if I have to be stationed here in Judea, at least we get to live in the splendor of Herod's palaces."

Claudia replied, "My favorite is the white marble palace in Caesarea built on the shore of the Mediterranean. But this place," she groaned, "is like living in a big marble mausoleum, and it's just as chilly. Oh, Pilate, I wish we were both back in Caesarea."

"I agree, and what's more, I wish I was anywhere else in the Empire except here in this god-infested Jerusalem! I'd rather be back in the saddle as an army officer, when I led my troops with strength and courage, instead of being a governor, which merely requires shrewdness and the political ability to please the crowds."

"Your Excellency, forgive me," said Marcus, who suddenly appeared in the hallway, "and you also, Lady Claudia."

"Granted, Marcus. What is it?"

"Excellency, a temple priest named Zechariah has just arrived and says it is most urgent that he see you at once, as he has a message from the High Priest. I had him wait in the atrium at the front door. Sir, your orders?"

"Thank you, Marcus. Go tell the priest that I shall see him shortly. After that, come meet me at the Audience Hall."

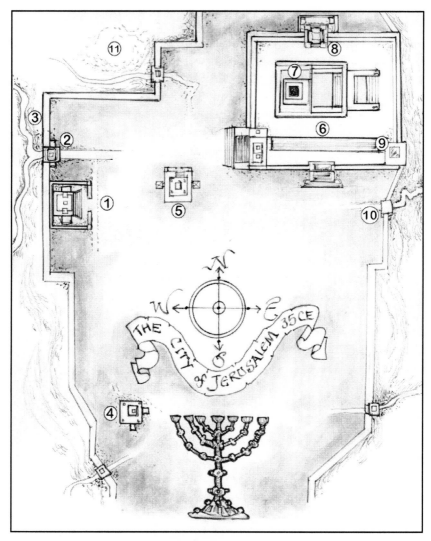

Map of Jerusalem

1. Herod's Palace
   ~*Gabbatha*: Roman Praetorium
2. Jaffa—Garden Gate
3. Road to Caesarea Maritima
4. Palace of Caiaphas & Annas
5. Herod Antipas Palace

6. King Herod's Temple
7. The Holy of Holies
8. Roman Fortress Antonia
9. Pinnacle of the Temple
10. Way to Mount of Olives
11. Golgotha—Skull Place

As Marcus departed, Pilate turned to his wife. "I'm sorry I have to end our visit so abruptly, but I must attend to business—and this time I fear it's serious. I'll see you later today."

Lady Claudia kissed him on the cheek and returned to her quarters, while Pilate walked to the Audience Hall. After entering the enormous room with its floor-to-ceiling marble walls, he walked to the eastern side and stood at one of the tall windows. He watched the morning sun glisten off the golden panels on the Temple as it flowed out in yellow waves over the brown rooftops of Jerusalem.

Pilate mused, *The Egyptians believed the sun to be a god, as do our simple Roman peasants and slaves. I've seen them greeting the rising sun with a deep bow of reverence while praying for its blessings. Maybe I should....* A knock at the door interrupted his reflection.

"Enter!"

"Excellency," said Marcus, "are you ready to receive the priest?"

"Give me a few moments to be seated, and then bring him in."

Pilate turned from the window and strode across the shining marble floors to the slightly elevated platform at the far end of the hall. In the center of the raised platform was a backless wooden curule chair with ornate curved legs used by Roman officials of superior rank. He seated himself upon it and had just finished adjusting the folds of his white toga when the Audience Hall door opened.

"Your Excellency," announced Marcus with a bow, "the priest Zechariah."

Into the huge hall walked a young temple priest whose pale face reminded Pilate of a white lump of unbaked bread. The priest's youthful scraggly beard and his long flowing priestly robes were annoying reminders to Pilate of his repugnance for the Jews and their religion. Aware that this disgust was rising up like vomit in his throat, Pilate at once lowered his eyes to the floor—an old tactic used by Roman judges lest their faces betray their real feelings to those standing before them.

The priest, after crossing the long hall and arriving at the platform where Pilate sat, gave a slight nod of his head instead of the full bow required of subjugated people. "Excellency, I am Zechariah,

24

a messenger of High Priest Caiaphas." He said this in a matter-of-fact voice devoid of respect. "He wishes you good health and a long life. He prays that the All Holy One, Blessed be His Name, will let His countenance shine upon...."

"Thank High Priest Caiaphas for being so concerned about my health," Pilate said sarcastically, as he momentarily raised his eyes and looked at the priest. "But surely, priest Zechariah, at this very early hour of the morning you haven't come all the way here merely to relay wishes for my well-being. I have much to do today; state your business!"

"High Priest Caiaphas wishes to inform you that he will be coming here this morning to personally meet with you. He will be accompanied by a delegation of the senior Sanhedrin members, members of the Temple priesthood, and the scribes, who are bringing a notorious public criminal for you to judge."

"On the eve of the Passover? I'm stunned to hear that High Priest Caiaphas and his cohort should enter this pagan dwelling to meet with me on such a day. How very unusual!"

"That, Sir, is the purpose of my visit. The High Priest and the elders request that you meet them outside this palace on the stone platform so they won't have to enter."

Pilate, knowing in advance of Caiaphas' visit, enlarged his eyes in mock shock, but before he could speak, the priest continued, "The High Priest said I was to inform you, and I quote, 'I feel confident you would agree to this minor inconvenience, knowing of your personal respect and that of Emperor Tiberius for our ancient religious beliefs and customs.'"

"Minor inconvenience?" snapped Pilate. "Does a defeated enemy dictate his choice of the place to meet his conqueror?"

Ignoring Pilate's question, Zechariah went on, "I am also to inform you that the Galilean prisoner they are bringing you has already been judged by the High Council of the Sanhedrin and found guilty of horrendous crimes against the Temple and the Laws of Moses. They have already passed judgment on him and sentenced him to...."

"Silence! Not only do I find it highly offensive that you are dictating to me what I shall or shall not do, I do not know why you are bringing this man to me! Why am I, Pontius Pilate, to pass judgment on a man when your religious court has already convicted him? That is," Pilate continued, as a thin smile crept across his face, "unless you Jews are finally acknowledging that even your religious decisions are subject to the authority of Rome."

Zechariah flinched slightly but continued, "I am to inform you that the Council of the Sanhedrin has decreed—since this Galilean's crimes are so horrendous—that his penalty is to be crucifixion! Only you as Governor have the authority to order a man to be crucified; that is why they are bringing this criminal to you to judge and condemn to the cross."

"Crucifixion?" snorted Pilate. "That's a Roman punishment! I've been told that according to your prophet Moses, your god Yahweh has decreed stoning to be the punishment for violations of the major prohibitions of your law. So, priest, if your god has decreed the penalty of stoning, why can't a group of your holy elders be found to stone him, or even some of you Temple priests; that is, unless you're impotent...."

Before Zechariah could respond, Pilate arose and strode over to a tall window, where he stood with his back to the priest in an authoritarian stance with his legs spread apart and his hands on his hips. As Zechariah waited for Pilate to finish his sentence, he was left to stew in anger over the accusation of being impotent.

The interminable silence echoed louder than thunder off the marble walls of the vast canyon of the palatial hall as Pilate fumed about having his behavior dictated to him by the temple authorities. Tired of waiting for Pilate to speak, Zechariah was just opening his mouth when Pilate whirled around to face him. At the sight of Pilate's livid face, Zechariah turned ashen and his eyes darted fearfully left and right as if he was afraid someone was about to pounce on him.

"Priest," shouted Pilate, as if giving a military order, "go back to your master and remind him that the Roman Empire is civilized, even if Judea isn't! Perhaps if Rome rules you Jews for another hundred years, you may become a civilized people and abandon your primitive desert laws...."

Abruptly stopping mid-sentence, Pilate whirled around again with his back to the priest and looked out the window. He sternly admonished himself, *I must think clearly — what should I do next? If Lucius were here, I know he would say my next step should be to calm my anger.* He prayed to the goddess Fortuna to cleanse his tongue of acid-tainted Jewish prejudice, lest he become deeply ensnared in this politically dangerous situation.

Having regained his composure, Pilate slowly turned to face the priest. "Return to High Priest Caiaphas," he said in a calm but authoritarian voice, "and tell him I appreciate this gesture of his friendship in informing me of his intentions prior to his arrival. Especially," he continued, smiling unkindly, "because by doing so he placed the soul of his priestly messenger in dire jeopardy by requiring him to enter into a defiled pagan's house on the eve of Passover."

Pilate walked back to the platform and seated himself in the curule chair as Zechariah shamefacedly looked down at the floor, acknowledging that by entering the palace this day he had indeed acquired ritual impurity.

"You also are to inform High Priest Caiaphas," Pilate said to him, "that I consent to his request to maintain religious purity and will meet with him and the others on the stone platform outside this palace. As the official representative of the Roman Empire here in Judea, I will listen to all the testimony in this case to see if the prisoner has broken any Roman laws. Then, after proper deliberation, in the name of the Emperor Tiberius, I will judge whether the accused is guilty or innocent. If he is found guilty of any crime, I shall then determine the appropriate punishment!"

Pilate leaned back slightly and closed his eyes. The priest Zechariah waited, until Pilate shouted, "Marcus!"

Bowing, Marcus stepped forward as Pilate gestured with his right hand toward the door and said curtly, "Show this man out!"

As the door closed behind the departing priest, Pilate smiled, feeling satisfied. Since he had been informed by his spy of Caiaphas' visit, he had held the high ground in this encounter. "I admit, I

27

enjoyed taunting Caiaphas' messenger," he said aloud to the vast empty hall. However, he regretted his outbursts about their religion. If Lucius had been there he would have been upset by the way Pilate allowed his emotions to overrule his prudence. Since Pilate was a youth, Lucius had lectured him about the need to control his emotions, repeating the words of Sophocles, "The greatest griefs are those we cause ourselves." He concluded that old Sophocles was right and resolved that when he confronted the clever Joseph Caiaphas later that morning he would guard his emotions and his speech.

As Pilate's left elbow rested on the arm of his chair, he raised his index finger and began to stroke his upper lip. Pondering that impending encounter, he thought, *I must discipline myself to be more tolerant of the Jews' strange beliefs and that desert wind god of theirs, who made as many religious laws as there are stars in the night sky. I've never heard of such a nomadic, sadistic god who must be placated daily by the slaughter of animals, whose blood cascades in red rivers down the temple steps. What other people on this earth have a god with a nose like this Jewish god, who enjoys the rancid stench of burning animal flesh?* Pilate shook his head. *Ah, you must stop, Pilate! You're digging your own grave with every shovel of your disgust for the Jews and their religion.*

Pilate continued to brood over the many prejudices he had against the Jews since he was a youth in Rome, but then admitted to himself, *Yet, part of me admires these Jews. They're willing to die for that god of theirs, and they are absolutely unbending in their religious convictions and beliefs. That's more than you can say about yourself, isn't it, Pilate?*

Standing up, he walked across the room to one of the windows and stood looking over the city. He continued to question himself: *So, Pontius Pilate, if these Jews believe fervently in their god to the point of dying for him, in whom or what do you believe?* After a long pause, he reflected, *Well, I certainly don't believe in the old Roman gods and goddesses, even if their temples are on every street corner in Rome. Yet didn't I go to pray at the Temple of Mars the Avenger before I departed from Rome for Judea?*

Mulling over these contradictions, he knew his visit to the Temple of Mars was no act of belief but merely the observance of an ancient custom for new governors about to depart from Rome. For Romans, daily life was intertwined with religion and the Empire, like the semi-religious cult of the reigning emperor. But he certainly didn't believe that Tiberius was divine!

Pilate was aware he was contradicting himself. Didn't he keep a statue of the Emperor in the center of his family altar and frequently refer to him as "the divine Tiberius"?

Reluctantly, Pilate acknowledged that he was a complex man. In fact, at times he felt there were legions of Pontius Pilates within him: one was ruthless and impatient, another believed in omens, and yet another believed that one could read the future in the stars. There was a Pilate who trusted the loyalty of his slaves and soldiers and another who was suspicious of everyone. However, although he kept a golden image of the Emperor on his family altar that was merely for political reasons, and if he referred to him as "divine," well, he didn't truly believe that Tiberius was a god!

Pilate's ruminations about the Emperor reminded him that a Roman denarius was considered a good luck charm, since it was engraved with the face of Emperor Tiberius. He recalled once hearing that criminals clutched a silver denarius in their hand as a sacred amulet to help them escape punishment.

Pilate reminded himself, *While the uneducated and lower classes believe Tiberius to be a god, the Emperor himself — being ever cautious never to offend the Senate — cleverly rejects the title of divinity. When he is called divine, he usually responds, "My temples are in your hearts." Then he changes the subject.*

Pilate placed his right hand over his heart and spoke to the wind, "In this temple of my heart, Caesar Tiberius, I reverence you, but my reverence isn't adoration!" Yet an inner voice inside him asked, "If you don't believe Tiberius is a god or that the old Roman or Greek gods exist, in what *do* you believe?" With his right hand still over his heart, he responded in a whisper, "I believe in Pontius Pilate, and in the Fates who control my destiny."

A soft tapping at the door interrupted the flow of his thoughts, and he knew it must be Lucius returning from the archives with his requested reports. As he called out for him to enter, Pilate chuckled to himself, saying, "I'd better have Lucius get a silver denarius for me."

Lucius entered, accompanied by Aristocles, who carried only one scroll. After bowing, Aristocles placed this scroll in Pilate's extended hand. After again bowing, he departed as Lucius sat on his stool next to Pilate's chair. "I'm sorry, Sir, but we found only one report dealing with Jesus of Galilee."

"Only one?" asked Pilate.

"Yes, Sir. Both Aristocles and I scoured the archives, but we only discovered this one report. The date on the scroll you're holding implies that Jesus didn't begin to teach and move about in Galilee until after Governor Gratus had departed from Judea."

"Since you're aware of its content, Lucius, summarize it for me."

"This single scroll is a report from one of our Galilean spies, who talks about the activity of a certain Jesus of Nazareth after the beheading of John the Baptizer."

"That was about three years ago, wasn't it?"

"Yes, Sir. The only report in our archives about Jesus is dated after you became Governor! I suspect that it was of only minor importance at the time, and you wouldn't have remembered it. In that report, our spy informed us about Jesus of Nazareth, a common village laborer, stonemason, and carpenter, whom the villagers said had been a disciple or admirer of John the Baptizer. After John's beheading, this Jesus became a wandering teacher and sage who drew small crowds that in time grew larger. It was reported that this Jesus is the son of peasant parents and like them is illiterate, yet he is a powerful speaker and storyteller who attracts people to him."

"Does the spy say anything in this report about the man inciting rebellion or claiming to be a king?"

"No, Sir. He only briefly details this man's disregard for many of the Jewish purity codes and his notorious custom of eating with prostitutes and with tax collectors employed by Rome. It seems that he has been denounced by the synagogue elders for associating with sinners, ritually unclean Jews, and Jews who associate with Romans and other gentiles."

"Lucius, I think I'm going to enjoy meeting this Galilean prisoner. He sounds like a very interesting man."

"He sounds unusual, Sir," replied Lucius, cautiously. "Yet there is more in the report that you will find interesting. Our informer refers to him as being a magician and healer who is gathering a small following of uneducated peasants and fishermen. While he is regarded by the people as a religious teacher, it is significant that there is not a single priest or scribe among his group of followers!"

Pilate lifted up the scroll. "When I have time I will read this carefully, but for now I'll ask again: Does our informer say anything about this uneducated, peasant laborer claiming to be a king?"

"No, Sir, he doesn't."

"Did he say anything about this Jesus making any coinage with his image on it? As you know, Lucius, the first thing new kings—even pretender kings—do is to make their own coinage."

"He makes no mention of it, Sir."

"I appreciate your overview of the report. The more knowledge I have about the prisoner, the better position I'll be in when he comes before me. Centurion Petronius should be here soon, and he may be of some help. He was previously stationed in Galilee, speaks Aramaic and some Hebrew, and has a good knowledge of these Jews and their customs. As my tutor, Lucius, you taught me Greek, along with the philosophies of Plato and Aristotle, and many plays of the Greek theater. I find my Greek most useful out here on the edge of the Empire while dealing with educated Jews, but at this trial I'll need someone who knows Aramaic and Hebrew. But this report has helped, and now I'm eager for Petronius to arrive."

"I'm pleased, Sir, that I was of some small assistance."

"If Petronius can provide me with additional information, I'll feel more confident when I duel with Caiaphas this morning. From what I've heard so far, it appears the Galilean is not guilty of claiming to be a king. I'm going to enjoy watching the faces of Caiaphas and the others when I pronounce him innocent."

"With your permission, Sir, your old teacher proposes that you cautiously approach your final verdict. As Publilius Syrus said, 'The judge is condemned when the criminal is absolved.'"

"Condemned? I don't understand. Only a madman would dare to claim to be the Imperial Caesar of Galilee, since there's only one Caesar, the Emperor Tiberius. Although Emperor Augustus made Herod Agrippa the King of Judea, that was only a token kingship bestowed on a minor potentate of a distant Roman province. As you can see," Pilate said, sweeping his hand at the palace's classic Roman architecture, "in his tastes and lifestyle, Herod was far more Roman than...." A knock on the door interrupted Pilate.

SCENE IV

THE PALACE AUDIENCE HALL

Mid Morning That Same Day

Pilate acknowledged the knock, and the tall doors opened. Marcus stepped in and bowed. "Your Excellency, Centurion Petronius is reporting as you requested."

"Wonderful — show him in, Marcus."

Through the open doorway walked a Roman centurion wearing a scarlet military cloak, molded brown leather chest armor, and a knee-length soldier's tunic. His sword hung from his belt on the left side, an indication he was an officer; most soldiers wore their swords on the right. In the crook of his folded left arm he carried his red plumed officer's helmet. Petronius was of average height but had a muscular build, a strong Roman face, and a head of deep black hair. He boldly strode across the room to where Pilate sat, then stopped and saluted him. Pilate stood, acknowledged his salutation, and greeted him.

"Petronius, good health and the blessings of the gods be with you. Thank you for coming so quickly at this early hour; I know you must be busy with the security precautions for the Passover Festival. I've called for you because I'm in need of some knowledge you acquired during your years of service in Galilee."

"Your Excellency honors me. I'm eager to be of assistance in any way possible. Allow me to begin by repeating how grateful I am to you for arranging to have me transferred from the staff of the prince Herod Antipas to your personal service. Whatever your needs, I am at your command."

"Petronius, be seated," Pilate said, gesturing toward an empty chair next to his. "You speak of being grateful for being assigned to my staff; instead, it is I who am grateful. I thank the gods who gifted me at birth with the genius to ask Herod Antipas to transfer you here. I had heard reports about you and the knowledge you acquired of the customs of the Jews while you served as the Roman advisor to Herod's court. I was in need of a personal military adviser versed in the ways of the Jews, and I was inspired to collect a favor that old fox of Galilee owed me. So I asked Antipas if I might have you transferred."

"Again, Sir, thank you for that honor."

"My officers told me that you were known in the army to have the most knowledge of the behaviors and beliefs of the Jews. I was also told that the Galilean Jews held you in high esteem because while you were stationed there you built them a synagogue. Is that true?"

"Yes, it is."

"Brilliant! It's a clever move to show that Rome is more than eager to accommodate itself to these people and their unfathomable religious beliefs. That was well done. Now, as for our business today, I have a special need of some information you may possess. Allow me to quickly lay out the field of combat: in a short while High Priest Caiaphas, along with a gang of elders and priests, are bringing a wandering Galilean teacher to me, named...uh...," he said, turning to Lucius.

"Jesus of Nazareth, Sir."

"Ah, yes, that's his name. Petronius, as if I had nothing more important to attend to today, Caiaphas is dragging this peasant to me whom they all claim is guilty of insurrection against Rome, and whom they wish to be crucified!"

"Insurrection?" asked Petronius, with a troubled expression. "Sir, I find such a charge most difficult to comprehend...that is, if the prisoner is the same Jesus with whom I'm acquainted. The Galilean I know by that name couldn't possibility be guilty of armed rebellion against Rome; in fact, he's renowned throughout Galilee for his strong opposition to all forms of violence. He even teaches that the mere thinking of violent thoughts against another is equivalent to murder!"

"Imagine, Lucius," exclaimed Pilate, "being crucified or beheaded for your thoughts!"

"Sir, during my years in Galilee," Petronius continued, "I've found that the Jewish people often exaggerate in their daily speech and use poetic embellishment. Yet I was told with assurance that Jesus wasn't exaggerating—he meant just what he said."

"Amazing! You mean this Galilean literally equates being angry with being guilty of murder?"

"Yes, Sir. I'm told he forbids his followers to engage in any form of violence in their thoughts, words, and deeds. I've also been told that in their Jewish moral code there is no parallel for such a prohibition."

"Petronius, you just confirmed my suspicions. This is going to be a typical Jewish case with entangled, trifling religious regulations all twisted together into knots. But enough of this; crafty old Caiaphas will be here soon, so let me summarize our situation."

Pilate stood up, and linking his hands together behind his back, began pacing in front of the tall windows. "This Galilean Jesus came to Jerusalem for the Passover festival, and last night at the Mount of Olives was arrested by the temple police on the orders of the Sanhedrin. According to my spy he was taken before the High Priest and the council of elders, who presented fake witnesses, and he was then judged guilty of treason against Rome. Now they are demanding that I, as Governor, crucify him today!"

"Today, Sir? On the eve of the Passover? But Jerusalem is crowded with...."

"I agree it is insane, Petronius. Crucifixions are always potentially dangerous, even when they don't commence on the eve of the Passover. Yet it seems the High Priest and his cohorts aren't concerned about the consequences—which makes me wonder if they're conspiring to use this situation as a trap to try to make me accountable for another messy riot."

Petronius gravely shook his head as Pilate returned to his chair and seated himself. "Petronius, search your memory of your years in Galilee. Do you know anything about this man Jesus that could be helpful to me?"

"Sir, I agree with you that a crucifixion at this time could become dangerously volatile. As for any insights into the prisoner...well, while stationed at the court of Tetrarch Herod Antipas, one of my duties was to oversee his network of spies. They passed information of any possible rabble-rousers or potential revolutionaries through me to the Prince. That included any person who attracted large gatherings of the people, as this man Jesus was beginning to do. In my time there, though, I never saw a single report that said anything about him agitating the Galileans to revolt against the Prince or the Emperor. He was simply a poor wandering teacher who went from village to village teaching many things — among them, that the people were actually to love their enemies."

"Love their enemies? We Romans are their enemies! Did he really expect them to love us?"

"It appears so, Sir. I saw one report in which someone in the crowd asked Jesus if his new rule of love applied to us Romans, and he replied that it did. So unless his teachings have radically changed, he couldn't be guilty of an uprising against Rome."

"Oh, Petronius, since coming here...." Pilate stood up and began to walk back and forth across the polished marbled floor of the Audience Hall. "Forgive my pacing; it's an old soldier's habit, and I think better on my feet. As I was saying, since coming here I've tried to be accepting of these Jews, but I haven't been able to escape my old Roman prejudices. Regardless of whether they call themselves Judeans, Galileans, or Samaritans, I lump them all together as Jews — who are detested in Rome!"

"I'm aware of that Jewish prejudice by Romans," affirmed Petronius, "who call them lazy for refusing to work on Saturdays by using the excuse that their god forbids it."

Pilate responded, "Romans also consider Jews to be cowards for refusing to perform their lawful duty to serve in the army. What I find despicable about them is that they're like fanatical peddlers trying to induce Romans to buy into their primitive desert beliefs. I'll never understand why any sane Roman citizen could be attracted to such a barbaric religion. Yet I know some Romans have adopted aspects of the Jews' religion without actually becoming Jews. I'm curious, Petronius, why do you think these Romans would do such a thing?"

"With your permission, Sir, uh...I believe the old Roman religions no longer nourish...uh...."

"Go on — speak freely, Petronius."

"Thank you, Sir. I'm hesitant to say it, but many educated Romans no longer believe in our ancient Roman gods and goddesses and see the worship of them as a ceremonial civic duty. The lower classes, being superstitious, have a need of the old gods, and they celebrate their festivals since they are occasions for feasting, rowdy drunkenness, merrymaking, and debauchery."

"But what do educated Romans find attractive in the Jewish religion?"

"Well, for one thing, it offers a belief in a life after death!"

"Petronius, isn't that true for only some of Jews? From what I understand, only the Pharisees believe in a life after death, while the Sadducees and Samaritans do not. Talk of life after death, I believe, is a subject that only elderly philosophers debate! Thanks to my old mentor," he nodded, smiling at Lucius, "I learned the wisdom of Publilius Syrus, who said, 'The fear of death is more to be dreaded than death itself.' He had another gem: 'Every day should be lived as if it were to be our last!' As a soldier I've tried to live without being afraid of death, so I have no need of a religion about life after death. And even if I did fear dying and what happens after we die, that wouldn't be sufficient for me to become a Jew!"

Pilate spat on the floor as he continued, "What real man wants to become a Jew, and who would take part in their painful ritual of cutting their manhood! It's so repulsive and yet...also fascinating." He mused further, "I once heard that circumcision makes Jews more sexually potent. Do you think that is true?" Not really wanting to know, Pilate went on, "No need to answer, Petronius. Even if it's true, I could never be circumcised! It's disgusting and so obviously shameful whenever one goes to the baths. I agree with Cicero, who said that Jews were 'a people born to be slaves.' That was easy for him to say, of course, because unlike us, he didn't have to live surrounded by them. If he had, he would have known Jews are anything but slaves...." Rapid, repeated knocking at the door interrupted Pilate.

"Enter!"

"Your Excellency," said Marcus, bowing, "High Priest Caiaphas and the others have just arrived and have sent word for you to come outside and meet them on the stone platform."

"Thank you, Marcus. I did agree to meet them out there so they wouldn't be 'ritually defiled.' Go out to our guests and inform them:

'Your Imperial Governor Pontius Pilate, being in an important conference, is presently unavailable. As soon as circumstances allow, he will come out and meet with you.'"

As Marcus bowed and departed, Petronius picked up his helmet and began to stand.

"Sit down, Petronius; there's no need to hurry. I intend to let them stand out there a while to remind them that Imperial Rome is their master. Now, you and I must use our time wisely before I face this Galilean prisoner. Do you know anything else about this man?"

"He's an illiterate peasant preacher who has an imposing physical presence. He's a good storyteller who uses simple words and easily understood examples, yet he speaks with authority and conviction. I saw him once from a distance in Tiberius when I commanded a detachment of our soldiers assigned to protect your wife, Lady Claudia, when she visited Galilee."

"Yes, I recall Claudia hadn't been feeling well, and it was suggested that she go and bathe in the healing hot springs at Tiberius on the shore of the Sea of Galilee. She told me that as she was being carried away from the baths in her litter, she heard jubilant shouting and saw a cheering crowd gathering. Ordering that her litter be stopped, she asked her slaves what was happening. They told her the crowd was joyfully shouting the praises of a man who had healed a cripple simply by the touch of his hand."

"Sir, I also was aware of that same healing in Tiberius and recalled it sometime later when my personal slave, Gaius, became deathly sick. The physicians weren't able to cure him, and I was desperate. Then I recalled the name of the healer at Tiberius and what I knew of him from our spy's reports. The elders owed me a favor for building their synagogue, so I asked them to petition Jesus to come and heal my beloved slave."

"Ah, yes, the ancient exchange of favors; I know that custom well. I'm governor here because of that very system. In exchange for a favor, my patron in Rome arranged with the Emperor Tiberius that I be appointed Governor of Judea...but I've interrupted your story."

Petronius continued, "The elders went to Jesus and told him my request—and also that I had built their synagogue—and he agreed to heal my slave. Typical of his unpredictability, he shocked the elders by saying he would come to my home to heal Gaius; yes, come to a pagan's dwelling! Upon hearing that Jesus was on his way to my home, I sent a slave to him with the message, 'Lord, as a gentile pagan, I'm not worthy that you should come under my roof; say the word and my slave will be healed. As a Roman centurion, I know the power of authority, for whenever I give an order, it is done. So I believe that whatever you order to be done, will be done!'"

Pilate was quite surprised. "Petronius, you addressed this Jew as 'Lord'? Is that not a title for someone superior to you? No matter — though I'm amazed you actually believed the Galilean could heal someone at a distance!"

"Sir, after they gave Jesus my message, I was told that he said, 'I have not found such faith in all of Israel!' And when my messenger returned, Gaius was already restored to full health! I never saw Jesus or had the opportunity to thank him for curing my slave. But, speaking of that incident at Tiberius, may I ask if you have told Lady Claudia that you must judge the same healer she saw there in person?"

"Not yet. I've been informed she isn't feeling well and is resting, and I didn't want to disturb her; I'll tell her later when she's feeling better. Now, before we go out to meet with Caiaphas, I have another question for you. When you were in Galilee, did you ever hear reports about the prisoner proclaiming some kind of a kingdom?"

"No; well, not precisely," Petronius replied, cautiously. "Talk of a coming new kingdom is common among the Jewish people. It's one of their prophetic dreams of a coming reign. Some versions describe it as a peaceable kingdom without violence, wars, armies, governors...or even an emperor."

"No armies or wars? Impossible! That's not a dream — it's a fantasy. There's only one kingdom on this earth, and that's the Imperial Empire of Tiberius Caesar! May the gods protect me, I'm about to sit in judgment on a ragtag peasant king of an empire of the insane. Now, I've kept Caiaphas and his gaggle of priests stewing out there in the sun long enough. It's time to go." Unconsciously, Pilate began rolling his signet ring around his finger, thinking he should pray to the goddess Fortuna as he went forth to meet a devious enemy in combat, naked of any armor except his wits.

Upon standing, Pilate, like a field commander, rapidly began giving orders: "Marcus, have Quintus and two others carry my curule chair out onto the front stone platform, along with a stool for Lucius. Petronius, see that my chair is placed in a prominent place in the middle of the platform, as close as possible to the top step of the stairs that lead up to it. Then station my personal guard of Roman legionaries across the front of the palace, and have a detachment of our foreign mercenary soldiers strategically placed along the outer colonnade of the courtyard."

After Petronius and Marcus departed, Pilate and Lucius were alone. Pilate stood discreetly beside a window, where he could observe the crowd gathering in front of the palace without being seen himself.

"Lucius, that's no small group of temple elders gathering out there; it's beginning to swell into a large crowd."

"Beware, Pilate. Remember what Horace called crowds: 'The many-headed beast.'"

"Yes, you're right to remind me. I'll do my best to keep my eye on whichever of its many heads appears to be the most dangerous."

"Pilate, may I presume to speak?" It was only when he and Pilate were alone that Lucius would address with such familiarity this man whom he loved as dearly as a son.

"I command you to speak. I need all the insights you can give me if I'm to be victorious in my combat with the crowd awaiting me."

Lucius said, "Remember that Emperor Tiberius appointed you procurator, not governor, of Judea. I know that's not unusual, because Rome had done the same for your predecessors Valerius Gratus, Annius Rufus, and the others they've sent out here to Judea. However, when the Emperor appointed you procurator, although you were not officially *given* the title of governor, he did give you both the powers and the right to *use* the title of governor."

"Ah, yes. Old Rome loves the imperial ladder of its hierarchy of power and relishes in creating countless distinctions of class and rank among its administrators. The rank of procurator, I know, is due historically to Judea's rebellious nature. But, regrettably, by being only a procurator, I have no Roman legions under my command. Instead, I have mercenary Syrian and Samaritan troops who lack the discipline of real Roman soldiers. Fortunately, they did give me a detail of Roman legionaries as my personal bodyguards."

"I do agree, Pilate — it is unfortunate you don't have the power of Roman legions, but here in Jerusalem you have something more useful. You have the power to nominate or depose the high priest! Don't forget that power when dealing with Caiaphas, for I can assure you Caiaphas hasn't forgotten it! And," Lucius said, looking into his eyes, "know how proud your old tutor is when he hears your troops and the populace address you as 'His Excellency Pontius Pilate, the Roman Governor of Judea.'"

"Lucius, you're my perpetual mentor, not my 'old' teacher! By reminding me of my official rank, I'll be more cautious in handling this trial, since as procurator I'm always subordinate to Vitellius, the Roman Legate of Syria. Speaking of which, I'm convinced that the greatest pleasure of these damn Jews — even more than sex — is to write letters critical of me to Vitellius — and, sadly, to the Emperor."

At that moment Petronius entered and saluted. "Sir, your chair is in place on the platform, and the troops are stationed as you requested."

Lucius arranged Pilate's toga, and as he was doing so, he discreetly slipped into Pilate's hand the silver denarius he'd requested. Then he gathered up his cuttlefish ink, iron pens, and a few empty scrolls with which to record the proceedings of the trial.

Pilate declared, "Let's go forth to encounter our foes as Ovid recommended, 'To see what we can learn from our enemies.'"

SCENE V

THE LIMESTONE PLATFORM
IN FRONT OF KING HEROD'S PALACE

Late Morning, 35 C.E.

Pontius Pilate sat regally in the imperial chair that had been placed in the center of the broad, stage-like limestone platform designed by King Herod for royal outdoor audiences. It was located on the east side of the palace at the west end of a paved courtyard surrounded by a circular stone colonnade.

The centurion Petronius stood on Pilate's left, and at his right Lucius was seated on a stool, ready to record the trial's proceedings. Marcus stood directly behind Pilate with his powerful arms folded across his chest. Behind them, stationed in front of the pillars of the palace, were the Roman legionaries of Pilate's personal guard. In front of Pilate, below the stone steps on the pavement, stood the High Priest Caiaphas, surrounded by ranking members of the Sanhedrin and the Temple priesthood. While Caiaphas was plump with a round, chubby face that reflected the good life of the Temple aristocratic elite, he also possessed a bearing and presence of one who was powerful. Behind the priests a large crowd was beginning to gather in the courtyard, and behind them, stationed along courtyard's stone colonnade, were Pilate's foreign mercenary soldiers.

The scene was set.

"Petronius," Pilate said out of the side of his mouth, "Caiaphas gave me no indication there would be a crowd. Look out at that swelling horde."

"Sir, I recognize several of them," Petronius said, leaning over. "They're hired agitators. I've seen them at previous disturbances. The temple priests often use them like a Greek chorus to shout whatever they want said."

"Sir," whispered Lucius, "I warn you to be on your guard. As honey draws flies, a crowd attracts crowds! That's as true here in Jerusalem as it is in Rome or Athens. Be prepared, for if this trial drags on the mob will swell, and by its sheer size it will attract even more curious spectators."

Pilate understood. He needed the gods to help him use his wits to maneuver this crowd to his own advantage, and not that of the priests.

As Petronius studied the faces of the High Priest and the highest elders of all Judaism, he thought, *Since coming to Judea I've been attracted to the Jews' religion. I find their holy writings ennobling, especially those that command them to care for the needs of widows, orphans, and the poor. They have a wonderful and simple moral code of just ten rules that tell them not to lie, steal, lust for what belongs to another, commit adultery, and most of all, not to kill! Yet here in front of me are the leaders of that religion who are lusting to kill this prisoner, who surely is innocent.*

Petronius' gaze then moved to their prisoner, who stood guarded beside the High Priest. He had never seen Jesus so close before and was impressed that he was at least a head and a half taller than the others gathered around him. He had the broad shoulders and strong body of a laborer. Even with his hands bound by rope in front of him he stood erect with his head held high, unlike the typical criminal who usually hung his head in fear or shame. The prisoner was looking straight ahead with his dark brown eyes fixed on Pilate. Then he looked up directly at Petronius with a gaze that sent a shiver through him. He felt as if Jesus was looking directly into his heart.

"Petronius, this does not look like your average Jewish prisoner," Pilate remarked. "His calm, almost regal composure makes me wonder which one of us is the prisoner today."

At that moment the sun broke through the gray overcast sky and shone directly down on the stone platform. Lifting his head up to look at the sun, Pilate thought, *It's an omen from Apollo, the sun god, shining down his favors upon me.* Smiling, he lowered his head as he ordered, "Centurion, declare this trial in session."

"In the name of the great Tiberius Caesar," Petronius announced loudly in Greek, the official language used by Rome in its eastern empire, "the August Emperor of Rome and the entire world, this Roman Court of Justice is now in session. His Excellency, Governor Pontius Pilate, is the presiding judge, and as required by Roman law, the proceedings of this trial will be recorded." Petronius then pointed at Jesus. "What is the name of the accused?"

Petronius' question dangled unanswered in the air as Jesus continued to stare at Pilate silently.

"The name of the prisoner," shouted High Priest Caiaphas, also in Greek, "is Jesus of Nazareth!" The crowd replied to this declaration with much hooting and booing.

"With what crime is this prisoner charged?" asked Petronius.

"This Jesus," shouted Caiaphas, "has been found guilty of many grievous crimes. He has incited a riot in God's holy Temple and has performed countless violations of the teachings of Moses. He threatens the authority of Rome by urging the people not to pay their taxes to Tiberius Caesar. For these, as well as numerous other crimes, he has been condemned to death!"

"Not by me," Pilate replied serenely in Greek. "In a Roman court all are presumed innocent until they are proven guilty. You who are his accusers must produce witnesses and evidence that the prisoner is guilty of encouraging the people not to pay their Roman taxes. Before you do, however," he said, raising his index finger in the air, "I warn you that the very opposite has been reported to me. I have heard eyewitness reports that when the prisoner was asked if Jews should pay taxes, he answered, 'Render to Caesar what is Caesar's'!"

This statement was followed by waves of murmurs from the crowd as the Sanhedrin elders began arguing among themselves. At this, his first defeat, Caiaphas remained expressionless, since he had avoided using false witnesses lest Pilate dismiss the entire case against Jesus.

"High Priest, your other accusations of the prisoner's violations of the Law of Moses are not a concern of Imperial Rome—they are the domain of the Temple authorities. Why are you wasting my time with them?"

Unseen by others, in his left hand Pilate was rubbing his silver denarius for good luck. As his thumb ran across the face of Emperor

Tiberius on the coin, he thought, *I need more than good luck in this verbal combat with crafty Caiaphas; I need the intercession of the gods.*

"Your Excellency," replied Caiaphas, after making a profound bow, "we the religious leaders of the Jewish people, in our humble attempts to serve as best we can the great Caesar Tiberius, ask your pardon if we appear to be wasting your time. However, we judge the Galilean prisoner standing before you to be a living affront to our August Emperor!"

"How is he a living insult to the Emperor Tiberius?"

"By brazenly claiming that he, Jesus of Nazareth, and not Tiberius Caesar...," Caiaphas replied, raising his voice to almost a shout, "...is the King of the Jews!"

On cue the crowd began shaking their fists in the air and screaming angry threats against Jesus. Tightly squeezing his denarius, Pilate knew that the most dangerous of charges now had been set loose on the wind, like a hawk escaping from its cage. He stoically stared ahead, waiting until the priests had quieted the mob.

"According to Roman law, the prisoner has the right to defend himself against the charges you have made against him. So, Galilean, you have heard the High Priest make a very treasonous allegation against you. Are you the King of the Jews?"

Jesus only stared silently at Pilate, while the crowd, like some great animal, leaned forward to hear how Jesus would respond.

"Then, you are the King of the Jews?" asked Pilate, this time louder.

Jesus did not reply.

"Centurion, translate my question to the prisoner into Aramaic."

"Are you asking me a question," Jesus replied in Greek, "or making a statement?"

"It is not I who accuse you," replied a slightly shaken Pilate, surprised that his peasant prisoner spoke and understood Greek. "It is these, your own people," he said, gesturing toward the priests and the crowd, "who say that you proclaim yourself to be their king." Then, lowering his gaze to Jesus' groin, he said, "I am not a Jew, am I? So, Galilean, how do you answer their accusation that you call yourself a king?"

Jesus replied only with his eyes as he continued to stare intently into Pilate's face. Pilate found Jesus' piercing gaze unnerving and hid his anxiety by adjusting the drape of his toga. Caiaphas was also anxious, now fearing that Pilate was about to ask for witnesses as required by Roman law.

"Your Excellency," said the High Priest after a profound bow, "I know you need witnesses, and they exist. Last night, this man stood before the entire high council of our most distinguished elders, including myself and the former high priest Annas, and all of us heard him boldly assert that he was 'the Son of God'!"

At that declaration, the crowd, like a many-headed beast, erupted into thunderously loud howls and shrieks. When they finally subsided, Caiaphas continued, "Along with his seditious crime of claiming to be a king, he blasphemed God by making himself equal to the All Holy One. The Law of Moses states that the penalty for the sin of blasphemy is death. So this prisoner is twice worthy to die on a cross, and...."

"High Priest," Pilate interrupted him, "I respect the judgment of your elders on the Law of Moses and religious issues. However, for the serious accusation of claiming to be a king, I need to hear the testimony of witnesses." Then, addressing the crowd, he said, "Surely, in such a large crowd as this, some Galilean pilgrims are visiting Jerusalem for the Passover. So I ask: Who is willing to testify that this man has claimed to be your king?"

Anxiously, Caiaphas turned around to look at the crowd. Pilate smiled at Lucius, who returned his grin with a generous nod of approval for this clever maneuver. But the crowd remained as quiet as a burial ground as Pilate saw faces in the horde whose lips appeared to be about to speak, but didn't. From both his army and civilian life he was aware of how fear can castrate tongues that possess the truth.

"Galilean pilgrims, do not be afraid to speak. Surely there must be some here who have heard this man speak in your villages or have witnessed his reported good works and healings. I ask you, is this Galilean prisoner guilty or innocent of claiming to be your king?"

Again, only condemning silence came from the crowded courtyard. So Pilate decided to pursue another tactic. "People of Jerusalem and Judea, in this large gathering, is there not someone who recently enthusiastically welcomed this man as a prophet as he rode into your city on a donkey? As your governor, if I am to judge him justly, I need to know what his own people have to say about him. Do you think he is innocent or guilty?"

"Guilty! He's guilty!" shouted the infiltrators in the crowd. Their chant soon spread to others, thus sealing the lips of any who might have been tempted to speak on behalf of Jesus. "He deserves to die on the cross! He's guilty! Guilty! Guilty!" howled the crowd, in a chant that grew louder and louder.

Pilate held up his hand for silence. Instantly the mob obeyed, as if it were a trained circus animal. The crowd became silent not out of respect for Pilate, but because the priests had jerked on the invisible strings of these, their puppets.

Pilate decided to try another legal move. "I shall now ask the prisoner himself to exercise his legal right to defend himself." Looking down, he challenged him, "Jesus of Nazareth, are you guilty or innocent as charged?" Pilate had sat in judgment of numerous criminals before in his life who, when asked, typically and loudly proclaimed their innocence—or pleaded for mercy. This prisoner said nothing. "Rome requires witnesses, and there are none. The accused will not condemn himself, and since Rome does not condemn to death those falsely accused...."

As the crowd interrupted him with loud, ferocious shouts, Pilate's fingers slowly traced across the words *Tiberivs Caesar Divi Avgvsti Filivis* inscribed on the silver denarius. As he touched those words, "Tiberius, Son of the Divine Augustus," he hoped they would bring him the good fortune he needed. Meanwhile, the crowd chanted for Jesus' death.

As Petronius looked out over the bloodthirsty mob, he realized that the individuals in the crowd were incapable of the hideous act of killing this man, so they wanted the Romans to do it. Petronius thought, *Every mob is a collection of cowards who, thinking they're faceless, believe they can kill without guilt, just as soldiers do in battle, without being accused of murder.* The thought of battle caused Petronius to glance down at a jagged scar at the top of his left hand that now rested on the hilt of his sword. The old battle scar was a constant reminder of a bloody hand-to-hand combat he was engaged in years ago. He won by killing the other man, as had happened in so many battles while he was at war. Yet he wasn't guilty for the deaths of the faceless, anonymous foreigners he had killed, because they were the enemies of Rome! The warrior who gave him that scar, however, was not like the others. His dark eyes were filled with terror as they begged Petronius not to kill him—but Petronius had showed him no mercy. Frequently in his dreams he saw those pleading eyes staring at him, and they brought back all the horrors of war—the filth, blood, and grime of the battlefield, and the stench and shrieks of the slaughtered. Looking down at his sword, he was grateful that it had been years since he had to use it, as being a military advisor had freed him from combat in battle. Now, serving in Judea, he felt himself being drawn to observe the Jewish moral code: "You shall not murder." Thus far he had been lucky that he'd never had to test his new resolution against his Roman officer's code.

"He's a blasphemer! Crucify him!" the crowd now began chanting.

"High Priest," Pilate shouted over the racket of the crowd, "if the prisoner is guilty of breaking one of your religious laws, then take him and administer the appropriate punishment yourselves."

"Your Excellency knows," Caiaphas shouted back, "we are a conquered people who lack the authority to crucify! That form of punishment is reserved for Rome, and so solely then to you as Governor!"

The crowd's shouts grew louder. "Crucify him, crucify him!" The words came thundering toward Pilate like a tidal wave and caused him to remember that regrettable riot in Caesarea. Images of it flashed across his mind as swiftly as a flight of birds. Hundreds of Jews from Jerusalem were marching to Caesarea, demanding that he remove the Roman Legion standards bearing the face of Tiberius Caesar. Pilate had hung those standards secretly by night on the walls of the Fortress Antonio, and when the Jews saw them at sunrise, they went into a frenzy. Learning that hordes of Jews were marching on his palace in Caesarea, Pilate ordered his Syrian and Samaritan mercenary soldiers to be disguised as ordinary Judeans who, when the mob arrived, were to be scattered among them. When he repeatedly refused to remove the standards, the mob gathered in front of his palace grew viciously angry and suddenly rushed screaming toward him. Frightened, Pilate had made a fatal mistake: he signaled the mercenaries, who, despising the Judeans, eagerly attack the unarmed crowd, slaughtering many and causing a stampede in which many more were killed.

Maliciously looking down at the High Priest and other priests in front of him, Pilate thought, *They proclaimed their outrage at the slaughter, but secretly, they were delighted!* They had written directly to Emperor Tiberius detailing the entire incident with the numbers of those killed, and they relished telling him how incompetent Pilate was, demanding that he be replaced with a new governor. Tiberius, who was notorious for his violent temper, wrote Pilate an irate official letter reprimanding him for his incompetent handling of the incident. He warned Pilate that since this was the second grave accusation by the Jews of his inability to govern (the first being when the people learned of his covert use of temple funds to build an aqueduct), it was to be the last! The shame of the Emperor's reprimand and his threat of removing him still festered in Pilate's heart.

That memory of the Caesarea riot caused Pilate to fear that this unruly mob might also become so enraged it would rush him. Marcus, sensing that same fear, quickly moved to stand directly behind the curule chair. With a snap of his fingers Pilate signaled Petronius, who raised his right arm, signaling the soldiers stationed along the stone colonnade of the courtyard to draw their swords. The loud racket of their weapons being drawn caused the crowd and the temple authorities to turn toward the soldiers. In the confusion that followed, Lucius leaned over and whispered to Pilate, who nodded in agreement.

As an ocean wave, once it has crested, quickly recedes, so the crowd quickly grew still…either because of the soldiers' display of swords or because of tugs on the strings being pulled by the priests.

Regardless, the mob, while now quieted, was far from peaceful. It was trembling with the primitive energy of a great beast about to pounce.

"This is not a chariot race or gladiator contest!" shouted Pilate. "This is a Roman court of justice! Because of your disruptions, you make it impossible for me to properly question this prisoner. Therefore, I will continue my interrogation in the quiet of the palace."

Caiaphas and the elders, unprepared for this surprise maneuver by Pilate, began arguing among themselves. The crowd was stunned and disappointed that they were now robbed of the spectacle of the trial, and the hired instigators scattered among them waited for a sign from the elders.

"Centurion, escort the Galilean prisoner inside the palace," said Pilate. With a sarcastic smile and a sweep of his hand toward the priests and Sanhedrin elders, he continued, "If any of you wish to join us inside to listen to my interrogation of the prisoner, please be my guests."

The scarlet-cloaked Petronius and four of the Roman legionaries quickly descended the stone stairs, and taking Jesus by the arm, began climbing the steps up to the top of the platform. As they did, Pilate stood to go back inside the palace. As he did, he said quietly, "Lucius, old friend, thank you."

At the sight of the legionaries escorting Jesus up the steps, the crowd angrily stamped their feet and screamed, "Crucify him! Crucify him! Crucify him!"

SCENE VI

THE AUDIENCE HALL
INSIDE KING HEROD'S PALACE

Immediately Afterward

As Pilate stood facing a silent Jesus, he thought, *Although I've judged all manner of thieves, rebels, and mutinous soldiers, this is the first time I've had to judge a man who claims to be divine – a son of a god! This peasant certainly doesn't look like a god – but then, Pilate, you don't believe in the gods anyway, do you?*

Pilate, his arms folded across his chest, stood with his legs spread apart in a stance of power as he and his prisoner stood face to face in the center of the vast audience hall. Although Pilate was in full control, he was ill at ease, and thought, *I find it intimidating to stand face to face with this man. It puts me at a distinct disadvantage to be in a position of equality with someone who is my prisoner.* Whirling around, he started walking toward his chair by the window, saying, "Escort the prisoner to my chair, where I shall continue the trial."

Once Pilate was seated, Jesus, his head erect and his hands still bound by rope, walked over to where Pilate sat. He stood silently in front of him, flanked by two brawny soldiers.

Pilate said, "Personally, Galilean, I don't care a fig about the religious bickering among you Jews regarding who you can or cannot dine with or whether you work on your Sabbath. What *does* concern me is when someone makes an audacious claim that he is a king, because that is a grievous offense against the Emperor Tiberius Caesar. Out there, when I asked you if you were a king, you implied it was others who said that about you. So I will ask you a direct question: Are you, Jesus of Galilee, a king?"

Jesus stood as still as a marble statue. His silence inside the cavernous marbled hall felt louder than the shouts of the crowd outside. Lucius sat patiently with his pen ready, until for Pilate the silence became unbearable.

"Why do you refuse to either affirm your innocence or admit your guilt? Does your silence imply you are indifferent to your fate, or is it an act of defiance against me and the authority of Rome? I ask you again, are you guilty or innocent of the accusation of claiming to be a king?"

In the silence that followed his question, Pilate had the following insight: *The steadfast silence of his prisoner is an act of passive resistance, a muted mutiny against the power of Imperial Rome! He's using the same tactic my spy said he used to confront the power of the Sanhedrin. I'll have to find a way to overcome it.*

"Don't you realize," Pilate demanded, "that as Governor of Judea I have the power to have you crucified? You must be aware of that manner of death. You've seen bandits and rebels nailed on Roman crosses and slowly dying along Galilean roadsides, haven't you?"

Jesus said nothing, his eyes never straying from Pilate's face.

"You have no answer, Galilean? Perhaps you've forgotten; let me refresh your memory. The condemned criminal is stripped naked and his clothes are confiscated, which would be shameful for anyone, but especially for you Jews. Next a nail rips through the flesh of his hands and feet as he is hammered to the cross, and the shock causes him to lose control of his bowels, shaming him even more as he is smeared with his own excrement and urine."

Pilate paused to allow this graphic description to fill his prisoner's mind. Meanwhile, Petronius looked down at the scar on his left hand and thought, *I had to close my eyes when I was assigned to supervise a crucifixion rather than witness the hideous atrocity of such a horrible death.*

As Pilate spoke, Jesus thought, *I don't need Pilate to tell me about the horrors of crucifixion. Since I was a child, I've seen dying Galilean men dangling from Roman crosses countless times. After the Roman general Varus crushed a Galilean revolt led by the rebel Judas, he crucified 2,000 Galileans along our roads to leave a lasting impression on us of the fate of those who attempt to revolt against Rome. Last night, my most painful agony as I prayed in the olive grove was seeing myself hanging on a cross, dying in shame and disgrace.*

"And remember," Pilate's voice catapulted Jesus back to present, "how crucifixions draw crowds eager to indulge in the depraved pleasure of watching the victim's dying torture. Think of the shame of your family to see you so disgraced. Imagine dying from a slow, agonizing suffocation that causes you to cry out loudly in pain."

I will not cry out! Jesus thought. *Whatever suffering is meted out to me, even if it includes dying naked while nailed to a cross, I shall maintain the silence of a man. As a child I learned from my father Joseph how to endure harsh punishment, as did all sons whose fathers followed the ancient law, "As the twig is bent, so grows the tree." As a youth I learned how to silently embrace physical pain so when I was grown I would truly be a man, capable of enduring suffering in stoic silence. I also learned from my father Joseph to obey without hesitating, complaining, asking questions, or knowing why I had to suffer. It was my childhood training in Nazareth that made it possible for me to conquer the temptation last night in the olive grove to run away from the cross by escaping to Galilee.*

"There's more shame after you die," Pilate said, again jerking Jesus back to the present moment, "for another disgrace, the ultimate disgrace, awaits you! You will be denied an honorable burial alongside your dead ancestors, which I know for you Jews is a truly great dishonor. After you're crucified, your body will be dumped into a common trash ditch along with the decaying bodies of executed murderers and robbers, to be feasted upon by wild dogs and birds of prey. Have you heard enough? I ask you again: Are you innocent or guilty?"

As Pilate waited, Jesus silently prayed, *Father, deliver me from the fear of being shamed, so I can obediently accept the death you've decreed for me, regardless of how ugly, painful, or disgraceful it may be.*

Jesus, realizing how his thoughts and prayer had extended the silence after Pilate's question, felt the touch of the Spirit, and he inhaled deeply. In an unemotional voice, he said, "I am not a king! Even a village idiot can see I am only a common peasant! Yet God's Spirit has anointed me a prince, priest, and prophet in my Father's kingdom. I know you will ask, 'Where is that kingdom?' It is here," he tapped his toe on the marble floor, "hidden like a buried treasure, small as a mustard seed."

"Ah, good," said Pilate, clapping his hands together, "the prisoner has found his tongue! I'm delighted, even if I was lost in his mishmash of poetic words. So then, Jesus, in plain Greek, without poetic words or riddles, tell me, where is your kingdom? My centurion Petronius has told me that the long-awaited peaceful kingdom of God you Jews dream about has no kings, slaves, or masters," he said, smiling sarcastically, "and no wars or violence. Where on this earth would I go to find such a kingdom?"

"God's kingdom is not here, yet it is right here this very moment."

"You are more confusing than the Delphi oracle. While I won't even try to unravel that last riddle, am I to understand that you are saying, albeit in a poetic manner, that you are a king?"

"The reason I was born, my destiny, was to testify to the truth. Everyone who belongs to the truth listens to me."

"Ah, truth!" Pilate sarcastically replied. "Tell me, O wise one, what is truth?"

Jesus stared silently at him.

"Has the peasant sage from the Galilean hill country again lost his tongue, or does his silence imply that he doesn't know the answer to my question? Don't answer — it's really not important. As far as I'm concerned, like individual immortality or the existence of the gods, truth is only a vaporous theoretical concept, and trying to understand it is like wrestling with the fog. My tutor Lucius long ago schooled me in the Greek and Roman philosophers who loved to debate such murky subjects for hours and even days on end. But I'm a man of action! I leave philosophical musings to old men too weak for battle or manual labor."

Jesus stood silently and continued to stare at Pilate, which was embarrassing because it made him appear helpless in front of Petronius, Lucius, and Marcus.

"The High Priest and those others," Pilate said, deciding to strike from another direction, "accused you of encouraging the people to reject their ancient religious codes by what you go about teaching in Judea and Galilee...." Pilate stopped short after he said "Galilee," slowly closed his lips, and smiled broadly.

"Petronius, the gods have just given me a gift! Go out at once to Caiaphas and the elders and inform them that their Governor has decided to transfer this trial to its rightful legal venue: The court of the tetrarch of Galilee, Prince Herod Antipas!"

From his scroll Lucius looked up with surprise and then smiled; Petronius frowned with confusion, while Jesus appeared bewildered.

"Petronius, the accused prisoner is a Galilean! As such he is a subject of Prince Herod Antipas, who, fortunately for us, is here in Jerusalem for the Passover Festival. Petronius, inform the High Priest of my decision and, with an armed guard, take our prisoner across the city of Jerusalem to the old Asmonean Palace where Prince Antipas is residing, so he can pass judgment on this subject of his."

SCENE VII

THE SAME

After Petronius Departed with Jesus

"Marvelously ingenious, Pilate," said Lucius, as the door closed behind the departing Jesus and his military escort.

"A gift from the divine Tiberius, Lucius," Pilate said, kissing the image of Tiberius on his silver denarius. "That stroke of genius to have Antipas judge the prisoner almost makes me believe old Tiberius actually is divine."

"I congratulate you for devising a clever solution to your problem. I could feel your struggle as you tried to prevent the prisoner from condemning himself to a cross—yet he appears to have no desire to escape it."

"Yes, it is confounding; he almost seems to *want* to die on a cross. But I'm overjoyed by this stroke of luck from the gods, or as you Greeks say, 'the immortal ones,' that has released me from this convoluted affair."

"You were clever to make Prince Antipas the judge in this case. Not only did you avoid becoming a pawn of the priests, but you simultaneously acknowledged, if not elevated, the status of Prince Herod Antipas. Dear Pilate, you've won a threefold victory."

"Your affirmation means a lot to me, Lucius. I also wonder if I may have given another gift to Herod Antipas, for he is fascinated with magicians and wonder workers, and I know he's been eager to meet this miracle worker of Nazareth. I'm sure his spies have reported to him the stories of Jesus changing water into wine and even, some say, his ability to walk on water!"

"I agree—it doesn't take the Oracle of Delphi to predict that Prince Antipas will ask him to perform some magical tricks."

Pilate called out for Marcus, who opened the door and stepped inside the room.

"Excellency, how can I be of service?"

"Go ask my wife Claudia to join me while I await the prisoner's return."

"Excellency, her maid told me that your wife isn't feeling well and is presently resting. Shall I have her maid awaken her?"

"No, let her rest. I only wanted to tell her about Jesus of Nazareth being here and the charges of insurrection made against him by the priests."

"She already knows, Excellency. She heard the noise of the crowd out in the courtyard, asked her maid what was happening, and was told about the Galilean prisoner. Indeed, Sir, all the household slaves are talking about what happened this morning."

"No secrets in this house, eh, Marcus? Lucius and I will make good use of the time as I wait for the prisoner to return by dictating some letters; that is, if he returns. Antipas may imprison him in the dungeon under the old Asmonean Palace. Whichever way this affair goes, Marcus, I want you to stay nearby, for this is not your usual Friday morning. That's all for now."

After the door closed, Pilate said, "I would add a fourth element, Lucius, to that three-pronged victory of which you spoke. Sending Jesus to Antipas was a tactical maneuver, if I may speak like an old cavalry officer again. By this move I also was able to extend the time that unwashed rabble and those arrogant priests are forced to stand and wait in the sun. Today, time is on my side; this the eve of their Passover Preparation Day, and soon they will need to be on their way home to attend to their detailed preparations for the Passover."

"I'm proud of you, Pilate. Knowing you as I do, I suspect you would have preferred to wade out into the midst of that mob with your sword to teach them some respect for Rome's authority and for Emperor Tiberius Caesar."

"You know me well, Lucius. Yes, my palms itched to take my sword and use it to remind that rowdy rabble who their master is."

"I understand, but as Cicero said, 'Men whose civil capacity is to direct the affairs of the nation render no less important service than those who conduct its wars. Diplomacy in the friendly settlement of controversies is more desirable than courage in settling them on the battlefield.'" With his eyes closed, Lucius recited Cicero's words as if he saw them imprinted on the inside of his closed eyelids.

"Those are inspiring words for an old soldier, Lucius; they feel like a healing balm for my itchiness to resolve conflicts with my sword instead of my mind. I know Cicero is right, yet for me the skill of diplomacy is as slippery as an eel. I know I'm too rash, but since I was a youth I have practiced the dictum, 'Act now; theorize afterward.'"

"But Pilate, I've seen you grow wiser. I know your natural inclination is to resort to physical strength, if not military arms, but Tiberius said...um...."

"Yes, Lucius, continue."

"We all know the Great Tiberius is, uh...complicated; in fact, he has many faces. He requires his governors in the provinces to be strong and never compromise Rome's authority, yet he also says, and I quote, 'A governor should be a good shepherd.'"

"I agree that Tiberius has many sides to him, Lucius. But how do I act like a kindly shepherd to that hostile mob and those scheming priests?"

"I'd best let Cicero answer that," said Lucius, who again closed his eyes as he quoted. "To discover some time in advance what is going to happen, whether for good or ill, and what must be done in any possible event, so as never to be reduced to having to say, 'I hadn't thought of that.'"

"What a wonderful quote! Repeat it, Lucius; I must memorize Cicero's advice."

After Lucius had repeated Cicero's words, Pilate sat quietly thinking and then shared his thoughts. "I can't stop thinking about what went wrong with the arrangement I had with Caiaphas. He told me in advance that some Galilean religious radical was coming to the city for the Passover. We agreed that I wouldn't be involved in how the Council dealt with him, and I oiled his palm with a bribe—in fact, a bigger one than usual."

Then Pilate stood and began silently pacing across the marble floor with his hands linked behind his back as he pondered Cicero's words, "I hadn't thought of that...," inwardly searching for any hidden possibilities in this situation. He stopped and faced Lucius. "At last night's trial our prisoner must have surprised the High Priest by saying something that transformed him from an itinerant Galilean preacher into a dangerous threat to the power of old Caiaphas. It reminds me of the desert ascetic madman named John the bather who was attracting large crowds at the Jordan when I first arrived here. From all reports he was a fanatical mad man."

"To some he may have appeared to be mad," Lucius agreed, "but the spy reports in our archives say the common people considered him a prophet of their god. Great throngs were going to hear him preach and to have their sins forgiven by his ritual bath in the river."

"You'll laugh at this, Lucius, but I think I could have been one of his disciples, since I loved his description of the temple priesthood as 'a nest of poisonous vipers'! What a wonderful description of them: Vipers! I wish I could have called them that this morning." He paused and said, "Lucius, I just thought of something very curious. If this John was so fiercely opposed to the temple priests that he called them vipers to their faces, why didn't they try to have him crucified as they're trying to do with Jesus, who is far less radical?"

Pilate stopped walking near a window so he wouldn't be visible to the crowd. "Out there during the trial, Joseph Caiaphas appeared to be in control of the elders and priests and even of that noisy rabble, yet he seemed as much a prisoner of this affair as I am."

SCENE VIII

THE SAME

Early Afternoon the Same Day

"Your Excellency, I've returned with the prisoner," Petronius said, as he entered the room and saluted. Pilate stood, returned his salute, and then reseated himself. Outside, the sun stood high overhead.

"Returned with him? What was Prince Herod's verdict?"

"None, Sir! He has returned Jesus to you."

"I don't understand. What happened?"

"As soon as we arrived, Antipas ordered that several large water jars be placed in front of the prisoner and asked him to change the water into wine."

"Ah, then what happened?"

"Prince Antipas and all his royal courtiers were hushed in expectation, but Jesus did nothing and only stared at Antipas. Despite repeated orders from the Prince, he refused to perform any kind of magic. Disappointed, Antipas decided to play a game with the prisoner."

"A game?"

"Sir, allow me to show you." Turning, he called out, "Marcus, have the guards bring in the Galilean prisoner."

"What a transformation!" exclaimed an astonished Pilate, upon seeing Jesus now dressed in a dazzling white robe. "Our village carpenter now actually looks like a king! But go on."

"Well, Sir, we weren't alone when I presented Jesus to King Antipas. When Caiaphas heard that the prisoner was being sent to Antipas, he had a group of priests and elders follow us there. They repeated to Prince Antipas the various religious crimes of the prisoner and their accusation that he claimed to be King of the Jews. Upon hearing that accusation, Antipas burst into laughter, as did all his royal court."

"Old Antipas is a fox, all right; it was very clever of him to make a joke out of that treasonous charge of kingship."

"Sir, Antipas then asked the prisoner if he were a king; and as he did with you, Jesus silently refused to either deny or affirm the accusation. I had the feeling that Prince Antipas, being surrounded by his royal court, found this prolonged silence of Jesus intimidating, so decided to gain the upper hand. To assert his control, he ordered one of his own regal robes be brought to him, and then ordered his attendants to robe Jesus in it. The sight of Jesus attired as a king provoked much hilarity among his court. Herod Antipas let the joke play out until all had grown tired of it, and then he ordered me to return the prisoner in his kingly robe to you."

"But didn't Antipas pronounce any verdict on him at all?"

"None, Sir. His refusal to do so greatly distressed the priests and elders, who quickly departed ahead of us and rushed back to inform Caiaphas what had happened. But while the priests left empty-handed, I didn't! Before we left, Antipas ordered an attendant to retrieve something for him; then he called me up to his throne and gave me this." Petronius placed in Pilate's hand an exquisite ivory carving of the god Apollo encircled with large pearls. "As he gave it to me, Antipas said, 'This is a gift for my good friend, Pontius Pilate.'"

"It's beautiful, Petronius, and very precious; it must be worth a fortune. However, the gift I would have preferred was a verdict of guilty or innocent!"

"Sir," Lucius said quietly, "the Prince may actually have given you a gift by *not* pronouncing him guilty! If he had, wouldn't you, as governor, had to crucify him?"

"Yes, that's true." Pilate thought a moment. "The act of costuming a peasant so-called king in the splendorous robes of a real king is typically Oriental, yet I'm curious. Prisoner, why do you think Prince Antipas robed you thus?"

Jesus, his face devoid of any expression stood as still and silent as a statue. While he remained mute, inside he was raging. *I'm shamed to my bones to be dressed up as an object of ridicule. As God's chosen one, I expected to suffer, yet I never imagined the intense agony of humiliation when, by being dressed in Antipas' robe, I was made into a fool. I wear no silk robe but one of painful, galling mortification.*

In the face of Jesus' silence, Pilate said, "Since the prisoner refuses to speak, I will ask you, Petronius; what do you think was his purpose in costuming the prisoner like this?"

Petronius replied, "Since I've been stationed here, I've learned that these Judaic people dread shame more than they do death and are always on their guard against any possible loss of honor. One possibility is that Antipas dressed the prisoner in one of his own kingly robes to shame him, as it surely must have, or...." He paused briefly. "Or maybe the Prince did it to taunt and shame the priests and elders."

"Brilliantly decoded, Petronius! You know these Jewish people well. Yes, the old Fox must have been taunting those Temple priests, not with words but with regal symbols that screamed loudly at the Temple hierarchy, 'I know you secretly want to be ruled by your own Jewish king and not by some puppet prince like myself, and especially not by any Roman Caesar. So here, Temple priests and elders, I present to you your long-desired King of the Jews!' I wish I could have seen their faces."

"Sir," Lucius commented, "besides giving you that ivory carving, the Prince could have given you another gift by making the accused prisoner into a kind of a clown—a fool king."

"Go ahead, Lucius—you've got my attention. Explain to me how Antipas gifted me by returning the prisoner dressed like this?"

"Could it be, Sir, that the prince was cleverly transforming the deadly serious tragedy of Jesus' trial into a laughing farce...."

"Sir, I believe Lucius is right," said Petronius. "Having Jesus made into a fool can be of great assistance to you. In their holy writings, the Jews are admonished to be compassionate to the poor, the orphan, and the weak minded! The Prince's hidden gift may be the notion that if an illiterate, common peasant laborer claims he is the King of the Jews, then he must be crazy!"

"Wonderful, Petronius! Fools are to be pitied, not crucified. The Roman Empire crucifies rebels, not the insane, does it not?"

"Yes, and I know there's additional support for your defense. While in Galilee, I heard that because Jesus had become a poor wandering teacher and because of the things he was saying, his own family thought he was out of his mind and came to take charge of him. Added to that, the scribes themselves publicly called him mad, saying he was possessed by a demon."

"That is supporting evidence indeed, if any is needed of the state of mind of a peasant carpenter-stonemason with dirty fingernails who thinks he's Caesar. Yet while we discuss the fate of our prisoner, he remains silent; has he gone deaf as well as mad?"

"He hears you, Sir," said Petronius. "His refusal to speak could be his attempt to live out another prophecy about the Expected One, or 'Messiah,' who is predicted to come save Israel."

"I've heard that name Messiah before, but what does it mean?"

"The title is ambiguous. I've heard some say he will be a savior king and a great military commander who will come leading heavenly armies, while others say he will be a gentle prince of peace. Among those predictions is one that says he will be as silent as a lamb when he is approaching his sacrificial death. By his silence, he could be attempting to live out that prediction—but perhaps you should ask him?"

"Jesus, even if the prophets said you wouldn't speak, I, Pontius Pilate, now order you to do so. If you're thinking of not speaking, do not forget that I have the power to set you free or to send you to your death on a cross."

Suddenly breaking his silence, Jesus said, "The only power you have comes from above! You have no power to set me free from dying on a cross, for God has willed it!" Raising his voice, he continued, "The ancient prophesies of my death will be fulfilled! You, Pilate, are no more able to prevent my death on a cross than you are to prevent the sun from setting at the end of this day! You and Caiaphas are merely actors playing out your assigned roles in a drama written ages ago by the All Holy One, even if you don't wear the masks and costumes of Greek performers. Oh, I know about your pagan theatrical plays, for years ago I worked on repairing the Greek amphitheater in a village near Nazareth, and in this particular prophetic drama, fate has cast you, Pilate, in the role of the villain! You are impotent to rewrite what has been decreed."

"You are wrong, Jesus of Galilee," Pilate replied, recovering his composure after being taken aback by his prisoner's sudden outburst and the authority with which he spoke. "I am not impotent! Here in Judea; I, Governor Pontius Pilate, decree what will or will not occur! We have delayed long enough over this religious gibberish about what your prophets have said and what your god decrees; it is time we go out and confront the High Priest and his motley rabble. Petronius, the prisoner shall remain dressed in Antipas' regal robe as we go out to the High Priest; I plan to use his majestic attire to my advantage."

SCENE IX

THE STONE PLATFORM
IN FRONT OF THE PALACE

After Pilate Presents Jesus to the Courtyard Multitude

As if someone had stolen their tongues, the raucous crowd immediately fell silent when they saw Jesus attired in the stunning white robe. Pilate took special pleasure in seeing their shock, and pointing to Jesus, he shouted, "Judeans; behold your king! Your own Prince Herod Antipas, after having heard the accusations made against him, has sent him back to you dressed in this royal robe."

It was then that Pilate noticed a lavish litter with drawn curtains at the end of the southern colonnade of the courtyard. He knew that it belonged to the previous high priest, Annas. Ten years before Pilate came to Judea, his predecessor, Governor Valerius Gratus, had deposed Annas from his office as high priest. Apparently while Pilate had been inside the palace waiting for Jesus' return, Annas had come personally to observe how his son-in-law Joseph Caiaphas was handling the trial. His presence removed any doubt that Annas was the hidden instigator of the plot to have Jesus crucified. Although he was no longer the high priest, among the temple elite he was the acknowledged leader of the Sadducee party and continued to control the Temple priesthood.

"People of Jerusalem and of all Judea," said Pilate, after sitting in his imperial curule chair, "this prisoner, being a Galilean, is a subject of the tetrarch of Galilee, Prince Antipas. Thus I sent him to be judged by the Prince, who, after hearing that the prisoner was charged with claiming kingship, has found him *not guilty!*"

Like the rumble of far-off thunder, the crowd began to object and then erupted into a great roar. Looking down at Caiaphas, Pilate thought, *I can tell by his composure that this was hardly news to Caiaphas, but he's taking it very calmly; he must have a new tactic planned to spring on me. And I don't like surprise attacks.*

"People of Jerusalem and Passover pilgrims," Pilate said, as he secretly rubbed his silver denarius, "this prisoner is clearly not sane in claiming to be King of the Jews. If he really is a king, where are his legions to defend him? Why haven't his loyal Jewish subjects rushed here to rescue him? Prince Herod Antipas, by his robing this Galilean peasant as a king, has loudly declared his judgment that this man is an imbecile and therefore not guilty, and I concur with his judgment. Rome is a civilized empire; it does not crucify the feeble-minded. Thus, in the name of the Emperor Tiberius Caesar, as Governor of Judea, I declare this prisoner not guilty by reason of insanity."

Pilate had prepared himself for the reaction he surmised would follow his judgment of not guilty, and he sat serenely—almost regally—as the temple priests signaled their agitators.

On signal, the crowd thundered loudly, "Crucify him! Crucify him! Crucify him!"

"Why should this man be crucified?" asked Pilate, when their shouts finally subsided. "Based on my reports, he goes about doing a great deal of good: healing the sick, feeding the hungry...."

The crowd interrupted Pilate and continued their chant of "Crucify him! Crucify him!" Some began wildly shaking their walking staffs in the air, and others started to stomp their feet. Pilate grew fearful that the mob was on the edge of a bloody civil riot, which awakened a memory of another riot: *This reminds me of when I wanted to build a Roman aqueduct to bring fresh water to Jerusalem, as the Roman emperors had channeled water through aqueducts to Rome for the fountains. I needed money to pay for it, and so I made a secret deal with Caiaphas to temporarily appropriate funds from the Temple treasury, which I would replace with money from taxes. My intent to built my aqueduct with Temple money was — not by accident, I'm sure — discovered by the people, resulting in a massive anti-Roman disturbance, for which I was reported to the Emperor.*

"Excellency," Quintus whispered in Pilate's ear, recalling him to the present, "your wife Claudia has sent you this message: 'Avoid condemning the Galilean healer. My voices have told me he's innocent. I'm praying to the gods for you, Pilate.'"

Pilate thought, *Claudia's message is troubling; I've learned not to disregard her intuition. The day before I was appointed Governor of Judea, her voices told her it would be so. Is her intuition today a message to me from the gods?*

As the chanting of the mob thundered in Pilate's ears, he pondered Claudia's warning, *Still, I must do something to prevent this trial from turning into a riot, or it will end my career. I must act quickly to drain the venom from this many-headed beast before it attacks me!*

Lucius, leaning over to him, and whispered, "Sir, flogging the prisoner might satisfy this blood-thirsty mob."

Pilate, nodding, remembered that scourging often replaced crucifixion; because it was so agonizingly painful, being flogged in itself often was considered adequate punishment. He proclaimed, "You the people have unanimously judged this man guilty and are demanding that he be punished. And so I sentence the prisoner to a punishment so excruciating it is forbidden to be used on Roman citizens and is reserved for criminals and runaway slaves. I hereby order that the prisoner be scourged so you all can witness it."

The many-tongued beast yelped with glee as Caiaphas and the elders huddled to consult about this new twist in the trial.

SCENE X

THE SAME

The Soldiers Prepare to Scourge Jesus

"Centurion," ordered Pilate, "bring the prisoner here, have your soldiers strip him of his kingly robe, and then flog him until I give the signal to stop!"

Reluctantly, Petronius obeyed, recalling how Jesus had healed his favorite slave. Jesus was quickly stripped of his white robe by the Syrian and Samaritan mercenary soldiers, leaving him naked except for a small loincloth. Another soldier rolled a large wooden barrel in front of Pilate and forced Jesus to bend over it. Two soldiers firmly held Jesus' arms in front of him as a burly Syrian soldier stepped forward. With a whip made of leather lashes tipped with bits of bone and lead, he began flogging Jesus. The mob responded with wild hoots and jeers as a stoic-faced Petronius counted each blow.

By the time he reached, "twenty, twenty-one, twenty-two..." streams of blood were trickling down Jesus' back. As Pilate watched the prisoner's blood form an expanding pool on the stone pavement in front of him, he thought, *It's the very likeness of that bloody omen I saw this morning in my shaving bowl. O Jupiter, Father of the gods, I pray that the omen I saw at dawn today was only a portent of this flogging, and not one of anything worse to come.*

Jesus, with tightly shut eyes and gritted teeth, prayed as each strike of the lash took a bite out of his flesh, *O Father, seal my lips so I'll not cry out in agony.*

"Thirty...thirty-one...thirty-two...." Petronius counted more and more slowly as the Syrian soldier flogging Jesus grew weary. Before ordering another man take his place, Petronius glanced pleadingly over at Pilate, whose face remained as expressionless as that of Emperor Tiberius on a denarius.

"You, soldier," ordered Petronius, pointing to the one holding Jesus' right arm. "Take the place of this Syrian, and continue the prisoner's punishment."

The soldiers exchanged places, and the flogging of Jesus resumed. When the count reached, "thirty-nine…forty…forty-one…," Pilate calculated how ruthless he should make the scourging. It was the custom that it shouldn't be too severe if, after the flogging, the condemned man was to be crucified, because he needed to be able to carry his crossbeam. If, on the other hand, the flogging was to be the only punishment, then it had to be properly brutal to fit the crime and to satisfy the crowd. As Pilate looked into the eyes of the mob in front of him, he saw only a greedy lust for more torture, not any pity for the bleeding prisoner. *Horace spoke the truth,* Pilate thought, *this is indeed "a many-headed beast," and one whose appetite for inflicting pain is insatiable. We Romans have always detested mobs – the unwashed rabble of the masses. This mob of Jews is no different from other mobs I've seen in Rome.*

"Forty-eight…forty-nine…fifty…." At "fifty," Pilate raised his hand and snapped his fingers. Instantly the flogging ceased.

"Please, sir," begged a Syrian soldier, who knelt on one knee before Petronius, "may we have your permission to honor this prisoner as befits a king?"

Petronius turned to Pilate, who nodded his consent. As an old army officer, Pilate knew about the wretched game in which a captured enemy was comically and sadistically mocked as a king. *It's harmless play,* thought Pilate, *a release of tension for soldiers who often have to obey unreasonable orders given by inept officers. And in this case it may help gratify the mob.*

Two soldiers lifted the stunned, bleeding prisoner up off the barrel and sat him on a wooden stool that was quickly brought forward. Another soldier draped a tattered red military cloak around Jesus' bleeding shoulders. Then a Samaritan mercenary came forward with a crown he had woven out of thorn branches during the flogging. The crown was jammed on top of Jesus' head in a clownish imitation of the green laurel wreaths worn by the Caesars. The crowd clapped and loudly roared its approval of the humiliating coronation, delighting in this unexpected military comic theater that added to the shaming of the prisoner. Then one by one the soldiers knelt in front of Jesus and slapped him or spit in his face as they repeatedly shouted, "Hail to the King of the Jews! Hail to the Caesar of the Jews!"

After several minutes, Pilate snapped his fingers and the game ended abruptly, causing the mob to hiss and boo. They were not the only ones who were disappointed; the hired foreign mercenaries in Roman army uniforms didn't want their game to end, either. Being Samaritans and Syrians, they had taken great pleasure in scourging and mocking a Judean. With the game over, Petronius ordered the soldiers to take Jesus, wearing the crown of thorns and the red military cloak, to stand next to Pilate's chair.

Pilate stood up, extended his right hand toward Jesus, and loudly proclaimed, "Behold the man!"

A semi-naked Jesus stood before them, blood trickling down his forehead from the crown of twisted thorn branches and a wilted bent reed that served as a comic scepter stuck in his bound hands. At the sight of his blood-splattered, bruised body, the mob responded with screaming taunts. As they screamed, Pilate thought, *Even naked and flogged, this man stands before this mob as regal as any king! He shows the same strength as the bloodied gladiators who endured pain and even defeat with dignity in the Roman Coliseum.*

Looking down at Caiaphas and the elders, Pilate said, "I have had the prisoner flogged for no other crime than being insane! I have had him brutally punished and ridiculed to satisfy your desire for blood, and now I shall obey your own god's commandment, 'You shall not kill!' Therefore, I...."

Caiaphas shouted, "Moses also commanded that those guilty of blasphemy must die!"

On cue, the mob chanted, "Crucify him! Crucify him!"shaking their fists in the air.

"High Priest, why must he be crucified?"

"Excellency, this Galilean commoner claims he is a king, and we Judean people have only one king, the great Caesar Tiberius! If you allow this criminal to go free, you, Pontius Pilate, are *no friend of Caesar!*"

Quickly the mob seized upon the condemning indictment of the High Priest and began to chant, "No friend of Caesar! No friend of Caesar!" As that damning denunciation grew louder, Pilate studied the pavement at his feet so that no one could see the fear in his eyes. Caiaphas had shot his sharpest arrow at Pilate's Achilles heel — the allegation of being complicit in treason against the Emperor. No more lethal or perilous accusation could be made against any Roman governor than that he was "no friend of Caesar." To permit anyone to be king other than the Emperor, especially one as unpredictable as Tiberius Caesar, was to forfeit forever that coveted political title, "friend of Caesar."

Pilate's mind quickly explored the consequences of that accusation. *When I was appointed governor, I became a 'friend of Caesar' and entered into the inner circle of those whom Tiberius favors. Anyone who is no longer in his favor is ejected from that chosen circle, and they might as well be dead. I have two options; I can condemn this man to be crucified, or since he is innocent, I can do the right thing and release him. But to free him isn't a realistic choice, even if I use the justifiable grounds that he's insane; any pretender, sane or crazy, is a living threat to the Emperor.* Squeezing his denarius tightly, Pilate thought, *It's suicidal not to crucify him. What am I to do?*

A small voice from the left side of his head said, "Pilate, your political career has just begun, and it's far more important than the fate of this insignificant Galilean peasant. Don't forget that Rome does not tolerate the anarchy of mob violence; public order and the good of the majority take unquestioned precedence over the life of a common peasant."

Another small voice from the right side of his head said, "Pilate, remember the law; as a Roman judge, you possess the authority, if you deem it necessary, to legally adjourn a trial until proper witnesses can be summoned."

As Pilate anguished over which of these two voices to obey, he heard a faint third voice whisper, "Remember the old Roman law: Should a judge discern that the present venue of a trial isn't suitable for a proper and just hearing, he has the legal power to transfer the site of the trial to another place." Pilate's heart jumped with excitement, and he was convinced that this third voice had come directly from the gods. *Yes,* he thought, *I have the authority to transfer this trial of the Galilean to Caesarea, where I can question the prisoner in a proper setting.*

Meanwhile, the mob, having grown impatient, was chanting even louder. Over the racket, Pilate shouted, "Petronius, go tell High Priest Caiaphas that I wish to speak to him privately."

Pilate then instructed Lucius and Marcus to move back so he could speak privately with Caiaphas, and he had the soldiers move Jesus a short distance away. A plump, round-faced Caiaphas, holding up the hem of his robes, slowly mounted the stairs and stopped one step below the platform where Pilate sat. Then the two men leaned forward slightly to confer.

"Joseph," said Pilate, in a quiet, almost intimate voice, "why do you and your priests provoke these people into demanding that this prisoner must die? He's already dead. He's been completely discredited as a sage and teacher of the people by being so publicly shamed. He has lost all his influence among the common people; he's no longer a threat to you!"

"More is required!" whispered Caiaphas. "Annas has decreed that he must be silenced permanently, and the only way to do that is by a death so ugly that it will forever tarnish the memory of him and his teachings!"

"Why? Are your priests and elders jealous of his ability to draw hundreds to listen to him teach about your god? I assure you, this man has ceased to be a thorn in your sides."

"Annas demands that he be crucified! Any decision other than the cross is not in my hands." Caiaphas turned to descend the steps.

"Wait, Caiaphas. You and Annas want him dead, and I assure you he *will* die, only not today and not here in Jerusalem. I intend to use my legal authority to move the site of this trial to my residence at Caesarea, where I can conduct his trial without the risk of a riot. Trust me, Caiaphas, and don't voice any opposition to my transfer of this trial to Caesarea. As for Annas, I know he's orchestrating this entire affair from behind the scenes. However, we both know that mobs like this one can't always be controlled. I'm sure neither of you want this Passover of yours to be spoiled by bloody riots. I shall silence this Galilean as Annas desires, but I will do it my own way, not on the eve of Passover in Jerusalem."

"Your solution seems best," replied Caiaphas, cautiously, "especially since, as you say, it's the eve of the Passover, but I'll have to consult with Annas...."

"We don't have time! Besides, think of your image in the eyes of this large crowd; you don't want to appear to be a puppet of your father-in-law, do you?"

Caiaphas anxiously glanced over at the curtained litter of Annas, and then turned back to Pilate. "You're right; I can't be seen obtaining permission from Annas publicly. It's risky to irritate him, but.... Very well, Pilate, I agree with your plan."

"Good. Now, I've thought through this affair, and as on the battlefield, we need a misleading maneuver to distract the enemy. As it happens, three rebel bandits who have been condemned to be crucified are being held in prison; we can disguise one of them as Jesus, so the people will believe it is the Galilean who is being crucified. Don't frown—it's a plausible deception. The prisoner isn't that recognizable here in Jerusalem. Didn't you have to use a traitor disciple of his to identify him so he could be arrested? Trust me, I've thought this through. I'll have the selected rebel scourged, and he'll wear the crown of thorns the Galilean wore. I'll also give strict orders to my soldiers to keep all spectators a good distance away from the three crosses on Mount Calvary."

"But Pilate, surely his disciples will notice that their Jesus isn't the one being crucified!"

"My spies have reported that all of his closest disciples have already fled Jerusalem with their tails between their legs. None of them will be here to actually witness his crucifixion and so they, along with everyone else, will assume that Jesus was one of the three men crucified."

"Yes, but I'm afraid...."

"Don't be! To ensure the success of our deception, I'll delay the march of the condemned prisoners to Calvary until late afternoon. By that hour, the majority of the crowd will be hurrying home to prepare for the Passover."

"Well, it seems as though you've thought of every detail, but there's another factor to consider. We've heard reports that this Jesus predicted he would be raised from the tomb after his death."

"There will be no tomb, Joseph. I intend to follow the custom of dumping the corpses of rebels in the smoldering trash ravine outside the city walls. Wild dogs and birds of prey will see to it there is no body to resurrect! Caiaphas, the Galilean will no longer cause you, Annas, or your elders any more trouble, but," he paused and looked directly into Caiaphas' eyes, "I'll dispose of him my way."

The two men continued to speak in hushed whispers, and then, leaning back, Pilate said, "Trust me, Joseph, my way is best. You have my pledge: Jesus of Galilee will die! Now go and tell your elders and priests that I'm taking the prisoner away to his death."

Caiaphas nodded, turned, and began to descend the steps when Pilate quickly added, "Caiaphas!" The priest stopped and turned around. "Don't forget our agreement! No letters to the Emperor Tiberius, and none to the Syrian Legate Vitellius, or else...!" Caiaphas nodded, turned, and with great dignity descended the steps to the priests and elders.

"People of Jerusalem!" shouted Pilate, as the priests and scribes huddled around Caiaphas. "You have spoken, and I consent to your will and that of the Sanhedrin." A hush fell over the crowd as Pilate glanced toward the former high priest Annas' drawn curtained litter. Pilate continued, "I condemn to death this prisoner named Jesus of Nazareth! He is to be crucified with two rebel bandits this day!"

With an enormous roar the mob shouted its approval of this verdict. Then, glancing up in the sky, they saw that the sun was now in the far western sky. Since the trial had dragged on for so long, the day was now far gone. Quickly, like water running out of a sieve, they began departing the courtyard for their homes to prepare for the Seder rituals before sunset.

"Centurion," ordered Pilate, "have the legionaries escort the prisoner back inside the palace."

SCENE XI

INSIDE THE GREAT HALL
OF KING HEROD'S PALACE

Upon the Return of Pilate and Jesus to the Great Hall

Inside Herod's marbled great hall opposite the tall windows, Pilate stood with Petronius beside him. Lucius was seated on his secretarial stool, and a short distance away from them was Jesus, surrounded by four guards. "Excellency, I know you were trapped," said Petronius. "I'm sure it wasn't easy to condemn an innocent and good man to the cross."

"Ah, but I escaped the trap, Petronius," beamed Pilate, as he seated himself. "The gods smiled on me out there. The prisoner is not going to die," he said, pausing theatrically, "at least not today! I made a deal with the High Priest to transfer his trial to Caesarea!"

"You can't!" screamed Jesus with such fierceness that, in spite of his wounds, he was able to break free from the grip of his guards. "You fool," he yelled as he rushed toward Pilate, his two bound hands raised high above his head as if he was about to bring them down on Pilate's head. "You must crucify me today!"

Petronius shouted, the guards scrambled to seize hold of Jesus, and Marcus leapt in front of Pilate, accidentally knocking Lucius off his stool onto the floor.

"You must crucify me!" shouted Jesus, as he struggled to break loose from the four guards restraining him. "I must die here, in Jerusalem, just as the prophets foretold...."

"Silence him," shouted Petronius, as one soldier placed his hand over Jesus' mouth.

Shouting through the guard's fingers, Jesus said, "Isaiah foretold, 'He will be pierced for our sins, though he did no wrong...the Lord was pleased to crush him.' And I myself prophesied to my disciples that I'd be handed over to evil men, and...."

As the soldier pressed his hand even more firmly over Jesus' mouth, he jerked his head backward and broke loose of the soldier's hand, continuing, "And on the third day I would rise from the grave." Petronius shouted at another soldier, who then clamped his hand tightly on top of the other soldier's hand, finally silencing Jesus.

Pilate said with a grin, "Prophet of Galilee, now that my men have stopped your ranting, kindly allow me, your savior, to say a few words. First, regarding your prediction to your disciples, I fear your muse has once again misinformed you; in three days you'll arise not from a tomb but from a sleeping pad in your prison cell in Caesarea!" Securely held by the guards, the muted Jesus could now only defiantly shake his head in denial. "As for those old Jewish prophets you quoted, it seems they must have been thinking of another Jew instead of you." Shaking his finger as if to a naughty child, he said, "Whatever happened to Jesus the meek? You're actually shaking with anger! You surprise me—for a teacher who is renowned for his nonviolence, you're boiling with rage. You're also very ungrateful. In the past, whenever I pardoned men who were condemned to die, they always wept with gratitude."

By mustering all his will power, Jesus forced himself to drain his heart of the anger that raged there, and he stopped struggling with his guards.

Pilate said, "I see the prisoner has gained control of himself. Guards, release your hands from his mouth, but keep his arms secure. If he begins to rant again, silence him!"

"Pilate, I beg you to allow the Scriptures to be fulfilled and crucify me," Jesus said, in an anguished voice. "For the world to be redeemed, I must die as a sacrificial victim on the cross. God has spoken of me through the prophets, saying, 'He surrendered himself to death and shall take away the sins of many.'"

As he stood before Jesus with his hands on hips and his elbows extended outward, Pilate said, "Notice, Petronius, how our silent sacrificial lamb has found his lost tongue. I confess, never before have I met anyone so eager to die, especially on a cross!"

Falling to his knees on the marble floor in front of Pilate, Jesus said, "Please, Governor, I beg you to order that I be executed today, along with the other men you spoke of. Since the beginning of the world my sacrificial death has been destined to occur today; it is God's will!"

Pilate replied, "Oh, you *will* die—but I, not some god, will decide the day and place of your death."

"No!" Jesus retorted. "It must be today—I must die as a Passover sacrifice, carrying upon myself all the sins of the people; it is God's will...."

Pilate interrupted, "Ah, but it's not my will! And here in Judea, it is *my* will that is done."

Jesus silently slumped his shoulders in despair. With brisk military authority, Pilate ordered, "Petronius, go down to the dungeon, where you will find three rebel prisoners I have condemned to be executed. Select one of them who is about the same stature as the Galilean and have your soldiers scourge him, and then place on his head the same crown of thorns worn by our prisoner here."

A bewildered Petronius replied, "Sir, I don't understand the reason for your command, but it shall be done."

Pilate continued, "And, Petronius, this is extremely critical: Post some soldiers along the route to Cavalry and have them keep all spectators a good distance away from the three condemned men, so that Jesus' substitute will not recognized."

"Substitute?" asked Petronius.

"Forgive me, Petronius. In my haste and excitement I forgot to fill you in on my little Passover hoax. Out there on the platform the gods gifted me with the idea for a deceptive maneuver by which Jesus will be secretly transported to Caesarea instead of being crucified today!"

"To Caesarea?" asked a wide-eyed Petronius.

Pilate then explained his plan to Petronius and Lucius and noted how he managed to convince Caiaphas to go along with it. After they marveled at his ingenuity and congratulated him on his inspired plan, Pilate resumed giving orders. "You also have a part in my plot, Lucius. I need you to prepare a wooden board with my execution order. In Greek, Latin and Hebrew, you shall inscribe on it, 'Jesus of Nazareth, King of the Jews.' Then," Pilate said, smiling at Jesus, "give it to Petronius so his men can nail it to the top of the cross of the *real* scapegoat."

"Eloi, Eloi, lema sabachthani!" Jesus wailed, again falling to his knees.

Pilate asked, "Petronius, what's he saying?"

"Sir, he's calling out in his native Aramaic, 'My God, my God, why have you forsaken me?'"

"In Aramaic? Doesn't his god understand Greek or Latin?" Turning to Jesus, Pilate said, "Clearly, if your god does exist, he has deserted you! You've been rescued like a crippled bird from the paws of a hungry cat, not by any act of your god, but by the ingenuity of a pagan."

"Eloi, Eloi, lema sabachthani!" Jesus screamed even louder.

"Guards, take the prisoner to a cell in the dungeon until it is time to move him to Caesarea. I want two of you to stand guard outside his cell and the other two inside. You are to guard the prisoner constantly to prevent him from taking his own life, as he appears determined to die today."

As the four soldiers moved to drag Jesus out of the room, Pilate shouted, "And soldiers: Hear me!" They stopped and turned toward him. "No harm of any kind is to come to this prisoner, and I won't have you playing any more of your little games with him. If you violate my orders, I'll have you flogged seven times longer than he was himself. I repeat: No harm or abuse shall come to him unless I personally order it."

The guards nodded their understanding and then removed Jesus, who had resumed kicking and screaming in protest. Pilate said, "Quintus, go at once to Lady Claudia and tell her that she and I are departing tonight to return to Caesarea, and that I will explain all this to her later. Also inform her that the Jewish healer from Galilee will be going to Caesarea with us. And Quintus, this is important: Tell her to keep my plans for the prisoner a secret. Then supervise the household slaves as they pack our belongings for our return trip to Caesarea." Quintus bowed and departed.

"Marcus, have my curule chair properly packed for transport back to Caesarea. After that, supervise the packing of the gods of our family shrine and all of my personal items."

Marcus bowed and left. Pilate said to Lucius and Petronius, "I'm almost drunk with glee over the inspired way I resolved the dilemma of the Galilean's fate — not to mention my own. Now that we're alone, old comrades, let me tell you more about the magnificent gift I was given by the gods."

Raising his Roman denarius to his lips, Pilate kissed it twice, saying, "My good fortune must have been a gift from the divine Tiberius. As I was rubbing his image on this very denarius, I recalled that I had the legal authority to move the trial to Caesarea. The only snag was convincing old Caiaphas, but thanks be to the gods I was able to make a deal with the High Priest to transfer the prisoner's trial."

"Excellency," said Lucius, "that was an inspired idea, but I'm concerned about what will happen if the Emperor hears of this case of a Galilean pretender king."

Pilate replied, "I made Caiaphas promise that no letters would be sent to the Emperor or to Vitellius, and he knows if that happens I will depose him from the high priesthood just as my predecessor, Governor Gratus, deposed his father-in-law Annas."

"But Sir," added Lucius, "what about today's report to Rome, which will contain the account of his trial and the accusation of him claiming to be a king, and...."

"Lucius, that's the next critical step in our scheme. After completing the indictment board of the cross for the prisoner's stand-in, you must carefully edit out of today's report any reference to the charge that the prisoner called himself 'King of the Jews.' You needn't have any qualms about doing so; no evidence or witnesses were ever presented to support that accusation. Let the record of the trial reflect only the religious charges made against the prisoner."

"I shall edit the trial records as you've ordered."

"Good. And I shall write a personal letter to the Emperor to accompany the report, in which I'll tell him about the trial in very broad terms. I'll explain that because Jerusalem was in a very incendiary state, I moved the trial and the prisoner to Caesarea to avert any possible riots. I'm sure Tiberius will approve of that prudence."

"Yes, Sir. But with your permission...."

"No permission is required, Lucius—go ahead."

"I salute your creative solution and am pleased that the mob didn't succeed in pressuring you to act contrary to your conscience. You showed yourself to be a true statesman and not a politician. However...."

"However what, Lucius?"

"Having known you since you were a child, I suspect you have a secret motive for changing the venue of the trial. Otherwise, why would you risk your political career to save the life of some peasant?"

"Ah, Lucius, will I ever to be able to fool you?" Pilate replied, smiling. "I confess; I moved the trial to Caesarea to delay judging the Galilean so I can spend some more time with him. It is amazing, isn't it, that I—Pontius Pilate, of all people—should find a peasant Jew fascinating and desire to have further conversations with him?"

"Just as I suspected," said a nodding, smiling Lucius.

"Sir," said Petronius, "we know the Emperor has spies here in Jerusalem and in Judea. What if they report back to him about a crucified rebel whose execution order said, 'Jesus of Nazareth, king of the Jews?'"

"I've also thought of that, Petronius. If it should happen, I intend to inform the Emperor that the name of Jesus is a common one in this Judean Province, and pretender kings like this man characteristically pop up at almost every Passover." Lucius smiled with pride that Pilate had so well assimilated the wisdom of Cicero. "I'll tell the Emperor that the prisoner I brought to Caesarea and the rebel bandit crucified in Jerusalem were not the same man—which will be the truth!"

"Sir, you have foreseen every possibility," said a smiling Petronius. "I ask you now to excuse me, for I must attend to the details of the bandits' execution and our departure after sunset for Caesarea."

"Good. I want to depart once the Jews have begun to celebrate the Passover and slip through the main western gate just north of here; we should go unnoticed, because no decent Jew will be out on the streets tonight. In case anyone *is* out, Petronius, see to it that the prisoner is bound and gagged and transported under guard inside a carruca, one of our leather-covered wagons, so he will not be seen by anyone."

"Excellent idea, Sir."

"So the carruca carrying the prisoner doesn't draw any attention, we shall include in the convoy three other wagons. You can fill them with household articles and my curule chair. Lady Claudia will travel in her curtained litter with a military escort of my personal bodyguard of Roman legionaries. I shall lead the caravan on horseback at the head of a cavalry detail of our most trusted Syrian troops."

"Yes, Sir," Petronius saluted. "All shall be as you have ordered. I'll be eager for us to be on our way."

"Ah, but Petronius, you will not be accompanying us tonight! I wish you to be my deputy here in Jerusalem and command the garrison at the Fortress Antonio."

A stunned Petronius dropped his head to hide his bitter disappointment, and Lucius graciously looked the other way to save him from embarrassment.

"I know you would prefer to go with us because you've been so deeply involved in this entire affair with the prisoner, but I must have a prudent and trusted military officer in command of the city during Passover. After the Passover is over you can return to Caesarea with the troops we brought here for the festival." Placing his hand on Petronius' shoulder, he said, "My friend, your return to me will not be a day too soon."

"Sir, it shall be done as you've commanded." Petronius saluted. As he reached the door, however, he turned to face Pilate. "Sir, I would feel better if I were to personally escort you back to Caesarea. It could be dangerous, as you'll be traveling by night and there's always the possibility of attacks by rebels." Then he inhaled deeply. "But I understand that you need my services here, and I shall remain on duty in Jerusalem." Petronius saluted again, and as he opened the door he added, "And Sir, I will pray that God will protect you."

As the door closed behind him, Pilate said, "Did my centurion just say he would pray that *God* will protect me?"

ACT II

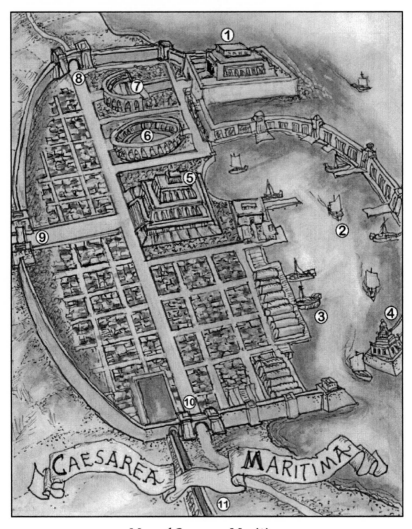

Map of Caesarea Maritima

1. Herod's Palace
   ~Residence of Pontius Pilate
2. Harbor Port of Caesarea
3. Warehouses and Docks
4. Harbor Lighthouse
5. Temple of Caesar Augustus
6. Roman Amphitheater

7. Roman Theater
8. Gate to Lydda and Jerusalem
9. Galilee Gate
   (to the eastern trade routes)
10. Gate to Tyre and Sidon
11. Roman Aqueduct

SCENE I

TERRACE OF HEROD'S PALACE
AT CAESAREA

Two Weeks after Passover in the Year 35 C.E.

"Isn't it stunning?" Pilate asked Jesus, who, with four guards, stood beside him on the palace's open terrace that overlooked the shimmering blue waters of the Mediterranean. "After bathing and in that clean robe, you're looking better than when you arrived here."

Pilate had summoned Jesus to show him the marvels of Caesarea, trusting that the beauty of the palace and the landscape would make his recalcitrant prisoner more amenable to conversation. "King Herod named his masterpiece of this city Caesarea Maritima, and it's second in magnificence only to his Temple in Jerusalem. He had this palace constructed on the only rocky promontory that extends out into the sea along this entire coastline. Over there to the north, you can see the massive artificial harbor port he created by constructing a sea wall some 800 feet out into the ocean. It's an architectural wonder that covers over 40 acres. It was built on piers of the new Roman concrete, made of volcanic sand Herod had shipped here from Naples. Ever the politician, Herod named this engineering marvel 'Sebastos' in honor of the Emperor; and since you know some Greek, you are aware that means, 'Augustus.' Have you ever seen anything as magnificent as this great harbor and city?"

Jesus remained silent as he stood gazing out over the harbor with its countless white-sailed merchant ships. For a few minutes Pilate waited for some comment on the fascinating view and then decided to change the subject.

"When you first arrived, I was concerned about your wounds, so I sent my physician to treat them. I trust that by now they are less painful."

Jesus made no reply but thought, *The wounds on my body are healing, but not my hidden scars of shame. They are as painful today as when I was stripped, whipped, and mocked back in Jerusalem.*

Pilate continued, "Look at all those ships down in the harbor. They're being loaded to go to Rome with products from Judea and all kinds of exotic goods from the Eastern world. When Herod created this massive harbor, he caused a major realignment of the trading routes of the East, including those that passed through your province of Galilee. He constructed this most ambitious project and the city itself to demonstrate his love for Rome. When he was finished he made Caesarea his capital, not Jerusalem. You could say that the Roman design and architecture of Caesarea was a token of his gratitude—if you excuse the irony—for the Roman Senate bestowing on him the royal title, 'King of the Jews!'"

Jesus made no response, so Pilate continued, "Look at that enormous temple over to your right. Because of its colossal size, it's the first thing seen by travelers arriving by ship and by land. Herod placed two gigantic statues inside it, one of the Emperor Augustus and the other of the goddess Roma. Now look northward beyond the harbor; parallel to the sea along the coast, that large stone aqueduct brings fresh water to Caesarea. And I have yet more marvels to show you—let's walk."

Flanked by his guards, Jesus followed Pilate until the two stood at the waist-high wall at the eastern end of the terrace. Pilate exclaimed, "Look at that city! Have you ever seen anything so breathtaking? Compare the dirty, twisting narrow lanes in Jerusalem to the broad Roman thoroughfare that passes through the city's center. That road leads to the Roman theater and the great amphitheater where athletic events and extravagant shows are staged. Ingeniously, King Herod laid out the sites of the theater and amphitheater so they directly faced his palace, where we now stand. He designed it that way so everyone attending the spectacular events would know who had sponsored them." Pilate's remarks were met with silence. "I confess, Jesus, you have disappointed me. I expected a peasant from the Galilean hill country to be in awe of the splendors of

Caesarea and this great port. Don't you have any comment or questions about what I've shown you?"

Jesus replied, "Yes, I have a question. Where in this fake Roman city do you intend to crucify me? Perhaps over there in that great amphitheater?"

Pilate retorted, "You're like a dog with his bone! You just can't let go of your obsession with dying on a cross, can you? Forget about the cross! Aren't you impressed by all this magnificence?"

Jesus responded, "I care nothing for Herod's fantasies of Roman glory. My only concern is doing the will of God. When do you plan to resume my trial?"

"Patience—first things first! I wanted to show you these sights since you arrived in Caesarea inside a covered carruca in the darkness of night and could see nothing of this fabulous city or the splendors of my home. Now, I have more for you to see."

"Guards, escort our...uh...guest alongside me as we walk. You will notice, Jesus, that this palace is made of splendid white marble. And this is its stunning jewel—a 60 by 120 foot pool of fresh spring water for swimming and bathing, with a marble colonnaded courtyard." Pointing to the serene blue pool, Pilate remarked, "Herod had this pool carved out of the solid rock on which this palace is built."

Jesus stood silently, looking down into the pool's crystal waters.

"It's nothing like the muddy waters of the Jordan that you were plunged into by that deranged soothsayer John, is it?"

Jesus made no response, but inwardly he was shocked by the sight of his reflection in the water. It had been a long time since he had seen his image reflected back to him, and he was taken aback by how old he looked.

Pilate continued, "I could offer you a bath in this beautiful pool, but I know you would refuse, so follow me, and we'll continue to tour the public section of the palace. Notice the wide tile walkway of inlayed mosaics that surround this oblong pool and the flourishing trees and flowering shrubs planted in these lovely marble tubs." They had now reached the end of the pool's walkway. "There to our right on the western side of the palace is the outdoor terrace where we began our tour. This terrace is the main room of the palace that, in Roman architecture, is called a 'Triclinium,' or dining area. King Herod designed this stunning setting for his sunset banquets so his dinner guests could enjoy both the sunset with its ocean breezes and the shimmering pool and its lush indoor gardens. In addition to dining, this terrace area is also used for casual visiting and relaxing. Don't you think this will be an ideal setting for us to visit?"

Jesus silently absorbed his surroundings as Pilate waited.

"Come, Jesus—I'm curious what a Galilean mud-hut dweller has to say about this marble palace, which was once the residence of King Herod and is now my home." Pilate paused. "Well, since you won't comment on the palace, perhaps you'll tell me what you think of your living quarters. It's a prison cell, true, but certainly no ordinary one. We believe that Herod must have created it as a place to imprison a son or royal family member he suspected of treachery. It's not your usual dark, stinking dungeon, is it, with its window that looks out to the sea."

His face set hard as flint, Jesus silently stared into Pilate's eyes.

Pilate said, "You don't need to be so defensive now that we're away from that raucous mob in Jerusalem, you know. I'm losing my patience, so I'll give you one last opportunity to say something."

Jesus replied, "Ah, a last opportunity! By 'last,' Pilate, do you mean that if I don't speak you'll order my execution?"

"Enough of this nonsense! I've tried to be civil with you. I'm sending you back to your cell, where you will remain until you're ready to speak to me. I don't care if it takes weeks or even years if necessary. Guards, take the prisoner to his cell, and we'll see if the bitter medicine of isolation will loosen his tongue."

SCENE II

THE SAME

Two Months after Passover, June, 35 C.E.

Pilate commented to Petronius, "I must say it's wonderful to be back in Caesarea. Even though it's been two months since I left the filthy stink of Jerusalem, being here hasn't ceased to be a delight."

"I agree, Sir, especially out here on the terrace with its warm sea breezes. Speaking of Jerusalem, may I ask how the prisoner Jesus is doing since you sentenced him to isolation?"

"I didn't sentence him! He sentenced himself by his stubborn refusal to speak to me about anything other than being crucified. When I first met him in Jerusalem, I found him rather fascinating and was intrigued at the prospect of discussing with him his ideas on life, death, and a whole range of other topics. But would he converse with me? No, he just stares, which does tend to make one uncomfortable."

"I'm still pondering that incident you mentioned about the bloodied, soiled garment he was wearing when he arrived here from Jerusalem. You said that after your slaves removed it, he refused to wear the Roman tunic you provided."

"Yes," replied Pilate, "Jesus told my slaves he'd rather go naked than wear the clothing of the foreign oppressors of his country! As I found the thought of visiting with a naked man unappealing, I sent a slave to the marketplace to procure not one but three Judean peasant's garments. I did that so he could have a laundered one each week, along with water for bathing. And what did I get for that unusual kindness to a prisoner, along with having my personal physician treat his wounds, and giving him a special cell with a window? Not a word of gratitude!"

"Sir, it is strange that he should be so ungrateful, especially for his cell. I've seen it before, with its window that looks out on the ocean. True, the window is narrow, being not more than three hands wide, so a grown man couldn't squeeze through it; still, it does provide fresh air and light...."

"Well, perhaps it was the window," Pilate mused, "or the warm June sea breezes that eventually caused him to change his mind."

"Change his mind, Sir?"

"Earlier today, before you arrived, Jesus sent me a message saying that he wanted to talk!"

"Congratulations, Sir. By being patient, you have won the battle."

"Not the battle, Petronius, but at least a decisive engagement. And you are overly generous to credit it to my patience—you know that's a gift I lack, as I am impetuous by nature. It's more than an undesirable trait; it's a curse for a governor of such a difficult province as Judea, which seems perpetually pregnant with soothsayers like that fanatical John of the Jordan. Speaking of prophets, Jesus is certainly beginning to look like a prophetic figure, with that long, gray, white-streaked beard of his."

Petronius replied, "Yes, he looks as if he's twenty years older than you, even though you're both around the same age."

"If he feels as old as he looks, maybe that explains his passionate desire to be crucified. Perhaps he's decided that he might as well die, since he's at the end of his life anyway. Regardless, I didn't want to crucify him."

"Why not, Sir, if I may ask?"

"It would have been stupid!" Pilate replied, definitively. "Executing charismatic leaders and religious visionaries only makes them into martyrs, so you don't remove your problem—you immortalize it! When these people die as martyrs you grant endless life to their ideas and words, as surely as if they had been chiseled in stone. Their ordinary human virtues become Olympian, while their weaknesses vanish like the morning mist. Take the great Julius Caesar; his enemies thought that by murdering him they would rid the empire of him. Instead, they only elevated him to the status of the immortals."

"I agree, Sir," replied Petronius. "The same thing was true of the prophet John. Our spies report that even though he was beheaded and died, he remains vividly alive among the common people. His disciples remain fiercely loyal to him and continue to preach his message of the need to repent before an apocalypse occurs — that's a Greek word, Sir, meaning 'a revelation,' but for the Jews it is used for the fiery final destruction of the world that they believed was now at hand. Stories abound of sightings of John's headless ghost roaming among the willows on the banks of the Jordan, and wandering in the palace of Herod Antipas."

"That's what I mean!" Pilate exclaimed. "When I arrived here I heard reports that this John was a raving religious eccentric. But now look at him; even without a head he's acclaimed as prophetic martyr! Herod Antipas was a fool to have beheaded him!"

"He does indeed live on, and the peasants now believe that every new charismatic preacher who appears is a reincarnation of John. Some have said that about our prisoner Jesus. But I'm curious — instead of killing John, what do you think he should have done about him?"

Pilate replied, "Since old Antipas had him in prison, he should have left him there to slowly rot to death. As for me, I think the best thing to do with political troublemakers and religious fanatics like John is to castrate them!"

"Castrate them?" Petronius asked, perplexed.

"Yes, if you can find some way to chop off the semi-godly status the people have bestowed on them, then they'll disappear like dust blowing away on the winds of time." Pausing, Pilate stroked his upper lip with his index finger and then said, "But, Petronius, my intuition tells me that our Galilean prisoner may be an exception to that kind of castration. Now that he's indicated he's ready to talk, I'll see him, but not right away. Perhaps delaying the visit will make him even more talkative."

SCENE III

THE SAME

Just Before Sunset, August, 35 C.E.

I'm surprised by how much Jesus has aged since the last time I saw him in Jerusalem, thought Petronius, as he and two soldiers escorted Jesus down the marbled walkway along the pool to the Triclinium.

"Your Excellency," said Petronius, as he and Jesus walked out onto the terrace, "as you ordered, here is the prisoner, Jesus of Nazareth."

"Thank you, Centurion," said Pilate, who was standing with his back to them, looking out over the blue Mediterranean Sea speckled with the white sails of Roman ships. "It's the end of a beautiful afternoon," he said, slowly turning around, "that promises an especially beautiful sunset. You guards are dismissed," he continued, "but stay within shouting distance at the far end of the hallway in case you are needed."

The two soldiers saluted and departed, leaving Pilate, Petronius, and Jesus standing alone on the terrace. Pilate said, "Jesus, I received your message that you were ready to talk, but official duties have prevented me from seeing you until today. What is it you wish to talk about?"

Jesus responded, "First, Pilate, I wanted to ask you to forgive me for my rudeness in failing to thank you for your many kindnesses. I'm truly grateful to you for providing me with good food and wine and a clean robe each week, sending your physician to treat my wounds, and giving me a cell with a window. I came to realize that...," he paused.

Pilate said, "Yes?"

Jesus continued, "Do you remember months ago, Pilate, when you were showing me this palace? We stood at that pool out there, and you remarked on how different it is from the muddy waters of the Jordan."

92

Pilate replied, "Yes, I remember; the differences between the two are striking."

Jesus said, "After weeks of silence, I realized that my heart had become as muddy as the brown waters of the Jordan; it was mucked up with my angry, hostile thoughts. After many days of sitting in silence, the waters of my heart began to grow clearer, until one day I could see to the bottom—and my true self. The silence cleared my vision so I could see my sins and errors, as well as my need to ask you to forgive me. I taught my disciples to ask forgiveness when they offended someone, and I realized that I needed to do the same. I fasted, which is why much of my food was returned uneaten, and I prayed. It was my fasting and prayer that prevented me from going mad."

"Mad?" Pilate asked. "What do you mean?"

Jesus explained, "I came to the realization that prolonged solitude could easily cause madness. I had spoken to no one for weeks on end, and I only saw the slave who came with my food and drink every other day. He never spoke, other than on his first visit, when he told me he was forbidden to talk to me. After that, he never said another word."

Pilate said, "I gave that order. I decided that since you refused to speak with me, you wouldn't speak with anyone."

Jesus replied, "I understand. Other than one time when I spent forty days alone in the desert, I had never been in utter solitude for such a prolonged time. I was frightened that being isolated from others would lead me to see mirages, but fortunately I was able to prevent that from happening."

"And how did you solve that problem?" Pilate asked.

"I spoke aloud to God every day. That's why I'm here, actually, for I was told to stop fasting...," he paused, "...not from food, but from speaking with you!"

Pilate replied, "While I approve your decision, I don't understand. You're in a solitary cell, so who told you to start talking again?"

"The Spirit."

"A spirit?" Pilate asked. "Do you mean to say the shades of the underworld have visited you?"

"No, it wasn't a shade of the netherworld," Jesus replied. "The voice I heard was that of the Spirit, my soul guide. I heard it the first time when I was coming up out of the water after John plunged me in the Jordan, when it said, 'You are my beloved son, in whom I am pleased.'"

"You're saying you heard a voice as clearly as you're now hearing mine?" asked an astonished Pilate.

"I didn't hear it with my ears, but here," Jesus said, tapping his heart. "It isn't like a human voice, yet it speaks like one; sometimes what I hear sounds reasonable, and at other times it's puzzling and contradictory."

Pilate replied, "I find that very interesting, because four months ago in Jerusalem as I was facing the mob screaming for your crucifixion, I too heard a voice. It's because I listened to it that you are alive today!"

Jesus said gravely, "The voice that told you not to crucify me didn't belong to the Spirit but to Beelzebub, the Prince of Lies, or to one of his demons!"

"Beelzebub?" Pilate asked.

"He's the Great Tempter," Jesus explained. "I too have heard his silky voice; he's so cunning that he's able to convince you that high noon is midnight. I first heard his sinister voice and those of his fiendish companions when I was alone during my forty days of solitude in the desert. And I've heard them here," Jesus said, tapping his toe on the marble floor, "down in my cell. I can see you don't believe me, but they're here inside your home, whispering their wickedness like hissing serpents."

At this talk of his home being infested by demons, Pilate anxiously began rotating his signet ring around his finger. "That's enough talk of evil spirits," he said, waving his hand as if shooing away flies. "Why cast a shadow over this beautiful time of the day?"

"If the Spirit of the Holy One had spoken to you in Jerusalem, Pilate, you would have been told to crucify me, just as the prophets had foretold."

"Prophets and soothsayers! We're also infested with them back in Rome, where they predict the future by poking around in bird guts.

94

It's such a hoax, for the future isn't determined by what they see there, but by what they *hope* to see going into their purses."

"Our prophets weren't soothsayers!" Jesus protested. "Isaiah, Jeremiah, and Ezekiel fearlessly proclaimed the will of God, even to kings!"

Pilate said, "Tiberius Caesar told me to learn about the people I govern, so since coming here I've learned something of the prophecies of your prophets. Whenever enemy armies were marching on Jerusalem, they predicted that unless you Jews faithfully returned to your god and kept all his commandments, Israel would be defeated, correct?"

"Yes," Jesus affirmed, "and for centuries they have correctly prophesized the defeats of Israel because of our infidelities to God's covenant."

Pilate said, "Jesus, I sense in you a quick and clever wit, even if you are illiterate. For the sake of discussion, let's say that every Jewish man, woman and child faithfully followed every commandment of Moses, including all the hundreds of prohibitions. Even if such perfect obedience was humanly possible, do you actually believe that Israel's scrawny little army could have been victorious over the enormous military might of the armies of the Egyptians, the Assyrians, the Babylonians, and...," he paused, grinning broadly, "that of the Imperial Roman Empire?"

"God could have...."

Pilate interrupted him. "Ah, yes, whenever you're trapped you employ the Greek device of the *deus ex machina* — the intervention of the gods — to resolve the plot. Be realistic! The reason Israel has been defeated again and again is because she's too small to fight against the world's great armed forces. You Jews have been victorious through your god's intervention only in your holy fables, such as your mythical escape from Egypt's great army at the Red Sea. In real life, such holy interventions never happen."

Jesus remained silent as Pilate seated himself on a couch. "Enough of the prophets; let's discuss more pleasant subjects. Come, sit on my right as my guest of honor, so we can visit as the sun disappears beneath the waves. Petronius, sit here on my left so we can hear your thoughts as well."

"I will stand!" Jesus responded with his arms folded across his chest. "Have you forgotten that I am a prisoner whom you are going to crucify, not your guest?"

"Indeed I had!" Pilate replied, amused. "But I thank you for reminding me of my official status. Let me rephrase my request: Prisoner, I now *order* you to sit down! And if you refuse, I'll have Petronius seat you!"

A glum-faced Jesus sat down reluctantly next to Pilate. Being seated on the dining couch reminded him of the night four months ago when he and his disciples shared their final meal in an upper room in Jerusalem. Jesus thought, *I vividly recall the last time I ate with my friends as we reclined on couches just like these. I wonder what Peter, Andrew, and especially John are doing right now?*

Pilate interrupted his thoughts by asking, "So, Jesus, how do you spend your days and nights in your cell?"

"I pray," Jesus replied, "or I stand at the window looking out at the ocean. Sometimes I walk back forth in my cell and talk to the walls!"

"Talk to the walls? Hmm...," Pilate said, as he wondered if his prisoner had spent too long in solitude and was perhaps losing his mind.

"Before I was arrested, I would frequently sneak away to be alone in the mountains, finding the solitude to be heavenly," Jesus said, pausing, "and now I find it hellish. Those stone walls have become like familiar friends, and in the absence of anyone else to speak with, I have found that talking to them helps keep me sane. And at night, I wrestle."

"Wrestle?" Pilate exclaimed. "Who do you wrestle with, as you're all alone in your cell?"

"With God...an angel...the wind."

"Uh-huh," Pilate responded. "And when you wrestle with a god or the wind, who wins?"

"Not me!" Jesus replied. "I always lose, for I'm wrestling with my destiny, which I'm impotent to achieve because of you, Pilate. Tell me, was it Satan who induced you to halt my crucifixion and thwart God's plan for the salvation of the world?"

"I must correct you, Jesus!" Pilate said, raising his index finger. "I've only decided not to crucify you *in Jerusalem!* But just now you used a word that's unknown to me: 'salvation.' What does that mean?"

"It means liberation from oppression — from the powers of evil, violence, and war. The release of the Israelites from Egyptian slavery was an act of salvation. For the liberation, the salvation, of the world, God requires my redemptive death as a sacrifice of atonement for the sin of Adam...."

"Adam?" Pilate interjected. "That's another name that is new to me. What did this Adam do that so grievously offended your god?"

"Sir, allow me to explain," said Petronius. "The prisoner is referring to a story in his people's holy writings about the first man and woman created by God, who were called Adam and Eve, and...."

"They disobeyed God!" Jesus interrupted, eagerly. "They ate an apple from a tree in the garden from which God had forbidden them to eat. They were tricked into eating the apple by a serpent, who told them they would become like God if they ate the tree's fruit, and it is that sin of Adam that requires atonement."

"A talking snake?" said Pilate mockingly. "It must be one of the Seven Wonders of the World! But your story about a forbidden apple reminds me of the Greek fable of the Golden Apple. It seems the goddess Eris was furious because she hadn't been invited to a feast with the other gods and goddesses, but she went anyway. Upon arriving, she tossed a golden apple into their midst on which she had written, 'For the most beautiful.' Now, each of the goddesses — Venus, Minerva, and Juno — claimed that the golden apple was intended for her. After much quarreling it was determined that it was intended for Venus, which made the other two goddesses so furious they caused the fall of legendary Troy — or so it is believed."

Jesus retorted, "Adam and Eve were real people, not characters in a myth! Their original sin of disobedience is the source of all of the world's wickedness and sins, and since their sin was a divine transgression, the only reparation possible was a divine sacrifice of atonement—which God has asked me, as his son, to perform."

"At least we Romans know the difference between a myth and reality," Pilate responded. "We don't try to appease the gods for a mistake committed in a mythical fable by killing a Roman citizen."

Jesus argued, "The story of Adam isn't a myth or a silly fable! He actually sinned against God, and I must atone for it and for all the sins of the Jewish people—indeed, for all the sins of the world."

"Stop!" Pilate commanded, holding up his hand. "You're confusing me with all this talk of atonement! Let me get this straight. It's not as if I haven't tried to educate myself about your beliefs regarding the removal of sins, such as your scapegoat ritual. Now, as I understand it, on the day of Atonement the high priest takes all the sins of the Jewish people and places them on a goat named...uh...."

"Azazel," Petronius offered.

"Thank you, Petronius. Its name got lost on its way to the tip of my tongue! Now, if I understand it correctly, this scapegoat who is carrying the sins of the people isn't slaughtered but is driven out into the desert wasteland, correct?"

Jesus nodded in agreement.

"And if I understand you, Jesus, you believe that, like Azazel, your destiny is to take upon yourself all the sins of world?" Jesus again nodded. Pilate continued, "And I suppose that when we first met in Jerusalem, in preparation for being crucified, you had already taken upon yourself the sins of the world?"

"Yes, for God has willed that I should carry them to my death."

Pilate asked, "Well then, how have I frustrated your destiny? Like the high priest, didn't I drive you out of Jerusalem, laden with all the sins of your people, into this pagan wasteland of Caesarea? The way I see it, as the new Azazel you have already taken away the sins of the people, so there's no need to be crucified!"

"You tricked me!" shouted Jesus angrily, jumping to his feet. "You made me identify myself with the scapegoat, when God requires much more from me!"

"Sit down, sit down," Pilate said, patting the coach next to him. "Look—the sun is still above the western horizon, and sunset won't come for a while."

With a scowl on his face and his lips clamped shut, Jesus slowly reseated himself, angry at himself for falling into Pilate's trap. Pilate, on the other hand, was having fun baiting his prisoner with questions about his religious beliefs.

"I have other questions for you, Jesus," Pilate said. "You've told me how your god, whom you call your father, willed—if not required—that you die on a cross to save the world. The three of us here have all seen crucifixions. Tell me, what kind of a sadistic father would require his son to die such a horrible death?"

Although he was looking out to sea, Jesus didn't see the setting sun, for his eyes were fixed inward at a new wound caused by Pilate's question, which exposed one of his secret, frustrating doubts. He himself had struggled with the contradiction of how a loving father could be so cruel, and finding his doubt unthinkable, if not sinful, he had suppressed it. He shuddered, feeling his heart sinking into an abyss, and he dreaded the coming days, for he knew he would be haunted by Pilate's question.

"Jesus, you look depressed. Don't be; you aren't a failure, even if you weren't crucified in Jerusalem. Petronius, tell him about the reports of our Galilean informer."

Petronius said to Jesus, "Pilate is referring to a report from one of our spies about your little group of followers in Galilee, who are saying that you *did* actually die on a cross in Jerusalem!"

Pilate enjoyed watching the shock on Jesus' face. He said, "Don't look so surprised. Our spy is reliable, and he's informed us that your disciples are going about the countryside saying that by your death on the cross, you have redeemed the world! So you see, you're not a failure!"

Stunned, Jesus attempted to grapple with the implications of this shocking news. What would his disciples do if they learned that he wasn't dead, but was alive as a prisoner in Caesarea? Or was this just another of Pilate's tricks?

Pilate continued, "I can see you're thinking that what I just told you can't be true, but I assure you it is! Even if not a single member of your little inner group personally witnessed your crucifixion, they firmly believe it happened just as they had heard. Our spy also told us that since your reported crucifixion was so devastatingly shameful, your disciples have cleansed it by making it a fulfillment of a prophecy. Apparently they've searched through the writings of the prophets and the psalms and were able to transform your death from a disaster into the victory of your so-called redemption."

"And Jesus," Petronius added, "your disciples are also publicly saying that even if you suffered the hideous death of crucifixion, you were truly the long-expected Messiah, the Christ!"

"No, it can't be!" Jesus protested. "I always denied that I was the Messiah! The Messiah is and has been the ancient dream of the oppressed Jewish people for the coming of a great military savior who will violently destroy...."

Pilate interrupted him, saying, "Look! The sun is dipping its toe in the ocean. Let's watch its graceful descent into the sea."

The three sat silently, watching the giant orb slowly descend into the cobalt blue sea. When it was only halfway submerged, Pilate commented, "According to Homer, the sun 'sees all things and hears all things.' So, Jesus, do you think Homer was correct? Did the setting sun actually hear what we've been discussing?"

Jesus replied, "In my youth, I learned, 'I saw under the sun that the race is not to the swift, nor the battle to the strong...but time and chance happen to them all.' So said the wise King Solomon."

"That's an interesting perspective," Pilate said. "However, as a former army officer, I don't agree, for I've found that the strong are always victorious. Petronius, in your experience, don't you believe the most powerful army is always victorious?"

Petronius responded, "Naturally, Sir, my military experience isn't as broad as yours, yet I can recall a time when the strongest force *wasn't* victorious. I was with a large force of our skilled Roman legionaries who far outnumbered a band of Nordic barbarians, yet we were defeated! Just as we were about to crush them, a great wind storm blew gigantic clouds of dirt and dust across the battlefield, blinding us. Thus we were forced to retreat, leaving the far less powerful barbarians victorious! At least in that engagement, King Solomon was correct, because chance gave the victory to those who were less strong."

Pilate remained silent as Petronius turned to Jesus. "I've heard you quoted as saying something similar: 'Fortunate are the meek, for they shall be victorious and possess the land,' or something like that."

"But that's ridiculous, Petronius!" interjected Pilate. "The spineless can never be victorious! The gods never favor the frail — that's why they die early. The gods only favor the strong, and throughout all of history the strong have always ruled over the weak, as it is here in Judea."

"Sir, by 'meek,' I don't believe Jesus means weak or cowardly, but...."

"Petronius, 'patient' is a better word for meek," Jesus commented, "and it is not the powerful but those who are patient who will be victorious in the end. So fortunate are those who, without growing weary, can endure suffering and oppression for years, even for centuries, for they will be triumphant by outlasting their oppressors!"

"Well, Jesus," said Pilate, "at least in your case, time and chance certainly have been in your favor. Now that the sun has disappeared beneath the waves, I propose we sit and watch for Venus, which will soon appear in the twilight sky."

As they sat in silence, Pilate thought, *I changed the subject to the coming of Venus because it was easy to see that I was on the losing side of our discussion. Petronius continues to surprise me by his familiarity with Jesus' teachings. Perhaps I shouldn't be surprised, for if I find Jesus compelling, why shouldn't he? Still, it was apparent at the trial that he was opposed to the scourging of Jesus, and clearly he didn't want him to be crucified. Could my loyal adviser actually be one of this man's secret disciples? If Lucius were here, he'd remind me of Cicero's advice, "Discover in advance what is going to happen, be it good or ill, so to be prepared. Never be reduced to saying, 'I hadn't thought of that.'"*

Pilate said, "I'm reminded that we've had more than three months of sunsets since your trial in Jerusalem, when I pledged to Caiaphas that I would resume your trial here in Caesarea. I should attend to my promise if I want to be remembered as a man of my word. What do you think?"

Jesus replied, "Do you actually intend to complete my trial and have me crucified?"

"You mean, a second time?" laughed Pilate. "Don't forget that your little band of Galilean disciples believe you've already been crucified. How could they explain that their teacher died twice by crucifixion? Although they seem to be skilled at finding old prophecies to explain things, justifying how a man can die twice would be as ridiculous an impossibility as finding a gray hair in Jupiter's bushy black beard. But fear not: I'm a very pliable judge and can arrange for you to have a clandestine crucifixion here in Caesarea, perhaps at the next eclipse."

Jesus sat stoically, though inwardly he was boiling in resentment at Pilate for mocking him and God's will.

"Look, Sir, there in the western sky," said Petronius, "it's Venus, the vesper star."

"Hail to the goddess Venus!" proclaimed Pilate playfully, as he saluted the sparkling planet. "Greetings, Venus, beautiful daughter of Jupiter, and divine founder of our Roman race!" Turning to Jesus, he said, "Her appearance signals that it is time for the evening meal. Soon Claudia and I will dine here on the terrace; for me, it's the finest hour in my day."

"But what about my trial and your promise to Caiaphas?"

"Ah, yes, my pledge to old Caiaphas to resume your trial for treason against the Empire. It's regrettable—yes, most regrettable," he said, with mock remorse, "but I fear it will have to wait until another time." Pilate stood, signaling the end of the visit. "You'll have to be more meek, Jesus; you are far too eager to be condemned. I urge you to practice that favored virtue of yours—long-suffering patience—because my tomorrow, as well as my foreseeable tomorrows, are all quite busy. I have to complete my annual tax report for Rome, and then I depart on an official visit to Samaria, and after that...," raising his hands in a gesture of unknowing, he said, "...who knows what I must deal with? You must be patient with your busy Governor. And now, I must prepare for the evening meal. Petronius, see that our Galilean guest is returned to his…uh…quarters." Before Petronius could respond, Pilate quickly added, "Oh, and Jesus, there's one more thing."

Jesus' closed his eyes, dreading what might be coming next.

"Now that you have agreed to speak with me and we can visit," Pilate said with a grin, "I'm giving orders to the slaves who bring you food and wine that they are now allowed to visit with you if they wish and it is agreeable to you. Too much isolation isn't good for the mind."

Jesus nodded graciously. Then Pilate silently gestured with his hand to Petronius. "Yes, Sir!" Petronius saluted and led Jesus off the terrace toward the hallway beside the pool. When they reached the walkway, Jesus stopped. Turning around, he looked back over his right shoulder at Pilate, and for a flicker of a moment their eyes met. Pilate was surprised to feel an unusual surge of emotion rising within him.

SCENE IV

JESUS' PRISON CELL
UNDERNEATH THE PALACE AT CAESAREA

An Evening at the End of August, 35 C.E.

Jesus sighed. "Another day is gone, to be added to all the others that have passed since I last talked with Pilate. Who is it—Pilate, or my Father—who continues to delay the fulfillment of my destiny?" Jesus' question drifted out the window on the early evening breeze. Turning to his cell, he continued, "I ask you, comrade walls; is it God or Pilate who delays my trial?" The chiseled cell walls only stared back at him, as silent as the walls of a tomb. "Jesus, listen to yourself. Now that you've lived alone for so long, with only a visit every other day from the slaves who bring your food," he patted the craggy stone walls, "you've made these stone walls of your cell your companion. You're so hungry to hear a human voice that you're talking to the walls just to hear yourself speak. When you were in solitude in the desert you didn't do such bizarre things. But that was for 40 days, and this time—well, it must be close to five months now."

He returned to the window and listened to the waves crash ashore on the giant boulders below, as they had done for endless centuries. Jesus thought about the full-length reflection of himself he saw in the waters of Herod's pool as he came back from his last visit with Pilate. "I know you stones are old," he remarked, gently patting the wall next to the window, "but I'm becoming old too! My hair and beard are streaked with white more than gray, and I'm not as tall as I once was. Plus in the mornings my knees and ankles are painful and stiff after a night of sleep."

He listened for some time to the relentless pounding of the surf below, and then spoke aloud, "You boulders seem untouched by the passage of time and the pounding of the waves, but that's not true of me! In the race against time I'm beginning to fear that death is gaining

104

on me. Before it catches me I must do everything in my power to be crucified!"

He turned and began pacing in his cell as he thought about his last conversation with Pilate. *It seems that Pilate has been gifted with the same cunning tongue as the Serpent, for he is tempting me to wonder if Adam and Eve really....* Jesus shook himself and said sternly, "Stop, Jesus! Don't question what has been written in the holy scrolls! Forgive me, Father, for questioning if Eden or Adam really existed."

Jesus stopped walking, for his swollen ankles were becoming painful. He reached down and rubbed them. "Pilate also cleverly trapped me into making myself into a scapegoat, and he mocked me, asking if I wanted to be crucified twice. O Father, come to the aid of this son of yours, who is so confused."

As no voice responded to his plea, Jesus returned to his sleeping pad and lay down. He closed his eyes so the darkness could gently encompass him, but his mind continued to race. *Pilate asked me how any loving father could want his son to suffer a hideous death by crucifixion – the very question that has haunted me for years.* Raising his head off the mat, he shouted into the darkness, "My God, you are a tender and loving Father! Didn't I teach that to my disciples? Didn't I tell the crowds that you were a compassionate God who was deeply moved when an insignificant sparrow fell to the earth? I told them you were not a stern judge or tyrant who punishes his children with crop failures, disasters, or diseases. 'Trust me,' I told them, 'I speak from personal experience of God as my "Abba," a loving and tender Father.' So then how can you want me to be crucified?" Finally, overcome by weariness of soul, he fell into a deep sleep.

Before long Jesus abruptly awakened to find his dungeon cell flooded with light, as if he had slept until high noon. Looking up, he was shocked to see an aged, white-bearded figure bending over him. "Peace be with you, Jesus," he said.

"Who are you? What hour of the day is it?"

"It isn't day, it's the dead of night—the time when deceased ancestors come to visit. I am Abraham, and I've come with an answer to your question."

"What question is that?"

"Your question of how a loving God can desire that you die by being crucified! And the answer is, God agrees!"

Confused, Jesus asked, "Phantom—or whatever you are—God agrees with whom?"

Abraham responded, "God agrees with Pilate, and with you! And I'm no phantom, I'm your ancestor Abraham. I've come to remind you what you yourself taught the crowds when you quoted the prophet Hosea, who said of God, 'I desire mercy, not sacrifice.'"

"I remember quoting those words of Hosea...." Then, closing his eyes, Jesus rubbed his forehead, as if trying to wipe away a bad dream.

Abraham continued, "Remember, Jesus, I also heard God's voice asking me to perform an unimaginable deed. I was told to take my only son, my beloved Isaac, to a distant mountain to make a holocaust of him! A holocaust, Jesus; my beloved Isaac was to be consumed by fire in an agonizing death!"

Jesus responded, "I know well the story of how Isaac climbed up the mountain, carrying the wood on his back for his own holocaust. I've thought of it whenever I have imagined myself carrying the wooden crossbeam of my cross to my sacrificial death."

"Yes, Isaac carried the wood and I the knife and a pot of hot embers for the fire, but I did not carry the desire! As I watched Isaac stacking up the wood of his own funeral pyre, I was drenched with doubt, tortured by how God could command me to make a human sacrifice of my only son. After he had stacked the firewood, my beloved son asked, 'Father, we've got the wood and the fire for our holocaust, but where is the animal to be sacrificed? Did you forget it?'"

Jesus observed, "As a father, you must have been in anguish."

Abraham replied, "Yes, it was almost too intense for me to bear. I couldn't look at Isaac lest he'd see I was crying, and so I looked the other way, mumbling, 'The Lord God will provide.' Then, before my resolve failed, I whirled around and seized my boy, tightly bound him with rope, and lifted him up on top of the pile of wood."

"And just as you raised your knife, God intervened, and an angel appeared...."

"Yes, and God said, 'Abraham, do not lay a hand on the boy; do nothing to harm your beloved son. Your willingness to make a holocaust of him is sufficient to prove your absolute obedience to me, your Lord God.'"

After speaking these words, Abraham vanished, plunging Jesus' cell back into darkness. Sitting up, Jesus leaned his back against the cold stone wall. He said aloud, "Surely that must have been a dream, yet it was so real! But even if it was a dream, in ages past, isn't that how God visited the ancient ones to speak to them? O God, whose ways are mysterious, does this visit mean that, just as you sent an angel to prevent Abraham from sacrificing his son, you used Pontius Pilate to do the same for me?"

Jesus didn't expect an answer, and for a long time he listened to the surf crashing below on the boulders along the coast. After a while, he said aloud, "Abba, are you telling me that just as Abraham's obedience, right up to the point of killing his son, was sufficient to prove his love for you, so my willingness to be captured and to die on a cross is all you required of me?"

SCENE V

THE TERRACE OF THE PALACE

Mid September, 35 C.E.

A cool morning breeze blew off the sea as Pilate was being shaved by Quintus and Lucius read a report from a spy. "Jesus' disciples are going about the countryside, saying that he died and was buried...," Lucius paused, pretending to clear his throat, "but that on the third day he rose from the tomb...."

At, "rose from the tomb," Quintus nimbly pulled back his razor just before Pilate jerked his head toward Lucius.

He exclaimed, "Rose from the tomb...what tomb? We typically leave the dead bodies of the crucified to hang rotting on their crosses. However, that being the eve of Passover, I made an exception for Caiaphas and ordered that their dead bodies be removed, but there was no honorable burial in a tomb, since they were rebels!"

"Ah, Excellency," Lucius said, laying the scroll in his lap, "legends are like children. As they grow older, they also tend to grow larger."

"And far more quickly than children! Look at how rapidly the story of Jesus' death has grown to almost mythic proportions; a dead man returning to life, like the Greek god Dionysus, is the stuff of myths. And it seems that Jesus' disciples are now making him into a Jewish Dionysus."

Nodding, Lucius picked up the scroll and continued, "His closest disciples report having seen the risen Jesus on several occasions."

"Seeing the dead Jesus? Lucius, does our informer say anything about him being seen by reliable eyewitnesses, such as the Temple priests, scribes, or the elders in Jerusalem? Have any of them claimed to have seen this dead man walking around alive?"

"He does not, Sir. From the report, it appears that only his disciples have witnessed these appearances."

"Enough of these peasant folk tales! Marcus, send word to the Centurion Petronius that I'm ready to resume the Galilean's trial.

Have him escort the prisoner up here to the terrace after our midday meal. Quintus, I want you to stay, and you also, Lucius, to record the proceedings."

SCENE VI

THE SAME

A Short While Later

"Ah, welcome, my Galilean scapegoat," Pilate said, as Jesus, escorted by Petronius, approached. Lucius sat next to Pilate, and Marcus and Quintus stood nearby.

"It's pleasant out here with the sea breezes, isn't it, Jesus? I've invited you up here to tell you some good news; I'm reopening your trial! But first, I have other news; two days ago a clandestine envoy from Caiaphas arrived here, enquiring if I had yet crucified you."

"Really? And what did you tell him?"

"The envoy was a Temple priest I've met before named Zechariah. I've always found him obnoxious, so after taunting him a bit I sent him back to old Caiaphas with a reply that was easy to remember: 'No, but he shall be in due time.'"

Jesus' heart leaped with joy, and he silently prayed, *Patience, Jesus. With persistent endurance, the will of God shall be done.*

Pilate continued, "Although I'm in no hurry, I've decided to reopen your trial this morning, which unfortunately has been postponed by of a series of demands on my time. While I'm not eager to see you die," Pilate smiled, "I know Annas and Caiaphas are."

"Sir," asked Lucius, "do you want me to keep a detailed record of this trial?"

"A detailed record isn't necessary; as is common in the provinces, I will conduct this trial *cognitio extra ordinem,* using only my governor's discretion as judge. But I do want an unofficial record kept so I can refer back to it if necessary." Then, clearing his throat, Pilate said, "In the name of the Emperor Tiberius, I officially resume your trial, Jesus, by repeating one of the charges leveled against you in Jerusalem. Do you claim to be 'The son of god'?"

"Yes!" Jesus replied, eagerly.

"I must caution you, Jesus; that's an imperial divine title reserved exclusively to the Emperor, as in, 'Tiberius, son of the divine Augustus.' For you or for anyone to use that title is a crime punishable by death! So, now that you're aware of the political consequences of claiming that imperial title, I'll ask you again: Are you the son of a god?"

"I am—and I believe that the Emperor Tiberius is also a son of God."

"The Divine Tiberius will be greatly pleased by your confession of his divinity," Pilate commented, dryly.

Jesus continued, "I also believe that you, Pilate, are a son of God, as is Petronius and your slaves Lucius, Marcus, and Quintus. All of us are children of God!"

Pilate replied, "What an incredible idea—not to mention ridiculous and impossible! How can I or Petronius, and especially my slaves, be the children of the gods, since we're mere mortals? But enough of that," he said, waving his hand as if blowing smoke away. "This talk is mere philosophical prattle, although not uncommon, for Homer said, 'All men need the gods.' I myself do not believe in the gods, but it is obvious, Jesus, that you do!"

"I do not doubt the existence of...."

"Never?" Pilate interrupted. "You've never, ever had even the tiniest sneaking doubt that the gods don't exist? Plato once said, 'A certain portion of mankind do not believe at all in the existence of the gods.' Since I belong to that portion of unbelievers, how comical is the mischief of the Fates to make me, a skeptic, the governor of this god-infested province!"

Pilate chuckled at his own joke, while Jesus remained steadfastly silent, determined not to say anything that might sidetrack Pilate from his trial.

Pilate continued, "The last time we spoke, you talked of wrestling at night with a god or some visionary being. I've been told that certain primitive peoples wait until midnight to feast, dance, and offer sacrifice to the spirits of their ancestors. Midnight, being the darkest time of night, is when their ancestors return from the Netherworld, and the living hope to learn the secret knowledge they've acquired down there. I think that's all foolishness, since the dead are dead; once departed, they're gone for good. But what about you? Do you believe there is...uh...*something* after death?"

"Yes...I think there's life after death," replied Jesus. Inwardly, he was shocked he had said "I think," instead of "I believe." He sighed in relief as he glanced over at Pilate, who showed no sign of hearing his unintentional slip, which implied a lack of conviction.

Pilate said, "I'm not surprised. But I'm afraid we're wandering away from your trial by this fruitless talk about life after death. As you know, I'm a former military man, and so I'm interested in practical things that can be seen with one's eyes. I confess that as a youth I wanted to go to the Orient like Alexander the Great and seek the wisdom of wise men, but unlike him I never made it to Persia or India to fulfill that youthful desire. Then last spring in Jerusalem I met you, and since some of your ideas were interesting, I rescued you from the cross and brought you to Caesarea. I hoped we could have some illuminating conversations, in spite of your mulish Judean behavior."

Jesus protested, "I'm a Galilean, not a Judean!"

Pilate replied, "Ah, yes, an important territorial distinction that was not lost on old Caiaphas and his aristocratic priests. They judge you Galileans to be what we Romans call *'paganus;'* illiterate, uncouth country people who are contaminated as Jews because you've adapted to the cultures of your gentile pagan conquerors, the Babylonians, Greeks, and we Romans." Grinning, he continued, "Your Galilean women fell in love with and married soldiers of the various foreign occupation armies.... But look how far the sun's golden chariot has traveled in the western sky! It appears we've run out of time. I don't have all day to devote to this trial, because many urgent matters are awaiting my attention. I'm afraid you'll have to wait until another day."

Jesus pleaded, "Please don't bring my trial to a premature end again! It wouldn't take a blink of an eye, Pilate, to pronounce me guilty and sentence me to death."

Pilate said, "I agree — pronouncing the words that condemn a man to death can be said as quickly as I can snap my fingers. But for a serious judge, sentencing a man to death requires time so the evidence may be properly weighed and judgment pondered. As I said, the sun tells me it is time that Lucius and I complete our daily report for Rome so it can depart on the evening mail boat. Then, Petronius and I must compose a report to be sent to Vitellius, the Syrian Roman legate, about our recent spy intelligence of civil unrest brewing in the district of Samaria."

Jesus said, "Please, Pilate, I beg you, don't send me back to my cell! If I spend much more time down there, I'm afraid I'll lose my resolve. Today I'm strongly committed to God's will that I be crucified, but tomorrow...I'm not sure what all this time alone will do to me. Please, don't delay...."

Pilate proclaimed, "I officially declare these proceedings of the trial of Jesus of Galilee to be adjourned! Petronius, have your guards escort the prisoner back to his quarters, and then return here, for we have much to do before sunset."

SCENE VII

THE SAME

Later That Same Day

"Petronius, I would like to hear your thoughts about our prisoner, Jesus," said Pilate. "Take a seat next to me here on the couch. I want you to be honest—what do you think of our Galilean?"

Petronius replied, "I keep thinking about his trial back in Jerusalem, when he stood before you and that mob in Jerusalem; the man I saw that day was more regal than the High Priest."

"I agree," Pilate said, "he's no ordinary looking Jew! But how did an uneducated peasant laborer acquire such a dignified bearing? In some ways he appears to be more Roman than Jewish."

"Your intuition is most likely correct, Sir. While I was in Galilee, I found it to be a district of half-breeds as a result of occupations by Greeks and other foreigners. Thirty to forty years ago the Syrian Legate dispatched Roman legionaries to crush a rebellion there, and some of our soldiers remained in Galilee afterward to maintain order. Naturally, as happens during occupations, some of our soldiers had affairs with Galilean women. As you know, mixed-blood children are a common sight after every war and military occupation. I went to Nazareth, Jesus' home village, while on an inspection tour for Prince Agrippa. While there I heard village rumors that Jesus may have been conceived out of wedlock in an affair with a Roman soldier."

Pilate responded, "Really! And did they know the name of his supposed Roman father?"

Petronius replied, "No. If the rumor is indeed true, it's impossible to know who the soldier was, because our Roman legionaries were recalled to Syria. Plus that was more than thirty-some years ago, so this gossip about Jesus had grown stale and was replaced with fresh rumors of indiscretions by other villagers."

"But Petronius, the stigma of being a bastard doesn't fade quickly, at least in Rome."

"I think that's true everywhere," Petronius said, thoughtfully, "especially in small villages where it becomes a shadow that follows a person his entire life. While I was on the staff of Prince Antipas, our Jesus was just becoming a popular figure in Galilee, and Antipas sent me to Nazareth to learn as much as I could about him. The villagers always referred to him as 'Jesus, son of Joseph,' because in their culture, connecting the father's name to the person grants legitimacy. This Joseph is now dead, but he had been a village craftsman and the husband of Mary, the mother of Jesus. The gossip among the older people in the village was that Joseph wasn't Jesus' natural father."

Pilate mused, "If our prisoner Jesus has Roman blood, that explains his physical stature and his strength of character. Petronius, our man Jesus is becoming more and more intriguing to me. What is your opinion of him?"

Petronius said, "I believe he's a good man. Whenever I asked about him in Galilee, everyone spoke of him as someone who went about doing good works. He's known as a folk healer and is said to have the power to drive out demons. While he was never trained as a scribe or rabbi—in fact, he's illiterate—he has a remarkable memory and is able to quote freely from the sayings of the Jewish prophets and the Law of Moses. As a result, the common people referred to him as rabbi, or teacher."

Pilate stood up, walked over to the terrace wall, and gazed northward toward the harbor wharfs, watching the ships being loaded and unloaded.

Petronius said, "Sir, if I'm not overstepping my position, may I ask if you intend to crucify Jesus?"

"Don't you mean *half*-crucify him?" Pilate asked. "If he is half-Roman, shouldn't he retain half the privilege of a Roman citizen not to be crucified? But seriously, I'm thinking of imitating Emperor Caesar Tiberius, who is known as the Great Procrastinator, and just leave our Jesus in our prison here for—well, who knows how long?"

"But Sir, what if the Emperor appoints you to be governor of another province and you leave here? What would be Jesus' fate under a new governor?"

"I don't anticipate receiving a promotion, Petronius; any chances that the Emperor will promote me to a better governorship are slim at best. By the graces of the goddess Fortuna, I'm been lucky to have survived as governor here for seven years. Tiberius, in his old age, procrastinates about making decisions, which explains his reluctance to change administrators. Governors who are competent are simply left where they are first posted. I've also heard that he has a low opinion of us governors, believing we're only interested in graft. Another possibility, one I hate even to say aloud, is that the Emperor could declare me *friget*—you know, cast out in the cold—if I were to make another political blunder. One more major mistake like trying to build that damn Jerusalem aqueduct, or bringing the imperial standards into Jerusalem, and he could easily renounce me. Tiberius is becoming known for recalling governors or army officers for minor accusations or even on mere suspicion, and some say he's begun to consider all offenses as capital crimes!"

"Sir, may you never become *friget*!"

"I hope not, Petronius."

"Sir, I must leave now, because I need to make preparations for our expedition down to Jericho from Jerusalem after the autumn festival of Sukkoth."

"Permission granted, Petronius. We'll need a substantial number of our troops in Jerusalem for Sukkoth, because it's another Exodus festival. Then we can depart on my official visitation to Jericho and from there down into that barren wasteland of the great Salt Sea to Qumran. I do thank you for your thoughts about our prisoner, which were most interesting. The goddess Fortuna indeed blessed me with great fortune in having a good soldier like you as my military aid—and friend."

Petronius departed, and Pilate turned back toward the harbor. While he stood in the warm autumn sun, he wrapped himself in warm thoughts about how best to avoid the chilling curse of imperial wrath.

SCENE VIII

JESUS' CELL IN THE DUNGEON

November, 35 A.D.

How much longer now until the final sunset of my life? Jesus mused, as he watched the bloated orange orb of the sun slowly descend into the sea, *I'd better be condemned to the cross soon. Having watched the changing faces of the moon, I estimate it's now been at least two months since Pilate went up to Jerusalem. I pray he quickly resumes my trial when he returns, so I can fulfill God's plan...if being crucified is what God really wills for me.* Striking the window ledge with his fist, Jesus exclaimed, "There it is again! That curse of spending so much time alone, which makes me wonder whether it's truly God's will for me to die on a cross!"

Being careful not to knock over his privy pot, Jesus began pacing in his cell. After some time he stopped, stood at the window again, and watched the amber sky slowly turn turquoise. Off to the north he could see gathering storm clouds, now edged pale yellow by the last rays of the sun below the horizon.

"Impossible!" Jesus cried aloud, upon remembering something Pilate had said to him. "Pilate said he heard a voice in Jerusalem telling him not to crucify me, but it *couldn't* have been the voice of God!"

"Why?" asked an inner voice. "Why is it impossible, Jesus, that the voice Pilate heard wasn't that of the Spirit of God?"

Pounding both his fists on the window ledge, Jesus shouted, "No. No. No!" Then he took a deep breath, saying, "Stop, Jesus! You can't beat the answer out of this stone ledge. As contradictory as it may seem, couldn't God have spoke to Pilate? Don't you believe that with God all things are possible?"

As those questions drifted off over the ocean, he heard the first distant rumbling of thunder, which was followed by blue-white flashes of lightening darting in and out of the storm clouds.

"Think about it, Jesus," spoke his inner voice. "In the past, haven't you heard that voice, as soft as a spider's web, whispering divine contradictions? God has given you inconsistent messages before, such as when he said, 'Tell the people to forget that once long ago I commanded "an eye be taken for an eye." Tell them that now I command them never to return evil for evil.'"

Jesus heard another rumbling of thunder, this time louder and closer. He thought, *As a small child I memorized God's command, "A life for a life, an eye for an eye, a hand for a hand," from the scroll of the Exodus. My mother was so proud of how I could repeat perfectly the law of Leviticus, "A limb for a limb, eye for eye, the same injury that a man gives another shall be inflicted on him in return," as well as almost the same words from the scroll of Deuteronomy.*

Emotionally drained, Jesus rested his throbbing head against the cold stone wall as the storm's reverberating thunder grew louder. He thought, *The storm that's approaching across the ocean isn't the only one raging tonight. My heart's in a tempest over Father Abraham's story about how God first demanded and then forbid him to make a holocaust of his son, Isaac. Am I another Isaac? As the ram in the thicket was Abraham's substitute for Isaac, was my substitute the rebel that Pilate crucified? Is my willingness to die on the cross sufficient to redeem the world?* "No!" he answered aloud, decisively. "I must actually *die* on a cross!"

Jesus could now feel the fierce winds that were swiftly driving the storm toward land. The rumble of the thunder grew louder and seemed almost directly overhead as he prayed over the roar of the storm, "O God, you've always been unchangeable, making me secure and giving me refuge! Now the chain of my trust in you has snapped and I'm adrift without an anchor, rudderless in this storm of my conflicting thoughts!"

The first raindrops spattered against his face as he continued to pray, "If I dare concede that you inspired Pilate alter what the prophets had foretold, then that means that you don't intend that I, Jesus of Galilee, be the savior of the world! Who then have you chosen? O God, speak to me; am I or am I not your chosen one?"

As if in response to his questions, Jesus heard a series of earsplitting thunderclaps as driving winds sent drenching rain through his window. Quickly, he turned away and found his way to his sleeping mat in the darkness. As he lay down, his rain-soaked robe feeling like a second skin, he waited for sleep to come. However, instead of sleep, a memory came of when the Pharisees and Scribes had come to him and demanded, "How dare you teach what contradicts the ageless words of God in the sacred writings?" Jesus felt a smile creep across his face as he remembered his inspired reply: "Did not the prophet say that God makes all things new? I am a teacher of God's new law." That memory faded into the darkness as he slowly fell asleep.

Jesus was awakened in the middle of the night by the need to relieve himself. He could tell by the pale moonlight through his window that the great thunderstorm had passed over and moved inland. By the feeble moonlight he made his way across the wet floor to his privy jar and then stood at the window, inhaling deeply of the sea air, which was pungent with the smell of seaweed and fish after the thunderstorm.

I wonder, he thought, *does tonight's air smell like it did after that great storm when old Jonah was washed ashore outside of Nineveh after being belched up by the great sea monster? As a youth I heard the story of God telling Jonah to go to Nineveh and preach repentance to those uncircumcised Assyrian pagans, and how he refused! That he refused was no surprise. As small children we had been taught to have nothing to do with uncircumcised pagans, not even to give them so much as a drink of water. Being a Galilean land-bound child, it was exciting to hear how Jonah boarded a ship sailing to a foreign port in the opposite direction of Nineveh. A great storm arose, perhaps like that one tonight, and the ship's sailors thought it was because the gods had cursed Jonah, and so they threw him overboard. He was swallowed by a great sea monster and was inside its belly for three days and nights, until it vomited him up on the seashore not far from the city of Nineveh.*

Pausing a moment in his childhood recollection, Jesus said aloud, "That's interesting. Three days and nights is how long the voice said I would spend in the tomb after I die. Companions," Jesus patted the stone walls, "do you think there was some reason that I remembered that tale of Jonah tonight? True, he was a prophet, albeit a begrudging one who finally did convert the people of pagan Nineveh to repent and turn to the ways of God."

Jesus returned to his sleeping mat and lay down; however, sleep evaded him. He rolled over again and again on his mat in an attempt to fall asleep, but his aching legs made sleep difficult. He thought, *Just like Jonah, I've unwillingly found myself here in pagan Caesarea. Does God want me, like Jonah, to proclaim God's love to these uncircumcised pagan Romans, including Pilate?* The darkness of his cell did not answer and Jesus tried to sleep, but the pains in his joints chased slumber away. He thought, *When the prophets foretold I would suffer revilement and torture, they forgot to include the pains of my swollen and aching joints that have afflicted me these past few years.*

Unable to sleep, Jesus rubbed his red and swollen knees, trying to bring some relief from the piercing pains. With difficulty he stood up and walked over to the window, looking at the stars that had been washed by the rain and seemed brighter than usual. Seeing an unusually bright star high in the sky, he spoke to it, saying, "You must be Venus, who Pilate said was named for a Roman goddess. He said you signal the time for the evening meal. Sparkling Venus, are you signaling to me that it's time for something, and if so, time for what? Heavenly Father, you who numbered all the stars and called each by name, did you name that bright star 'Venus'? O star, you whose true name is known only to God, guide me on the course I am to take."

SCENE IX

THE TERRACE AT THE
PALACE AT CAESAREA

Early March, 36 C.E.

Jesus will be here soon, thought Pilate, stroking his upper lip. *If you don't crucify him, what are you going to do with him? You can't just set him free to wander around Judea without putting your life into jeopardy. Remember what Cicero said; think what might happen, so you won't be taken by surprise. These past months you've never stopped to consider what you would do with him if you didn't crucify him. Don't delay any longer!*

Petronius said, "Your Excellency, the prisoner Jesus is here, whom you requested."

Pilate replied, "No, Petronius—whom I've invited. Dismiss those two soldiers, for we have no need of them." Jesus approached, shading his eyes from the bright sunlight with his right hand. Seated next to Pilate was Lucius, and Marcus and Quintus were standing nearby.

"Jesus," said Pilate, beckoning with his right hand, "come and be seated next to me. I regret it has been some time since you and I saw one another, but I had to go to Samaria to investigate rumors of potential trouble there. After leaving Samaria I made my annual official tour of Galilee. Since I've returned my hours have been filled with duties and reports, all of which have prevented me from returning to your trial."

Jesus nodded, acknowledging Pilate's explanation, but half of him wanted to scream about how his trial was plagued by endless delays. The other half, inspired by the Jonah story, now felt that he should be friendly with Pilate. These two sides of Jesus wrestled with one another as he thought, *I must demand that Pilate crucify me as soon as possible — yet if God has cast me upon the shores of Caesarea like Jonah to convert these gentiles, then I mustn't irritate Pilate. Grit your teeth, Jesus;*

you don't know what God is doing. Just surrender and wait patiently to be shown God's will.

Pilate remarked, "Before you arrived I reviewed Lucius' record of your trial and would like to return to our discussion about truth. According to Lucius' excellent notes, when I asked if you were a king, you replied, and I quote, 'I was born to testify to the truth, and those who belong to the truth hear my voice,' to which I replied...."

"What is truth?'" Jesus interjected. "Don't look so surprised that I remembered what you said, Pilate. Your question left a stain in my heart as enduring as purple dye."

"And how would you answer my question today?"

Jesus said, "After all this time thinking about it, I feel I understand more clearly what I said to you."

"You confuse me," Pilate responded. "You didn't know what you were saying when you said it?"

Jesus replied, "I trusted I would be told by the Spirit what to say, even if I didn't understand what it meant. I taught my disciples that whenever they were questioned before the authorities they shouldn't fret or try to prepare their answers but trust that the Spirit would tell them what to say."

Pilate observed, "But in Jerusalem when I asked you if you were a king, you said nothing! What happened? Didn't your...uh...*voice* tell you what to say then?"

"Oh, it did, Pilate! It told me to *say* nothing! It said just to remain silent, because 'Pilate doesn't desire to know what is truth.'"

"Your voice spoke correctly," Pilate noted. "At that moment, with a riot brewing, I didn't have the time to engage in a speculative discussion about anything. However, your so-called 'voice' was also incorrect; I did desire to know what is truth. So today, with no mob barking at my heels, I'll ask you again; Jesus, what is truth?"

"Truth is what is steadfast and unchangeable," Jesus replied. "Truth is enduring; it is something you can rely upon. For example, a 'true' peace is not simply a temporary pause in the fighting but an enduring period of peace. If someone is called truthful, that means they're steadfastly trustworthy. For another example, from what I've seen of your Centurion Petronius, I'd say he's a truthful man!"

Pilate responded, "I completely agree with your judgment. As for me, my understanding of truth is based on the word for it in Greek, *alethein,* meaning something unveiled—no longer concealed. From my old tutor Lucius here, I learned that in the Greek mind, truth and what is real are connected."

"I agree with your idea of truth, Pilate," Jesus said. "For me, too, what is true is real—something touchable. When I told you I was born to be a witness to the truth, I meant that in my life I have tried be a living, tangible witness to the steadfast love of God."

Pilate asked, "How is that possible, to witness in a material way to the love of a god who, being celestial, is logically not of this earthly world?"

"I witness by deeds," Jesus replied. "The children of God are to be witnesses to the love of God by acts of feeding the hungry, clothing the poor, and caring for the physical needs of others as best they can from their limited means. They also are witnesses to the heavenly Father's love by living in his providential care and not being anxious about tomorrow."

"Children of God!" Pilate exclaimed. "So we're back to your old theme of being a child of some god! Jesus, I'm a grown man; I can never be a child again even if I wanted to be. Tell me, how can a grown man become a child again?"

Jesus sat silently and brooded, *Pilate's done it again—it's almost as if he sees inside the deepest recesses of my heart and its secrets. With that question, he's once again unknowingly exposed one of my struggles—how can I, as an old man, relate to God as my father? I'm in the midst of the unpleasant harvest of aging; with my aches and pains and vision and hearing loss, my most cherished father-son relationship with God now seems no longer appropriate. Speak, Spirit; how am I to answer Pilate?*

As the awkward silence continued, Petronius, seated on the third couch, attempted to end it. "If I may, Sir, I have a question for the prisoner." Pilate nodded and Petronius said, "My question concerns your saying, 'The truth will set you free.' How does the truth that you and Pilate have been discussing set a person free?"

"Truth liberates those enslaved by illusion," Jesus replied, relieved by the question, since he had no answer to Pilate's query about being a child. "Truth frees you from error and therefore also from sin, which is but an error in making a choice between good and evil. I'll give you an example. You're very aware of the intense hatred the Jewish people have for you Romans, just as they also hated the Greeks, the Babylonians, and other foreign oppressors. My fellow countrymen see their hatred as something good—a sign of their great love for Israel—but that's an illusion! The truth is that their hatred isn't a sign of love and in fact enslaves them more than any foreign oppressor. The most domineering of all oppressors and tyrants is hatred!"

"I've never thought about hate as being an oppressor," said Petronius.

"It is the most oppressive, Centurion. That's why in my life I have passionately sought to be a free man; unlike my fellow countrymen, I have not hated you Romans or your military occupation."

"That's true, Sir," Petronius said. "While traveling across Galilee for Prince Antipas, I never once met anyone who quoted Jesus as expressing any hatred for us or calling for an uprising against Rome to get rid of us."

"Yet, Jesus, at your trial," said Pilate, "Caiaphas and the priests accused you of plotting the overthrow of Rome by making yourself the King of the Jews."

Jesus replied, "I never agitated to overthrow Rome or the Temple; I had no need to, because they will collapse under their own dead weight!"

A heavy tomblike stillness followed Jesus' statement, and Pilate's face spoke loudly of his angry resentment at what Jesus had just said. Jesus thought, *You stupid son of Mary, why did you lump together the Temple and Rome? Have you forgotten your resolution to try to befriend these pagans? Now you've offended and angered Pilate. True, what you said about the Temple and Rome collapsing is correct, but have the common sense, Jesus, to speak the truth only to those who can hear it!*

"Pilate, forgive me for that remark about Rome," Jesus said, quickly. "I know it surely offended you. I regret that I included Rome in my heated emotions about the Temple. It's the Temple and the religion connected with it that cause my soul to seethe because they so callously oppress the people, especially the poor."

As Jesus was speaking, Pilate was mulling over his comment about Rome. *As impossible as it sounds, he may be right about Rome collapsing. Rome is growing fat, soft, and corrupt. Love for the country and a sense of duty to Rome are disappearing, and her citizens are not interested in the decisions of the senate, nor are they zealous to defend the Empire. Most of them simply want to be entertained by bread and circuses. If what Jesus predicts happens, I hope I don't live long enough to see it.*

"I realized, Pilate," Jesus continued, "that the Temple is only a stone building, and it is the leeches clinging to it that anger me—the priests, scribes, and religious aristocrats who, with their temple tithes, rob the poor, along with those peddlers who exploit the pilgrims. The priests and aristocrats know this is how I feel about them and that I proclaim there is no need for a temple and its sacrifices; that's why they wanted to crucify me, and...," Jesus paused.

"Don't stop!" Pilate said. "Please continue; you're giving me a window into what was going on at your trial in Jerusalem. Although I'm not a religious man, as usual, you've aroused my curiosity. If you want to destroy the Temple and its rituals, aren't you doing away with religion?"

Jesus explained, "Temple religion, yes! For that is a religion where the priestly elite grind the poor into dust under the heavy millstones of religious tithes. The Temple priests aren't any different from wealthy landowners who greedily work their poor tenant farmers into their graves. I believe that once temple religion is overthrown, then the world can embrace the religion of the heart."

Pilate replied, "Religion of the heart? In Rome and in my travels I've come across many religions and mystery cults, but never a religion of the heart."

Jesus said, "I called it a religion, but it really isn't one because it doesn't have any temples, priests, or priestesses to act as intercessors to pray for you or pronounce you cleansed of sin."

"Well, if it's not a religion, what is it?" Pilate asked.

"It's a...a way of life. A new way of life for those who have repented and turned their lives around to live according to God's way. That is, by loving their neighbors as they love themselves and living daily as if the Kingdom of God has already arrived."

"What would be an example of this new way of living?" asked Pilate, who appeared truly interested.

Jesus said thoughtfully, "An example...well, the people who are living this new way no longer condemn the injustices of Rome and instead condemn their own injustices to one another! They desire a revolution not against Caesar but an uprising against their own greed, injustices, and sins of neglecting the poor."

"Hmmm," Pilate mused. "Well, while I would like to continue discussing this new kind of religion you want to bring to the people, your hostility toward the Temple and her priests remind me that it's time to go to Jerusalem for the Passover Festival. I'll be away for a couple of weeks, but during that time I'll reflect on this most interesting...."

"Pilate, please take me with you to Jerusalem, so I can die as...." Instantly Jesus stopped, ashamed for slipping back into his habit of badgering Pilate about being crucified.

"I'm sorry, Jesus; I can't break my promise to Caiaphas that he and Jerusalem would never again be troubled by the sight of you. With regard to your death on the cross, you'll just have to be patient."

"I understand. But while you are in Jerusalem, if you encounter High Priest Caiaphas and he asks if you have crucified me yet, what are you going to say?"

"I'll tell him what I just said to you: Be patient! We Romans have an old saying: 'Patience is the best remedy for every trouble.' So, Jesus, I suggest you go back to your cell and take your bitter medicine of patience. Centurion, see that the prisoner is escorted back to his quarters."

When Jesus and his escort reached the edge of hallway, Pilate called out. "Oh, I almost forgot." Jesus stopped and turned back toward Pilate. "For some time now my wife Claudia has wanted to meet you, and she asked if we could all have dinner together out here on the terrace some evening. I told her after I returned from the Passover in Jerusalem I would invite you, in her name, to dine with us. Lady Claudia would be greatly pleased if you would accept her invitation, but she is aware that in your culture men do not share meals with women, and also that she and I are gentile pagans. Unlike me, my wife is very sensitive. Because she's aware that we're pagans and her presence at the table presents a moral dilemma for you, she'll understand if you can't accept her invitation. I thought I'd tell you about her invitation now so you can have some time to think about it while I'm away."

Jesus replied, "I don't need any time! I already know my response. Please tell Lady Claudia that I accept her kind invitation."

SCENE X

JESUS' CELL

Early April Morning, 36 C.E.

Jesus struggled to get off his sleeping mat and felt a familiar painful stiffness in his knees and ankles. He was glad this was not one of those mornings when he felt so fatigued he didn't even want to get up. He pondered if these occasions of total exhaustion and the fact that recently he had no desire to eat could in any way be connected to the crippling pains in his joints. He hobbled over to his window.

I've watched the moon these past nights shrink from full to now only a slice, thought Jesus, as he meditated on the rising sun, which was casting dancing yellow beams on the waves. *The moon has told me that Passover is now long over. Surely Pilate has returned and may call for me, but I haven't yet solved the dilemma he raised at our last visit: "How can a grown man become as a child again?" I've prayed over it and still have no resolution to that problem Pilate unwittingly forced me to face.*

Closing his eyes, Jesus laid his forehead on the window ledge and allowed the stone's cooling touch to sooth him as he thought, *For years now, I've found closeness to God by addressing the All Holy One as, Abba, Father, finding reassurance and comfort in such a trusting, intimate name. But these past months I've become conscious that I'm now an old man, beset with the afflictions of old age.* Raising his head from the ledge, he mused, *I've felt the growing doubt of the appropriateness of my precious father-son relationship eating away at my soul like a rat gnawing on a turnip. It does feel odd for a grown man like me to address God as Abba, but if I'm not a child of God, what am I?*

One by one, each new wave coming ashore spoke of a new possibility: "Servant," said one, and then vanished into foam. "Messenger," said the next, followed by "witness," and then "prophet," as each of them, one by one, dissolved. Having not received an answer, Jesus prayed aloud, "O God, send me a truth-bearing wave that will speak of a new and suitable relationship with

128

you." After that brief prayer, each new wave that came ashore was disappointingly mute.

Jesus glumly shook his head as he turned away from the window and began to pace his cell. As he did so, he talked aloud to the walls, "Comrades of my imprisonment, my old stone friends, I didn't find the answer in the waves." He stopped, and in the quiet of his cell he felt his heart beating. "Do you think, old stones, I should ask my heart for a new name for God? It seems like a good place to begin, as it's the seat of love, and love is God. While I'm beginning to doubt many things, I have never questioned the powerful conviction that every time I've experienced love, I've also experienced the Holy One."

He stopped pacing and returned to the window, and as he looked out at the fathomless blue sea, he recalled a verse from the Song of Songs: *Deep waters cannot quench my love, nor floods sweep it away.* He repeated aloud, "'Deep waters cannot quench my love.'" He thought, *Indeed, true are those words about the invincible power of intimate love, for the deepest of waters couldn't quench my love for my youthful disciple John, which he returned by his steadfast loyalty and great affection.* Jesus paused, recalling their deep friendship. *While I loved all my disciples, John clearly was my favorite which made the others jealous that he was my....*

His thought abruptly ended as he suddenly said, "Friend! Yes, that's the name I've been searching for! My God, while you are indeed my Father, now you have become my beloved Friend, a perfect name for my adult, intimate relationship with you. Until now I never would have dared to address you by such an intimate name that implies equality, especially never in public, lest I be stoned to death! O God, you have been called *El Sabaoth* – Lord of Hosts, and *El Elyon* – God Most High, and Moses sternly forbid us to ever pronounce your holy name aloud, even in prayer. It was daring enough for me to address you in my prayers as Abba. I taught my disciples when they prayed to use that fatherly name to express their total dependence upon you, as would a small helpless child. It's only recently that I've grown to find it oddly unsuitable, when Pilate challenged me by his question of how a grown man could speak of you as a father."

As Jesus sensually inhaled ocean air, he felt ten years younger by this newest inspiration. He continued his conversation with God: "Calling you Abba was beautiful, but calling you 'My Beloved Friend' is even more intimate. 'Friend' fits our relationship, for a friend is another self, an affectionate companion, who shares your life. Friends are attracted to one another, as am I to you; and one depends upon a friend as I rely upon you. When you feel frightened or threatened, a friend is a safe refuge, as you are to me. You can trust that a friend will love you unconditionally, as I know you love me. And friends imitate each other, and oh, Beloved Friend, how I desire to be as much like you as possible!" Jesus' joy overflowed into prayer.

"My Beloved Friend, my heart is forever yours.
You are my sun and moon, the air I breathe.
Beloved Friend, you are my bread and wine,
whose affection feeds me with invigorating life.
Until this ocean becomes dry as a desert
and the sun burns into ashes, I will love you!"

SCENE XI

TRICLINIUM OF THE
PALACE AT CAESAREA

An Early Evening in May, 36 C.E.

"Jesus, come sit here on my left," said Pilate, who was attired in a white tunic. His wife, Claudia, was reclining on his right. On her right was Petronius, who wore a white Roman tunic instead of his uniform. A spring-laden breeze off the ocean blew across the terrace as Jesus stepped into the slightly moving yellow circle of light created by overhead oil lamps, which were gently swaying over the low table.

Pilate continued, "You know Petronius, whom I've invited to join us, but you haven't met my wife. Allow me to introduce you; this is Claudia Procula Pilate, the mistress of this house, and the one responsible for inviting you here tonight."

Jesus was struck by Claudia's beauty, highlighted by the golden yellow light of the overhead lamps, which caused her cream-colored complexion to shine. Her black hair had been carefully woven into rings like a crown atop her head. Her hairstyle imitated that of the empress, which was now the fashion among wealthy Roman women and the wives of Roman administrators. Claudia, as was the custom for Roman aristocratic women, wore a considerable amount of jewelry; her dangling golden pendant earrings were set with small pearls, while around her neck she wore several long strands of pearls and emeralds set in golden mesh chains. Entwined on her lower left arm was a golden bracelet made in the image of a coiled serpent with carved scales. She was wearing what appeared to be a silk or linen white tunic that had been pinned so that her right shoulder was bare. Draped over the silk tunic was a light-blue *stola* with intertwining red and gold designs on the borders, one end of which she had casually draped over her right arm.

Jesus had never before seen a woman so richly dressed, but he hid his astonishment by smiling as he graciously nodded to her and reclined on the couch. As soon as he did so, slaves stepped forward and washed Pilate's feet and hands; they then proceeded to do the same for the other three reclining at the table.

After the ritual washing ritual was completed, her brown oval eyes dancing, Claudia said, "Jesus of Galilee, I am told that according to ancient tradition, Jewish men never eat at the same table with women, even their own wives! Is my presence tonight at this table disconcerting to you?"

Jesus replied, "No, Lady Claudia, I don't observe that tradition."

"In fact, Claudia," Pilate said, smiling at her and taking great pride in the expensive jewelry he had acquired for her, "among the numerous accusations the Jerusalem religious authorities made against our guest was that he dined with women!"

"I'm curious," said Claudia. "Why don't you observe that tradition of your ancestors?"

"I believe God created men and women as equals, and so they should share life equally, eating at meals and sharing other aspects of daily life."

"Claudia, it has been reported to us," Pilate said, "that the women followers in Jesus' small group are indeed treated as equals, not only at their common meals but in all things, as we Romans do. That sounds very civilized, don't you think?"

"From what I've learned so far of the primitive customs of this province of Judea," replied Claudia, discreetly signaling the slaves to begin to serve the *gustatio,* the first course, "I am impressed, Jesus, by your progressive attitude toward women."

Slaves stepped forward and poured the first wine of the meal, customarily mixed with honey, into their cups. Pilate then held his cup out away from the table and poured some wine onto the floor. Seeing the bewildered look on Jesus' face, he said, "That's a libation to the gods by which we acknowledge their presence at this dinner; it's a sort of blessing or ritual of dedication."

"Jesus, what kind of ritual do the Jews use to begin their meals?" Claudia asked.

"We pray, Lady Claudia," Jesus replied. Then, picking up a piece of the round wheat bread, he pronounced over it the ritual blessing of bread in Hebrew. He broke off a large piece and handed it to Claudia, saying, "Break off a piece and eat it, and then pass the bread to Petronius." After Petronius broke off his piece he handed the bread across the table to Pilate, who apprehensively broke off a piece and ate it, handing the rest of the bread back to Jesus. After he had eaten his bread, Jesus lifted up his wine cup and pronounced in Hebrew the blessing of the wine; he leaned across the table and handed the cup to Claudia, saying, "Drink a little of it, and then pass the cup to Petronius." As she did so, Pilate's face betrayed his anxiety that very soon he was going to have to drink from the same cup a Jew had used. After drinking, Petronius handed the cup to Pilate, who, after taking the very slightest of sips, handed it to Jesus, who emptied the cup. Then he smiled at Claudia, "This is how we begin our meals."

Claudia, quickly attempting to cover her husband's obvious discomfort at being involved in a Jewish ritual, said, "Jesus, my husband has told me some things about your small group of followers in Galilee. He said that even though they believe you are dead, they still continue to meet together and that their numbers are actually growing."

"You are correct, Lady Claudia," Petronius quickly added, eager to assist her in hiding Pilate's discomfort. "Our spies report that the cult is indeed growing. It seems anyone can join their group; social outcasts, non-observant Jews, peasants, slaves, Jewish collectors of our Roman taxes, prostitutes, and...."

"Prostitutes!" Claudia said, interrupting him. "Do you mean temple prostitutes who provide communion with the gods, or women who provide a public service like bakers and wine merchants?"

"Lady Claudia, here in Judea," answered Jesus, "'prostitute' is a word used for women who offer their bodies for men's pleasure in exchange for money. Unlike in Greece and Rome, here in Israel, prostitution isn't an acceptable practice; our moral religious code condemns it as a grave sin before our God."

"How odd," replied Claudia, "that your god would judge as divinely offensive a respectable public service! For us Romans, prostitution is an ancient and respectful trade that provides the sexual satisfaction that is necessary for a healthy, well-ordered life. Prostitutes provide a much-needed service," she added, smiling at Pilate, "for those unfortunate men who can't find that pleasure at home."

"I'm aware, Lady Claudia, of that attitude from my contact with Greeks and Romans in Galilee," Jesus said. "I should explain that 'prostitute' can have two meanings: it can mean a woman who sells her body for a man's pleasure, or it can be used as an insulting slur for a woman who defies village social or religious codes. It is also used for a woman who, in public, freely speaks her mind and for women who are disciples and dine with their master, as do his male disciples."

Claudia smiled and said, "And of those two kinds of prostitutes, which are your disciples?"

"Both!" he said, smiling back at her. "God loves both kinds of these women unconditionally, and in imitation of God, I also unconditionally accept them. Besides, Lady Claudia, we both know how seductive is the enticement to prostitute oneself to achieve some personal gain."

Inwardly Pilate raged like a seething volcano about to erupt: *How crude of this Jew, who is a guest at my table, to disgrace my Claudia by comparing her to a common whore!* Just as he was about to challenge Jesus, he abruptly had a change of heart that caused his inner anger to evaporate as he thought, *But he's right! In politics and in the military, the need to prostitute oneself is essential for advancement! Have not I acted like a whore to advance my career, stooping before those who were my superiors to massage them with flattery, and obsequiously agreeing with whatever they said? Just now, Jesus implied to Claudia that he knew the temptation to prostitute oneself; I wonder when or to whom?*

"Lady Claudia, I share meals with women," Jesus said, "because I relish the company of those who are willing to bravely defy outdated village traditions and irrelevant religious laws restricting their rightful behavior. I'm drawn to free spirits, like you," he said, with a broad grin.

"I try to have a free spirit," said Claudia, as she extended her right hand across the table toward Jesus. "Do you see this silver ring on my index finger? I saw it among the wears of a jeweler and fell in love with it, and my generous husband purchased it for me, even if he had qualms about the inscription. Jesus, can you read what is engraved on it?"

"I regret, Lady Claudia, that I know little if any Latin. Would you translate the words for me?"

"*Libera Viva* means, 'May you live free.' I have made those two words my motto," she said, smiling again at Pilate, "which often can make life difficult for my husband."

"Our spies in Galilee," Petronius said, attempting to shift the conversation away from prostitutes and free-spirited women, "report that at the secret gatherings of Jesus' disciples, everyone is treated as an equal — the poor and the wealthy, peasants and their landholders, and even slaves and their masters."

"Remarkable!" said Claudia, as she dipped a piece of bread in a dish of wine and began nibbling on it. "Personally, I think that's going a bit too far! If daily life is to function properly, I believe that slaves and mistresses must stay in their appropriate stations in life." Then, graciously gesturing to the three men, she said, "Please help yourselves to our first course of olives, cheese, and these crackers." As she nibbled on a piece of cheese, she commented, "I can't even imagine how a decent household could function if the mistress and her slaves treated each other as equals."

"Lady Claudia," Jesus said, "I was pleased to hear Petronius say my followers practice equality, because that was our rule while I was still among them. No one was to be ranked as more important than another, and whoever was the leader was to be the slave of all. We were all to be one; male or female, gentile or Jew, slave or free." Turning to his right and smiling, he said, "Now Pilate, doesn't that sound civilized to you?"

Pilate covered his lack of response by holding a napkin over his mouth as he spit an olive pit into it. *Slaves equal with their masters!* he thought. *That's anarchy! May the gods help us if such insane lunacy should ever befall the Empire, as it would mean the end of civilization!* Then by slamming his empty wine cup down on the table he released some of his anger. A startled slave holding a wine jar jumped and rushed over to the table. He filled Pilate's cup with a different wine, as another slave placed a small pitcher of water on the table. Pilate picked up the pitcher and used this time to calm himself as he poured a little water into the wine in his cup.

"Jesus," he said, "the wine that is now being served is imported from Italy, and since it is more potent than Judean wines, it requires a little watering down."

Nodding, Jesus said, "I shall follow your example," and poured some water into his wine. As he drank from his cup, he thought, *What needs watering down to the point of being completed diluted is the slave-owning civilizations of Greece and Rome! I'm told that half or more of their people are enslaved as living tools to serve the needs and whims of the wealthy minority. But the time is coming....*

"Just now, Petronius reported that in your small group of followers, the slaves and masters treat each other as equals," said Pilate, smiling, as he dipped a piece of bread in the wine. "That's an interesting statement; I think it confirms that you Jews, like we Romans, own slaves?"

Jesus nodded silently in agreement, worried that a smiling Pilate was surely setting up another one of his traps for him, and he cautioned himself to be careful.

Pilate continued, "Yet I've gathered that you yourself highly disapprove of slavery. Am I correct in that assumption?"

"You are! I'm strongly opposed to slavery, because it's contrary to our dignity as...." Realizing he was about to say "the children of God," Jesus swallowed those words and said, "...the people of God."

"Yet, Jesus, while you strongly reject slavery as being opposed to the desires of your god, I find it unusual that, since you've forbidden your disciples to divorce, to return evil for evil, and to think angry thoughts about another, you've never forbidden them to own slaves." Pilate was growing more animated by the moment, as he was enjoying this verbal match. "Now, if you truly believe that slavery is such a grave evil, why haven't you condemned it to your disciples or to the crowds?"

Jesus sat in silence, waiting for the Spirit to give him the words to reply to Pilate's stinging and shaming accusation. None came; only silence.

"What, are you lost for words?" Pilate, drunk on victory, aggressively pushed forward his attack. "I'm curious why you didn't prophetically call for your Jewish people to overthrow this great evil of slavery, as did our Roman ex-gladiator Spartacus. Is it because you feared that, like Spartacus, you would be nailed to a cross? But that can't be the reason, because you wanted to be crucified; so, prophet of Galilee, why did you never condemn slavery?"

Jesus replied, "Enough, Pilate, enough! You've more than made your case clear; I know about your Roman Spartacus and how he attracted a great army of escaped slaves to join him in his ill-fated attempt to overthrow Roman slavery. But I'm no Spartacus! Unlike him and others like him, I don't believe you can change humanity by gathering a massive army of devoted supporters! I don't care how righteously motivated or vast be the numbers of those marching with you, they are impotent to ultimately change any great moral evil."

Pilate responded, "That's a bold and interesting declaration; why are they impotent?"

Jesus said, "Anger, even righteous anger, against any great evil is only the other face of the very evil you are attempting to overthrow. Evil can never overcome evil, so I have taught another way."

"As a military man, I wholeheartedly disagree with you that armed force is an evil," Pilate replied. "But I'm curious — what other way is there to deal with evil in the world?"

"The way I've taught is God's way, which I acknowledge is slower, yet ultimately it will be victorious. Armies of thousands who are angrily opposed to an evil like slavery can't overthrow it. You only change humanity slowly, one person at a time, by loving others as you love yourself — for true love makes slavery impossible."

"Ha — love!" sneered Pilate.

"Wonderful! Look, here come the dishes of the first course," announced Claudia, relieved to be able to change the conversation. Pilate and Jesus became silent as slaves stepped forward and washed their hands and then those of the others. After the slaves had dried their hands with towels, Claudia said, "Jesus, you really must taste this pickled asparagus or these artichokes, which are especially delicious."

"Jesus, I assure you," said Petronius, as he nibbled on a pickled carrot, "you will find that the meals at Lady Claudia's table are truly marvelous. I assure you they far exceed the chick pea and fava bean fare of us Roman legionaries." Claudia chuckled, smiling graciously at Petronius with gratitude for joining her in her attempt to redirect the conversation.

"Lady Claudia," said Jesus, "I agree with Centurion Petronius that this meal is delicious, and it far exceeds the usual bland ones of Galilean peasants. May I ask," he said, holding up a piece of food from a plate, "what is this?"

"Cauliflower. Taste it, Jesus; you'll find it to be delicious. However, I advise you to eat sparingly of these vegetables; they are only the first course of our dinner."

"I shall heed your advice, Lady Claudia, for if this food is only the beginning," Jesus said, raising his eyebrows in mock shock, "I can't imagine what is to follow." As Jesus nibbled on the cauliflower, he wondered, *I know Romans love to eat roasted pig; I pray, Beloved Friend, that is not the main dish of the dinner to follow.* Turning to his right, he said, "Pilate, before these delicious vegetables were served, you laughingly dismissed love. But love isn't comical; it's the most powerful revolutionary force in the world!"

"Revolutionary!" Pilate mumbled, his mouth full of artichoke. "Impossible! Love is only a feeling, and I assure you, Jesus, that feelings, regardless of how noble they may be, have never changed empires or history!"

"Pilate, I beg to differ!" Jesus replied. "Love is truly revolutionary, since it is the greatest force on earth in its power to level! Love has the power to lower those who are higher and elevate those who are lower until both are on the same level. Lovers and friends, in spite of their differences in age or even social positions, cannot truly be friends unless they meet as equals. No man who doesn't treat his wife as his equal can truly love her, and so love will be the powerful leveling force that ultimately will be victorious over slavery."

"Jesus, be practical!" Pilate retorted. "I'm a military man, and in my many years of serving the Empire in the army, I have never seen a single enemy or kingdom conquered by love! In the history of warfare, love has never conquered any empire; the sword, not emotions like love, is the greatest power!"

"Friend," Jesus said, placing his hand on Pilate's arm and gazing into his eyes, "you will see love be victorious, when God's Kingdom fully arrives!"

Pilate made no reply, for he was swamped by conflicting emotions caused by Jesus' unexpected gesture of touching him, gazing into his eyes, and calling him "friend."

"Allow me to explain, Pilate," Jesus continued. "Tonight this world is one vast field of prickly thorn bushes of aggression, wars, slavery, and violence. However, I foresee a day when there will appear a single, tightly curled flower bud in the middle of this ugly, thorn bush–infested world. When that flower bud unfolds and fully blooms into a breathtakingly beautiful flower, it will release the sweet, intoxicating perfume of peace and harmony. Then, as do all living things, it will age and die, but as it dies it will release its seeds. Then those seeds of that first flower will sprout one by one and bloom into beautiful flowers. Then in time they also will die and their seeds will be scattered across the earth. From them will spring hundreds and then thousands upon thousands of flowers like them, releasing the perfume of peace. Then the earth will be an endless field of beautiful flowers from horizon to horizon. When that day comes there will be no room left on this earth for the ugly, prickly thorn bushes of war and violence."

"Flowers?" Pilate snorted, as he struggled to shake off the feeling that, by Jesus' trance-weaving voice, he was being entangled like a fish in a net. "No, Jesus; the victor in this world will be the sword in the hands of the powerful, never fickle love or vulnerable, weak-stemmed flowers!"

Jesus glanced over at Claudia, and seeing her crestfallen face, he at once felt guilty for his part in destroying the mood of this meal. She, the mistress of the house, had tried to create a lovely evening meal of delicious foods and delightful conversation, and he and Pilate had spoiled it with their animated arguments over slavery and politics.

"Lady Claudia, I ask your pardon," Jesus said, slightly bowing to her. "Please forgive me for spoiling your wonderful dinner by discussing such controversial subjects. I apologize for being so thoughtless."

Pilate raised his napkin to his face and coughed. Although embarrassed about his part in the fiery debate, he wasn't able to publicly acknowledge any sense of guilt, and instead pointed up at the starry night sky over the ocean and said, "The night sky is so lovely tonight—a gift from the Roman Goddess Maia, for whom this month of May is named. Tonight she has gifted us with an enchanting, deep blue sea below that mirrors a dark-blue sky above in which in breathtaking beauty she has scattered handfuls of the brightest, sparkling stars."

"That's charming, Pilate, and so poetic," said Claudia, as she discreetly signaled the slaves to begin the hand washing before serving the dishes of the main course. "Now under this magical night sky, so creatively described by my husband, it is time for our next course."

As the slaves moved gracefully around the table, washing and drying each person's hands, Pilate thought, *She's right, my words were rather poetic; that's unusual for me. Maybe I was inspired by the Galilean's description of his fanciful rebellion as a field of beautiful flowers. Damn Jew! He thinks he's so original with his ideas about equality. We Romans commemorate the equality of all men at the winter solstice celebration of the god Saturn. An old Roman custom during Saturnalia is for the masters of the households to humble themselves by waiting on their slaves as they are seated at table. Once I was told that this radical reverse of roles reflected the natural equality among all men, and that the Saturnalia custom foreshadows the coming reign of the God Saturn when all men will be equal.*

As the slaves placed a great platter with a huge, steaming, fattened goose on the table, Pilate inwardly snorted, *Ha! The coming of the equality in the future reign of Saturn—that fable sounds like Jesus' coming fabled kingdom! No one takes seriously that equality between the master and his slaves at Saturnalia; it's just a time for jest and laughter, as part of the comical amusements of the festival. The next morning, for endless centuries, it's always been back to reality, when everyone returns to their proper stations!*

Jesus was relieved that the main dish was a fat roasted goose and not a stuffed roasted pig. He saw dishes of savory fish sauce and other spices surrounding the large platter of goose. Never before in his life until this night's gathering under the stars had he seen anything like this feast. As he enjoyed the flavorful and tender goose, he worried about whether he would have any room left for the third and final course he had been told was coming.

As Pilate devoured the succulent seasoned meal, he reflected, *I would have preferred roasted pig, but I know Claudia especially chose goose after inquiring from her Judean slaves about what foods Jews could and couldn't eat.* As Pilate ate a piece of goose, his mind was trying to digest Jesus' bizarre prediction about the end of slavery. *While parts of this evening have had their unpleasant side, this marvelous food has more than made up for the times Jesus contradicted and challenged me!* His thoughts about food caused Pilate to jump ahead to the evening's desert. Glancing over at the side tables, he saw on it bowls of grapes and other fruits and dishes filled with almonds, chestnuts, walnuts, and pine nuts. Finally, he saw his favorite desert of wheat cakes soaking in honey.

"You'll find it interesting, Lady Claudia," said Petronius, whose voice catapulted a distracted Pilate back to the present, "that it has been reported to us that the gatherings of Jesus' followers are centered on the secret ritual of eating a meal, which they call, 'The Breaking of the Bread.'"

"Secret? Petronius," she asked, "why do you think their ritual meals are kept clandestine?"

"I don't know, Lady Claudia, but I suspect the secrecy involved is because they don't want to risk being identified as Jesus' followers for fear of being arrested and maybe crucified. We have heard that these secret suppers are in remembrance of the last meal Jesus ate on the night he was arrested. What I know of their meals is limited to spy reports; perhaps you should ask Jesus why they're secret?"

"Everything I did," Jesus replied without being asked, "and that my followers did before I was arrested was done openly. While our teacher-disciple friendship meals were intimate, they were never secret. If my followers now gather secretly behind closed doors, I suspect the Centurion is correct, and they do so out of fear."

Pilate said, "Petronius, I have an obligation to be vigilant for any secretive, subversive groups within my jurisdiction, and that includes Galilee. So I must ask: Do you believe that some subversive activity is taking place in these secret gatherings of this Galilean cult?"

"Regretfully, Sir, I don't know that answer, nor do our spies! What does or doesn't happen at those secret meals is knowledge restricted to those who attend." Pausing, he added, "And the only ones allowed to attend are those who have been initiated in their water ritual."

"Is it possible, Petronius," interjected Claudia, "that these secret meals are a Jewish version of our Roman death memorial meals that are eaten by family and friends at the tombs of a dead family member?"

"I think a better explanation, Claudia," said Pilate, "about why they're clandestine is that they are engaging in magical rites of the dead by which they conjure up their dead leader."

Petronius said, "That's a very fascinating idea, Sir, especially as it's rumored that at some of these meals his disciples do experience the presence of their dead teacher Jesus!"

"Just as I thought!" smiled Pilate. "Do you think he returns as some kind of a phantom to pump up their courage?" Laying a goose leg on his plate and wiping his hands on his napkin, Pilate continued, "Petronius, I've got a feeling in my gut that this radical Jewish cult may be dangerous and needs watching. They are not, as I first surmised, simply a small gathering of simple-minded peasants and fishermen grieving the loss of their teacher. Yes, I can feel it down here...,"as he patted his stomach, "...something dangerously seditious is brewing up there in Galilee."

Petronius nodded, as Pilate resumed chewing on his goose leg. Then, after drinking some wine, he lifted and lowered his right hand. "Petronius, in this hand I've got those troubling rebellious Samaritans who eager for an uprising, and in this other hand," lifting his left higher, "I now have this potentially treacherous Jesus cult in Galilee."

"Yes, Sir. If I might use a figure of speech, it seems 'you have your hands full.'"

"Well put, Centurion! This Samaritan problem in my right hand is heavier than the one in my left, since we have excellent reports from spies of the activities of that wild religious prophet Simeon and his Samaritan followers. While in this other hand," again lifting his left hand higher, "I have a problem about which I know very little. In fact, there are only vague rumors and village hearsay! It is expedient, Petronius, that we get an informer inside that secret cult as soon as possible if we are to...."

"Jesus, earlier this evening in this 'pleasant' dinner," said Claudia, trying to redirect the table conversation away from threats of insurrection, "you enchantingly spoke of the power of love, comparing it to the unfolding of a flower bloom."

Pilate's unfinished sentence stuck like a fish bone in his throat, and he closed his lips and looked down at his plate, thinking, *You fool, Pilate! You've done it again! You're ruining her beautiful dinner with your ranting about your political problems of rebellion in Samaria and secret cults in Galilee. Be civilized! Stop ignoring Claudia's desire that this be a lovely dinner, and put aside your political problems until tomorrow morning. Now I'm going to give myself a direct order: "Pilate, place a sentry on duty at your mouth to keep your tongue from getting loose again!"*

"While the passionate love between two young lovers is beautiful," Claudia continued, "that love never has changed society. While I find your poetic teaching of the world filled with people who love each other to be ethically interesting, isn't it doomed?"

"Doomed?" ask Jesus.

"Yes, doomed by the passage of time. I see the top of the hourglass of love as being filled with water and the bottom half as being a cup full of ardent love. Day after day, drip after drip, time slowly dilutes the once-strong intoxicating romantic love," gesturing toward the water carafe, "just as we watered down this potent dinner wine. Since love loses its wild youthful vitality with the passage of time, don't you think the same will happen to your dream of the world being radically changed by love?"

"I agree with you, Lady Claudia; the vivacious youthful passion of lovers doesn't last forever. Yet it doesn't die! Just as youthful enthusiasm can mature into lifelong zeal, so youthful passionate love can and should mature into the enduring love of a committed lifelong companionship. Those lovers in my vision are committed for life to changing the world."

"Fascinating! As for myself, Jesus," she replied, "I have adopted the wisdom of Ovid, who said, 'To be loved, be lovable!' So I try to be as lovable a woman as possible so I will be loved."

"You have chosen an inspiring challenge," Jesus said. "I also have given myself a challenge; to strive as best I can to love the loveable as well as those who do not love me."

Claudia responded, "Why on earth would you want to love those who aren't lovable, and especially anyone who doesn't like you?"

Jesus said, "That is my goal because I believe we are all made in the image of God, and God is love! Therefore, our life's duty is to fulfill our birth image by loving as God loves, which means loving all—the loveable as well as the unlovable."

We're made in a god's image? thought Claudia, taking a sip of her wine. *What a strange idea. I've never thought of myself as being created in the image of the goddess Diana or Venus, and certainly never like any male god. I wonder if this god of love that Jesus speaks about is the Jewish version of Cupid, or Eros? For myself, I can't image myself being made in the image of a beautiful winged boy like Cupid. While I fail to comprehend much of what this Jesus says, he surely seems to know much about love.*

As she took another sip from her goblet, she looked over its rim across the table at Jesus. The light from the hanging oil lamps gave his face a golden glow and she pondered, *I wonder if Socrates or Plato were as captivating to their students as is this Jesus? He certainly looks like an old Greek philosopher with his white-streaked gray beard and hair and those compelling eyes. No wonder disciples followed him—and it's no surprise he had women disciples.*

"Jesus, as you and Lady Claudia have been discussing love," said Petronius, "I have a question about something you taught concerning love. Why did you teach, if not command, your disciples to love their enemies? Being an army man, I tend to think like one, so is your command a kind of reverse military maneuver? That is, by asking a disciple to love his enemy, are you actually challenging him to conquer himself and his natural urge in battle to injure and kill his enemy?"

Before Jesus could answer, Claudia said, "I recall, Petronius, that our great Roman poet Ovid said, 'Every lover is a warrior' and 'Love is a kind of warfare.' Until you asked your question just now, I never understood his words."

In the midst of this conversation Pilate was wrestling with the self-appointed guard he had stationed at his lips to ensure he wouldn't say anything to disturb the dinner. *What an insane idea*, he thought, *that love is like warfare. Only a man who has never been in battle could have dreamed up anything as ridiculous as that. Rumors say that Emperor Augustus exiled that old goat Ovid for his amusing poems on how best to seduce women. But who knows the real reason the Emperor exiled him, since only the gods know what incites imperial displeasure?*

"The poet Virgil, when speaking of love," said Claudia, "also used military language when he said, 'Love conquers all things; so let us surrender to love.'" She was delighted with this animated discussion on love and thought, *I deeply love Pilate; he is a good husband and father to our children. But he's never comfortable talking about love or his own personal emotions. What Pilate relishes is talk of battles, politics, the intrigues in the Roman Senate, and rumors about the Emperor.* Aware that her dinner companions were silent, she quickly ended her thoughts, saying, "Petronius, what is your opinion of Virgil's words, 'Love conquers all things'?"

"Lady Claudia, I'm no poet. Like your husband, I am a military man who is suited to more practical issues. However, in discussing love, I am fond of Aristotle's answer to the question, 'What is a friend?'"

"I know what you're about to say," interrupted Claudia. "Friends are 'a single soul dwelling in two bodies.' I find the idea of two lovers or two friends sharing a single soul to be such a beautiful thought."

145

Aware of Pilate's silent presence in the conversation, Claudia signaled the slaves to remove the plates. Then the slaves washed their hands and dried them in preparation for the desert course as other slaves placed on the table large bowls overflowing with grapes, figs, and dates, along with plates loaded with various berries and melons and dishes of nuts. Directly in front of Pilate, a slave placed his favorite, the mouth-watering honey-soaked wheat cakes.

"I hope you will help yourselves to whatever desserts appeal to you," said Claudia, as she leaned toward Jesus. "May I ask you, Jesus, what do you think about Aristotle's idea that two lovers share the same soul? Ah, but before you answer, I just thought of another question: When one lover dies, what happens? Does their single soul split in two when the dead lover departs into that bottomless pit of the netherworld? Or do you think that the dead friend takes their single soul into the emptiness of that pit, thus leaving the other soul-less?"

Jesus pondered her question for some time, and finally said, "Lady Claudia, I'm no Greek philosopher, even if tonight we dine reclining as the Greeks do. I'm an uneducated peasant laborer who lacks insights into the ideas of Roman poets and the wisdom of Aristotle. However, I have thoughts about what happens at death. I've come to believe that the emptiness of the pit, of the netherworld of which you speak, isn't truly empty! When death comes, indeed our life ends and we are plunged into that great abyss of nothingness, and yet…I believe that bottomless abyss is actually an abundantly fruitful womb!"

"The pit is a womb? That's a most fascinating idea," said Petronius. "I've never before heard that description of what happens after death. Does it come from the sayings of your prophets, the psalms, or from your ancient holy writings?"

Jesus responded, "Yes…and no! The contradiction of the great abyss being not a vacant pit but rather a womb isn't found in the prophets or the teachings of Moses. It is the fruit of my endless months of being buried alive in my cell, a kind of tomb carved out of solid rock on which this palace was built. The 'yes' part of my answer is an affirmation that the idea I proposed did grow out of the sacred writings. It comes from the opening words of the scroll of Genesis: 'In the beginning the earth was a formless mass and darkness filled the abyss.' Into that vast abyss the originator God spoke, 'Let there be light,' and there was light! And blindingly brilliant light suddenly consumed the darkness. I hope, Petronius, this explains my answer of both yes and no."

Petronius replied, "It does, and I appreciate knowing how you arrived at your idea. It may surprise you, Jesus, that as a soldier I haven't formed a final idea about what happens after death, but what you've said gives me much to think about."

"Lady Claudia," said Jesus, "you've patiently waited for an answer to your insightful question about what happens to the single soul of two lovers when death takes one of them. Death remains the great and inscrutable mystery! No one who has died has ever returned from the dead to tell us what happens. My own belief is that God gives each of us a unique soul, but that doesn't mean two lovers can't share a single soul, as the philosopher said. I feel he meant that love is great enough to intimately bond two people together; it is as if they shared a single soul."

Jesus and the other three each pondered their own thoughts about death to the sounds of the continuously crashing of the waves below and the sputtering of the oil lamps above.

Breaking the silence, Claudia said, "By their sputtering, the hanging lamps tell us not only that they are almost out of oil, but that it is time for us to conclude this lovely dinner. Jesus, I thank you for your willingness to join we three Gentiles tonight for dinner and for generously sharing your wisdom. Petronius, I'm grateful to you as well for the pleasure of your company and your insights. Now, I invite both of you to share in the old Roman custom of taking home …uh…to your quarters some of the leftover food in your napkins. This ritual expresses to your host and hostess how much you enjoyed the meal and your gratitude for being invited."

Jesus and Petronius nodded in appreciation to her and then put some bread, dates, and grapes into their napkins. As they were doing this, Claudia said, "Jesus, I have found your thoughts on love and death most fascinating. I would like to conclude by quoting our Roman poet Virgil, who may have spoken prophetically about you when he said, 'Your descendants shall gather your fruits.'" Turning, she nodded to Pilate, "And now I ask Pilate as our host if he would ritually conclude our dinner."

"I should explain, Jesus," said Pilate, "that the tradition of a Roman meal concludes customarily by the presenting of offerings to the Lares, the spirits of our ancestors and the spirits of this house." Then he nodded to the slaves, who stepped forward and handed Pilate a tray on which was a cake decorated with yellow saffron, a cup of the dinner wine, and a plate with pieces of the dinner's goose meat. Pilate lifted the tray above his head in a silent offertory, held it there for a moment, and then reverently placed it back on the table. After a moment of silence, he said, "I join with Lady Claudia in thanking you, Jesus, for sharing dinner with us. I myself appreciated your thoughtfulness in not bringing up that...ah...*issue* of yours, which wouldn't have been appropriate at a festival meal such as this. Thank you, Petronius. I always enjoy your presence at my table, and as a Roman, I need to explain the conspicuous absence this evening of a traditional Roman dinner custom of floral wreaths!"

Turning to Jesus, he continued, "It is customary, Jesus, that Roman dinners begin with the host and hostess presenting their guests with floral wreaths woven with green leafy branches, various flowers, and herbs. We believe these scented wreaths bring good health to the guest and also give the dinner the festive nature of a banquet. However, in preparing for this meal," he said, smiling at Claudia, "my wife and I decided we would not observe that custom tonight. We thought perhaps the wreaths would be an unpleasant reminder to you of that crude wreath of thorns you were forced to wear in Jerusalem."

Jesus nodded his appreciation to Pilate, as Claudia signaled the slaves to begin the final washing of hands that concluded the dinner.

SCENE XII

PILATE AND CLAUDIA'S
PRIVATE QUARTERS

Later That Night

In their opulent private quarters, before going to bed, Pilate and Claudia were enjoying the light Roman supper typical among the upper classes. Flickering oil lamps on a low table illuminated a large tray containing assorted breads, various fruits, and a bottle of wine. After pouring some wine into his cup, Pilate tasted it and licked his lips. "Delicious! I really like this sweet raisin wine."

"I found your prisoner fascinating," Claudia said, nibbling on a piece of sliced apple. "He has such a captivating presence, and even with his gray and white hair, I still think he's handsome. He looks much older tonight than when I saw him in Tiberius on my trip to the healing baths, although at that time I only saw him from a distance."

"You might not believe this, Claudia, but Jesus and I are about the same age."

"Really?" Claudia said, surprised. "He certainly looks much older than you, Pilate."

"The peasants here have a harsh life, and what with hard work and a poor diet, they age ten to twenty years faster than we Romans," Pilate said. "Did you notice how difficult it was for him to get up and onto his feet again after our long meal reclining on the couches? His knees and joints seem to have some affliction that causes him pain, although he never complains. I've watched him age rapidly since he came here to Caesarea, yet Petronius tells me he's fortunate just be alive at his age. Petronius says the majority of Galileans die before they're twenty-five years old!"

Claudia observed, "I've seen aging like that happen before. I've known older people who were fit until they reached a certain age, and then almost overnight they rapidly became infirm. At least in his case old age hasn't lessened his handsomeness; I find your Jesus very attractive."

Pilate smiled at her and said, "What you find attractive about him, dear, is his Roman half. Remember, I've told you he's a Galilean half-breed."

"Oh, yes, that story about his father likely being some Roman soldier," Claudia responded. "Regardless, he's a fine-looking man, and at dinner tonight I was tempted to ask him if he was married, but...."

"I did ask him that in one of our discussions," Pilate confided, picking up a slice of fruit.

"Really! I'm intrigued, dear — what did he say?"

Pilate said, "He answered cryptically, 'No!' And I wasn't sure if he meant he had never been married, or he wasn't now as his wife was dead, but who knows? These Jews, like all Easterners, can be as evasive as the Oracle of Delphi."

Claudia said decidedly, "I think he surely was married, because he speaks so knowingly about love, and you don't acquire such an intimate knowledge of love without having been *in* love."

"I agree," Pilate said, "and really, it would be almost impossible for him not to have been married at some time in his life. Judea is like the rest of the world; once children's bodies awaken to sex, their parents arrange marriages for them, and the young people don't have any choice about whether they wish to be married, or even to whom! Marriage is a business transaction between the children's fathers and their families. Besides, Petronius tells me that in their Hebrew and Aramaic languages, no word exists for 'bachelor.'"

"That confirms it!" Claudia said. "Speaking of our dinner, I want to thank you for inviting Jesus to dine with us; I'm sure that must have been complicated, with him being your prisoner and all." Placing her hand gently on his arm, she said, "And Pilate, I appreciated your willingness to allow him to dine with us as an equal."

"Not as an equal, Claudia!" Pilate exclaimed. "After all, he's a Jew! Oh, granted, he may have some Roman blood in him, but he's certainly no Roman, so he could never be our equal. Yet for a Jew I found him to be an acceptable dinner guest; at least he was able to engage in a civilized conversation, even if I didn't agree with some of his outlandish ideas. Besides, in my mind, I justified his presence at my table tonight as an act of obedience to Emperor Tiberius."

"Emperor Tiberius?" Claudia asked.

Pilate explained. "Yes, after one of my, shall we say, mistakes, our beloved Caesar rebuked me and lectured me about the need to educate myself in the customs of the Judeans he had sent me here to govern. So I considered dining with Jesus tonight to be part of my education. Thus, Claudia, not only were you pleased, but I wager old Tiberius would have been too!"

"You did well, Pilate," she said, picking up a peach. "I was proud of you, even if a couple of times you did slip from being Pilate the gracious host into Pilate the belligerent old cavalry officer."

"Ah, Claudia, other than Lucius, no one else knows my argumentative side as well as you. I pray that Lady Fortuna gifts me with many long years of marriage with you so you can make me as sweet as this raisin wine."

Claudia leaned over and kissed Pilate as the cool evening breezes rippled the sheer curtains hanging over the entrance to their balcony. They then retired, and as Pilate was drifting off to sleep, he recalled the events of that evening's meal. He relived the strong emotion he had felt when Jesus called him "friend" and the unexpected intimacy of his hand as it touched his arm. Then, slowly, sleep drew her silky-smooth curtains over his eyes and the events of the day.

SCENE XIII

JESUS' CELL

That Same Night

What a feast! Jesus thought to himself as he gradually lowered himself down onto his sleeping mat. *There were so many different dishes of food and cup after cup of wine, each more delicious than the one before. A single course of that dinner back in Galilee would have been a feast! I once recall hearing that the Romans like their meals sweet; well, that was confirmed tonight, especially with the sweet wine and those honey-soaked cakes.* Patting his stomach, he murmured to it silently, *Poor old stomach, after all that rich food, be prepared to be crabby tonight.*

"Son of Joseph!" he exclaimed aloud, "you should have relieved yourself before lying down for the night!" He slowly got to his feet, using his right hand to steady himself against the wall of his cell. As his legs grew stronger, he recalled that years ago in Nazareth he had heard some of the elders sitting around the village square complaining of their aching joints and knees. He had smiled when he overheard the village whisperers explain these problems by claiming that evil spirits had possessed the elders, or that they were the result of the sins in their younger days. While Jesus disregarded these superstitions, he wasn't smiling now as he pondered the source of this new excruciating burden he was forced to carry since he had become an elder himself.

He took a deep breath and then walked over to his privy pot. After he had relieved himself he went to the small window and stood looking out at the canopy of sparkling stars over the dark sea.

"Ancient sky nightlights," he said, conversing with the stars, "I like Claudia; she's an intelligent, inquisitive woman who asked some excellent questions. And whenever the conversation wandered onto dangerous grounds, the gallant Petronius would jump in and try to change the subject. He's a sensitive man, and even though he's an army officer, I sense he's a spiritual seeker. I can see a glint in his eyes when we're discussing serious issues."

Jesus stood silently listening to the calming repetitious sound of the waves crashing below on the rocks as he thought, *A beautiful night that can be enjoyed by rich or poor, slave or....* His thought stalled at the word "slave," as it released a memory of his final dinner with his disciples when, like a slave, he had washed their feet and told them they were to be slaves to one another. His mind jumped from that memory to the dinner that night with Pilate and Claudia.

"O Stars, I feel ashamed that real slaves washed my feet and hands tonight; actual enslaved men served my needs and waited upon me at dinner. Never before in my life have slaves waited upon me, and never before has anyone challenged me about why I never condemned slavery! It never would have occurred to my disciples to challenge me about it because, like everyone else, they unquestioningly accept slavery. To them it's a fact of life, like women and not men giving birth to children. No, Pilate was the first, other than...me, myself!" Tapping his index finger against the right side of his head, Jesus reflected, *Up here, I fiercely argued with myself over the sinful evil of slavery. In my heart I felt a burning shame that my own people, God's Chosen People, own slaves! God's Temple in Jerusalem isn't holy, because it's built on the site of the first temple that is polluted by King Solomon's use of slave labor to build it. We Jews, of all peoples, should not own slaves, since we once were enslaved in Egypt. Sadly, the Law of Moses permits slavery, as long we do not enslave fellow Jews. We should free all slaves, because God does not wish any man or woman to be enslaved.*

Resting his elbows on the stone window ledge, Jesus lowered his head into his cupped hands, moaning, "I've seen destitute Galilean fathers weeping as they were forced to sell their children into slavery, and destitute farmers actually selling themselves into slavery to pay off their debts! I despair that the sin of slavery may never ever be eliminated from this world because it's so deeply engrained in people—yet it must be! It's a despicable offence to human dignity, and it must be the most appalling sin in the eyes of God!"

Then Jesus heard a voice he recognized from past times when he challenged himself with such thoughts of slavery: "If this age-old

Edward Hays

practice is so grievously sinful, why didn't the prophets of old condemn it?"

Crushed by a deep sense of hopelessness, Jesus became silent and wordlessly stared up at the stars. The coolness of the night didn't diminish the seething anger in his heart about slavery and his shame at his own reluctance to condemn it.

"Could it be, Jesus," spoke a quiet inner voice, "that the prophets of old didn't condemn slavery because God intended that to be your prophetic destiny?"

"That sounds reassuring," Jesus responded, "but if that's true, then why didn't the Spirit inspire me to speak out against it or give me words to respond to Pilate?"

"Because, prophet of Galilee, you were destined to condemn slavery without using words!" answered the voice.

"How do you speak out against an evil without using words?" Jesus asked.

"I know you're confused because, other than by dying, you haven't thought about other ways you might redeem the world. But tonight the Spirit gave you a specific plan for how you can accomplish the liberation of the world from evil!"

"I don't remember being given any plan," Jesus objected.

"Unknowingly, you announced the divine design for how you are to accomplish the work given to you. It was in that story you told Pilate and the others about a tightly curled flower bud that slowly unfolds into full bloom and then is followed by other flowers of God's love. The Spirit unfolded that parable on your tongue tonight as you were telling it. And the parable was about you, Jesus of Nazareth—*you* are that prophetic blooming flower whose seeds will transform the world."

"If only I were that blooming flower," Jesus sighed. "In truth, I'm still a tightly curled bud, but I'm working as hard as I can to unfold and bloom."

"Jesus, flowers do not bloom by dogged self-determination!" the inner voice replied. "Their buds naturally and gradually mature, unfold, and bloom into stunningly beautiful blossoms. It is the same with holiness! You become Godlike not by rigorous spiritual

154

disciplines or by force of will power. You must allow God to slowly ripen you and accept that it will happen in ways you would never choose, and *then* you will bloom."

"There's nothing I can do?" Jesus asked.

"Yes," the voice replied, "you can passionately desire to be an unblemished pure mirror that will perfectly reflect God, in whose image you were made. By such ardent longing, you can quicken your blooming."

"I feel that's happening and that I'm becoming more Godlike. Like tonight, when I on impulse called Pilate, 'Friend!' I hadn't planned on doing that, nor did I plan to reach out to affectionately touch his arm—it just happened naturally. O God, Beloved Friend and Gardener of my Soul, please continue to ripen this flower of yours and bring it to full bloom."

SCENE XIV

PALACE TERRACE
AT CAESAREA

Early Morning, June, 36 C.E.

"Thank the gods, that chore is finished!" exclaimed Pilate, as Jesus was escorted out onto the terrace. "Lucius, I hope the Emperor never knows how tiresome I find it to write these daily reports to him." Lucius nodded in agreement.

"Welcome, Jesus," Pilate said. "I'm glad to see you on this warm, sunny June morning so I can explain my silence during part of our dinner together last…uh…let's see, that was.…"

"At least a couple of weeks ago," said Jesus, dejectedly.

"Really — that long ago? It doesn't seem that long since our meal. Well, anyway, I want explain why I was silent while you, Claudia, and Petronius discussed life after death. You see, I'm not a believer in those fables of dead heroes, such as Dionysus, being raised back to life from the dead." Pilate stood up and, walking over to the parapet, gazed at the harbor and continued without turning around. "Don't misunderstand me; I believe in death!" he chuckled. "It's the inescapable fate that awaits every man born of woman, and it's also the fate of the gods who, contrary to the myths, are not immortal."

Then, walking back, Pilate seated himself on his couch and gestured with his right hand for Jesus to sit next to him, "However, Jesus, I gather that you are a believer in life after death. Your poetic comments about death at our dinner intrigued me, especially the part about falling into the bottomless black abyss that suddenly becomes some sort of luminous womb of new birth. I didn't really grasp what you were talking about, but I found it interesting."

"Instead of speaking about death in general, Pilate," said Jesus, "isn't it time we talk about death in particular — specifically, mine?"

Pilate replied, "I got the impression that you weren't going to pressure me any longer about your desire to be crucified. Was I wrong?"

"You are correct, Pilate—I had reached a decision not to badger you and to patiently wait to be shown what God desired for me. But I'm tired of waiting, and although I don't want to pester you, perhaps I may politely ask when you will sentence me to die on a cross, as it is my destiny?"

"Ah, destiny!" replied Pilate, enthusiastically. "Now, there's a subject I do believe in! There's an old Roman saying, 'The Fates will lead a man who wills to be led, and to him who won't be led, they'll drag!'" Both men laughed, a rarity in their conversations. "My belief, Jesus, is that each of us travels a predestined road in life chosen by the fates; however, we're free to choose how we shall travel our unique road. The choices we make as we journey on that road influence our ultimate fate, and also the fates of others. Thanks to Fortuna, the goddess of luck, so far I've made some very good choices as I journeyed down my road. Yet there are those who say luck is not some gift from the gods but a state of the mind. What do you think?"

Jesus replied, "Your Roman saying is like one of our old Jewish sayings, 'If a man is destined to drown, he'll drown in a spoonful of water.'" Again both men were amused. Jesus then said, "But seriously, Pilate, your life road has led you here to Judea and placed in your hands my divine fate to redeem the world by dying on a cross."

Pilate said playfully, "So does your folk proverb mean that if I block you from dying on a cross, you'll accomplish it on a spoon?" Jesus smiled as Pilate continued. "For the sake of discussion, which I relish, let me propose another destiny for you. I'm aware that you Jews believe your god is all powerful, and that everything that happens is an act of his divine will—storms, crop failures, victories, deformed children, health, sickness, and even death, correct?"

"That is the common belief," Jesus replied.

"For the sake of discussion—forgetting for the moment your all-powerful god—tell me, why do you think there is suffering and death?"

After pausing, Jesus said, "I believe…I want to believe…that in the beginning God originally designed a better world than this one we live in. It was a beautiful world without war, sickness, suffering, and most of all, death. I've also come to believe that in our life God wants each of us to do whatever we can to restore this sadly flawed world back to its original beauty and harmony."

"Jesus, be patient with me as I try to unravel what you just said. Do you mean that your god doesn't will sickness and suffering, but rather a world free of them?"

"Yes, you've heard correctly," Jesus replied.

"Then, Jesus," Pilate beamed, "aren't I doing my little part to make this defective world a better and more beautiful place, at least for you, by delaying your death on a cross?"

Once again Jesus had failed to anticipate Pilate's clever trap and could only violently shake his head wordlessly, signifying a resounding "No!"

"It's just a thought, Jesus! Don't be so serious—I'm just having a little fun with you. I'm actually fascinated by your idea of a single man being willing to die for the good of the many. As a soldier, naturally I find such act of unselfish heroism most admirable. Yet at the same time, I find it unthinkable that in today's civilized world, anyone would make a human sacrifice of himself to one of the gods! I know Romans sacrifice birds and sheep as offerings to the gods, which I think is silly. But we're not so primitive as to sacrifice one of our very own to placate some mythical offense against the gods."

For some time Jesus sat silently thinking. Then he asked quietly, "Pilate, why don't you want to crucify me?"

Now it was Pilate's turn to be wordless. Finally he said, "Because, Jesus, I like you! I've grown fond of you, and I enjoy our playful fencing with words and ideas. Why would I want to see someone whom I admired die on a cross, especially a friend who…."

An awkward silence followed his unfinished sentence. Pilate recovered from his surprise at referring to Jesus as his friend and quickly attempted to camouflage his unconscious error by saying briskly, "The real reason I don't kill you, Jesus, is that I have no intention of making you into a martyr like John the Baptizer, even if that ragtag remnant of your followers is trying to do just that."

"Excellency, excuse me for interrupting you," said Marcus, "but Centurion Petronius is here."

"Show him in at once, Marcus," ordered Pilate.

Petronius entered and saluted, removing his helmet and placing it in the crook of his left arm as he walked over to Pilate. "Sir, I've brought the correspondence from Rome, which just arrived on the mail ship."

"Petronius, did you happen to notice if any of the scrolls in the mail contained the Emperor's seal? Jesus, forgive me, I've been expecting a reply from the Emperor for some time now."

Jesus nodded, wondering if the reply from the Emperor might have something to do with him.

"None did, Sir, but among them was one bearing the seal of Vitellius the Syrian Legate, as I presumed I had your permission to sort through the mail to see if the Emperor had written back to you. It's been over a year now since you wrote him about transferring the trial and the prisoner from Jerusalem here to Caesarea."

"Petronius, you were right to scan through my mail. Our two fates are intertwined in the Empire like the serpents on the staff of Mercury."

"Thank you, Sir, I feel the same. But why hasn't the Emperor responded?"

"Ten years ago I would have asked that same question," Pilate said, as he broke the seal on the scroll from the Legate, "but not today. In recent years, the Emperor has become an endless procrastinator, and I'm told he incessantly delays appointing new governors and resolving matters of state. He also delays the trials of prisoners who have offended him, leaving them to rot away for years in dungeons. If some Roman bureaucrat ever challenges me about delaying the trial of Jesus so long, I've decided I'm going to respond that as an admirer of Caesar Tiberius, I have adapted his Imperial style of delayed trials with long imprisonments! "

"But why do you think the Emperor delays the trials of those he's imprisoned?"

"My contacts in Rome claim it's another sign of his increasing malice. Tiberius enjoys torturing those who have displeased him by making them endure agonizing years wondering what ingeniously painful deaths he's preparing for them. Excuse me while I quickly read this letter from the Legate Vitellius."

As Pilate read the letter, Jesus reflected on his long imprisonment here in Caesarea. *I've got decent quarters, good food and drink, and for the first time in years the closest thing to a home, as I was a wandering poor teacher with only passing places of lodging.* Sighing inwardly, he thought, *But the isolation and solitude is taking its toll, and this old body of mine is telling me it's past time for me to die.*

Holding the scroll, Pilate said, "This is only a formal acknowledgement that he's received my letter about the political disturbances in Samaria. Petronius, you'll find this humorous; Vitellius encourages me, and I quote, 'to be tactfully diplomatic in your dealings with the Samaritans.' What nonsense!"

Dropping the scroll in his lap, Pilate curled his right hand into a fist and then slammed it into the cupped palm of his left hand, "That's how I'd like to deal with those damn rebellious Samaritans! As the great Pompey said, 'A dead man cannot bite!'"

"Then, Pilate, crucify me," Jesus interjected, "so Rome can't bite you!"

Pilate responded irritably, "I thought we weren't going to talk about that, but since you can't keep from doing so — guards, take this prisoner down to his cell!"

After Jesus had been led away, Petronius said, "Sir, I too disagree with the advice the Legate gave you. We continue to receive reports of Samaritan thugs attacking and robbing Galilean pilgrims as they pass through Samaria on pilgrimage to and from the temple in Jerusalem. The feuding between Samaritan Jews and the Jews in Galilee and Judea is ageless."

"So I've heard, Petronius, and in my letter to Vitellius I told him about these recurring ambushes by bandits, which I see as another expression of their resistance to our Roman authority. Yet to the question of how I'm to respond to these attacks of the Samaritans, the Legate only lectures me to act 'discreetly.' Since they are in his jurisdiction, it's obvious that Vitellius wants to avoid any kind of armed conflict with them, fearing that he will incur the disfavor of the Emperor."

"I believe you're correct in that judgment about the Legate, but if I could return to my former question, why hasn't the Emperor responded one way or another about transferring the case of Jesus here to Caesarea?"

Pilate said, "When it comes to attending to the details of ruling the Empire, Old Tiberius isn't as attentive as he once was, and that's in our favor. It was my hope when I sent him my letter about transferring the trial of Jesus to Caesarea that it would get buried under the avalanche of reports from all over the empire. The Emperor's secretaries scan them and only send the most significant reports to him. Seeing mine from this insignificant province of Judea, they likely just tossed it onto the heap of irrelevant reports. Caesar Tiberius, whose good fortune it was to become the adopted stepson of the Great Augustus, has been emperor now over nineteen years. That would make him about sixty-nine years old, and rumors say he now often does the very opposite of what he once would have done."

"Aging changes people, even emperors, it seems," commented Petronius.

"It isn't his advancing years that has aged him," Pilate replied, "it's fear! He's grown obsessed that senators, army officers, and others are conspiring to secretly murder him, and he fears that an assassin may be lurking behind every pillar. That's one reason he's retreated from Rome to live in seclusion in his palatial villa on the island of Capri south of the bay of Naples. But Petronius, why the frown?"

"Sir, it's what you just said about the Emperor being obsessed about others plotting against him. If that's true, and he hears about our Jesus being accused of claiming to be a king and that he is here in your custody...."

"I never tied those two things together before; I appreciate your insight." Pilate began stroking his upper lip as he pondered the logic of how a paranoid Tiberius would interpret Jesus as a dangerous threat. After juggling his various options, he said, "Because I didn't crucify Jesus at once, Tiberius will instantly judge me as being a co-conspirator in this Jewish plot to overthrow him. On the other hand, since Tiberius is secluded on the Island of Capri, he most likely will never learn about Jesus."

Petronius asked, "Why is he so secluded from the world?"

Pilate replied, "Being securely hidden away on his island, Tiberius can cavort with young girls—and boys! No wonder in Rome he is becoming known as 'The Old Goat!'"

"That's truly disgusting, Sir," Petronius said with distaste.

"Yes, and they say that in addition to his licentiousness, Tiberius has also become a heavy drinker. Yet drunk or sober, the lower classes consider him divine and call him 'Tiberius, the son of god.' But instead of talking about Rome's son of god, let's talk about our own son of god here in Caesarea."

"Who still wants to be crucified?" Petronius asked.

"He does and he doesn't; it's confusing," Pilate confessed. "In our recent visits with him, have you noticed that Jesus seems less enthusiastic about being crucified, and less antagonistic? He's stopped constantly harping about wanting to be crucified, other than a couple of slips like today. Something has changed, or rather is changing in him, and I don't know what it is."

ACT III

SCENE I

PALACE TERRACE
AT CAESAREA

A Night in September, 36 C.E.

After dismissing the two guards who brought Jesus to the terrace, Pilate said, "Are you surprised that it's just the two of us out here tonight? Come and be seated next to me so we can visit." As Jesus seated himself under the gently swaying oil lamps, Pilate continued, "I'll explain later why I've asked you up here tonight, but first, how are you?"

Jesus replied, "As well as can be for old man who wonders how many more years he has left. Like those sputtering lamps above us, I sometimes feel like I'm running out of oil."

Pilate responded, "Jesus, may we both live as long as the Emperor, who is close to seventy, which makes him almost twice as old as you and I."

"If the afflictions of aging increase as you grow older, who wants to live that long?" Jesus replied.

"Yet even in his old age the Emperor remains robust and...uh...sexually active enough to engage in debauchery," Pilate observed. "I myself think that's detestable, but an Imperial Caesar belongs to a privileged class who are beyond judgment, except by the gods."

"Nonsense!" Jesus retorted. "Emperors, princes, and high priests are no more privileged than a simple peasant. No matter how high their rank, their behavior is never 'beyond judgment.' God makes no exemptions for Caesar," Jesus smiled, "or his governors."

"Now there's a fiery retort, which no doubt comes from the Roman blood in your veins!" Pilate exclaimed.

"Roman blood? I'm a Galilean Jew, and proud of it!"

"Proud of being a Galilean?" Pilate asked. "Wasn't the fact that you were a Galilean the reason why the Jerusalem Temple purebloods considered you to be only a nobody, along with the shadow that hung over you of being illegitimate?"

"I'm not a nobody!" Jesus exclaimed.

"I agree, Jesus," replied Pilate, relishing the rich give and take of their conversation. "You're hardly a nobody, since you're a king!" Pilate extended his hand toward him. "Behold the King of the Nobodies—of sinners, prostitutes, tax collectors, slaves, the riffraff, outcasts, and other half-breeds." Lowering his hand, he continued, "As far as I'm concerned, as Emperor of the Kingdom of the Unwashed and the Uneducated, you are no threat to Tiberius Caesar!" Then shaking his head, he reflected, "On the other hand, Tiberius Caesar lives in dread of the appearance of a rival to his throne, so you and I must pray that he never learns of your existence. If he ever does, Jesus, not only will you be crucified, but I will lose my head as a conspirator in a supposed Judean plot to overthrow him. So what am I to do with you?"

"I never want any harm to come to you because of me, Pilate."

"I'm glad to hear that we share the same desire. However, if the folk rumors about you are true, we have even more reason to fear the Emperor's imperial wrath. Petronius told me that some village rumors say your mother was impregnated by a sprite or the spirit of your Jewish god," Pilate said, jokingly shaking his index finger at Jesus, "which makes you semi-divine! If Tiberius ever hears the story of your conception, he'll smash you like a bug. While Tiberius cleverly rejects being called divine, he nonetheless secretly thinks he was conceived by the gods!"

"He's not alone," Jesus responded. "All children are conceived by the Spirit of God—you, Pilate; your servants whom you call slaves; indeed, everyone. The Spirit is directly involved in every act of creation, whether it be the conception of a child, a star, or a flower."

Pilate replied, "I must say you have the most bizarre ideas I've ever heard; perhaps that's what makes visiting with you so much of an adventure! But regarding your peculiar proposal that the gods are directly involved in our births, it is your father's station in life when you're born that determines your destiny: kings come from kings, peasants from peasants, and slaves from slaves! Now, I greatly value my slaves; I actually love dear old Lucius, who's a treasure greater than gold, and Marcus and Quintus are like my left and right arms— yet they are still slaves! If I were to accept that they were conceived somehow godlike, that would mean the end of the ancient system of slavery, and also the entire Roman civilization...."

Pilate, becoming animated by his feelings, unconsciously jumped to his feet. Then he quickly regained his composure and slowly reseated himself.

"You see the effect you have on me, Jesus? This has been a very stimulating conversation, and you didn't disappoint me, even if I believe some of your ideas verge on madness. At any rate, I wanted to let you know why I asked you up here to visit tonight. Tomorrow at sunrise I'm departing for Jerusalem and will not be back for some time."

"Please, Pilate, take me with you to the Holy City so I can fulfill...," Jesus quickly closed his mouth, remembering his vow not to pester Pilate about being crucified and patiently leave his fate in God's hands.

"Unlike you, Jesus, I don't have the least desire to go to Jerusalem; I actually detest having to spend time there. I'd rather stay here in clean and civilized Roman Caesarea, but as Governor, duty demands that I go to ensure public order at the fall festival. As you can tell, it's autumn, which means it's time once again for the festival of Sukkoth, when Jerusalem's narrow streets will be overflowing with mobs of pilgrims waving green palm branches. And as is always the case, hidden among those pious pilgrims will be some mischief-hungry rebels."

"When will you return?" Jesus sighed sadly. "My trial has dragged on now for months and months; it must be close to two years now."

Pilate replied, "I regret that, and I know it must be frustrating. Now, to your question about how long I'll be away: I must depart after Sukkoth from Jerusalem to go to Jericho on my official inspection tour of that southern part of my province. After I leave

Jericho, I'll go down into the Judean wilderness to the area of Asphaltites, the Salt Sea; an expedition of that length should take two or three months. Centurion Petronius and Lucius, who will write the reports of my survey of the Jericho region, and Marcus will accompany me. As it is truly a godforsaken wilderness pockmarked with the cave hideouts of bandits, we'll be escorted by a cavalry unit and heavily armed soldiers."

"I know what a barren wilderness it is," Jesus said.

"Yes, according to spy reports you spent an extended period of time in seclusion there after your ritual bath in the Jordan by that wild man, John. But Jesus," Pilate said, chuckling, "I assure you I'm not going down to the Jordan to take a bath! High Priest Caiaphas has sent me numerous warnings about a dangerous seditious community called the Essenes living at Qumran on the shores of the Asphaltites. Caiaphas says they're plotting an uprising against our Roman occupation."

"I know the Essenes; I've visited them," Jesus protested. "They are good and pious men dedicated to holiness and are in no way plotting against you or Rome!"

Pilate said, "I hope you are right, for Caiaphas has sent me messages quoting them as calling for 'a war between the sons of light and the sons of darkness,' which he says clearly refers to we Romans. He also says these Essenes are a threat in my jurisdiction by claiming that priestly authority of the Temple is unlawful. As Governor, I must officially investigate this strange Jewish religious community, whom I'm told all dress in white garments, share their property in common, have no slaves, and even more incredible, have no sexual relations!"

Jesus responded, "Caiaphas was right that the Essenes challenge the legitimacy of the Temple priesthood, especially the present ruling high priests, as being invalidly installed, and...."

Pilate said decisively, "No, Jesus, not tonight! Don't even try to explain to me why Caiaphas or old Annas are invalid high priests. I don't have the time or the desire to get mired in that quagmire of Jewish religious politics, but I have appreciated your insights about the Essenes. Now, the hour is late, and I've much work to attend to before tomorrow's sunrise departure for Jerusalem." Standing up, he signaled the end of their visit; however, Jesus remained seated.

"When you're in Jerusalem for Sukkoth," he said, looking up at Pilate, "I would think you would meet with High Priest Caiaphas, even if only as a formality. If he asks you if you've crucified me yet, what will you say?"

"I'll politely inform him that a more than usual number of official duties have delayed my pronouncing the...um, final verdict. If he presses me as to precisely when I intend to crucify you, I'll ask him just one question." Pilate paused briefly, almost theatrically, and then said, "Joseph Caiaphas, do you enjoy the office of high priest?"

Pilate then called out to the guards standing in the darkened hallway to come and escort Jesus back to his cell.

SCENE II

THE SAME

Pilate Returns from Jerusalem, November, 36 C.E.

"Petronius, I feel like I have half of the dust of the roads between here and Jerusalem on me," Pilate said, vigorously shaking his dusty military cloak.

"And I, Sir, have the other half," replied Petronius, who stood with Pilate on the terrace after they had arrived back in Caesarea from their long expedition. "It feels good to be back here, and I'm grateful there were no troubling disturbances during Sukkoth."

"For that, we have the priests to thank. I'm always prepared for trouble at Sukkoth, as it commemorates the time that the Jews lived in makeshift tents in the desert after their Egyptian revolt, and so it is forever pregnant with the possibility of a new rebellion. However, the priests have drained off those dangerous memories of their old slave revolt with prayers and songs that emphasize Sukkoth more as a harvest festival. It always amazes me how those priests, with their rituals and festivals, continue to persuade the Jews that that this poor, barren land of thorns and thistles is the Promised Land!"

"I'm grateful there was no bloodshed and continue to be amazed by the size of the crowds that flock to the Temple to worship," Petronius commented.

"And I continue to be disgusted by all the holy butchering that goes on at that big marble butcher shop," Pilate said, glancing over his shoulder and lowering his voice. "Friend, forget you heard that stupid remark about the temple, since Emperor Tiberius has the priests daily sacrifice a bull and two lambs for his safety."

"Sir, I'm as deaf as these marble walls. I've never asked you, before but I'm curious; why does our Roman Emperor have sacrifices offered daily for him to a Jewish god?"

"It's either another superstitious quirk, or like King Herod the Great, he's cleverly ingratiating himself with the Jews. Herod shrewdly offered sacrifices in Jerusalem at the Temple, and when he was in Rome he did the same at the Temple of Jupiter. At any rate, Petronius, you and I are both covered in dust and tired from our long journey. I would enjoy a good long bath; first, however, I must go see how Lucius is doing."

Petronius observed, "He looked very sick when we arrived here and they carried him to his room. In fact, he looked sickly upon our arrival in Jerusalem from Jericho, but I thought perhaps he was simply exhausted from the long journey."

"I thought the same; that is, until just before we departed there for Caesarea, when Marcus told me that Lucius was complaining of chest pains. Although Lucius resisted, I ordered him to be carried in a litter back here to Caesarea. Upon our arrival I sent my own physician to attend to him with the hope he could heal Lucius of whatever is afflicting him. Now, Petronius, have a good bath, and a good night."

SCENE III

PILATE'S QUARTERS
AT THE PALACE

The Next Day

"Excellency, Lucius is very sick and won't be able to take dictation today," said Quintus, when he arrived early the next morning to shave Pilate.

Pilate replied gravely, "I had hoped he would be better this morning, but I knew there wasn't much chance of that. Late last night my physician came to tell me he was baffled by whatever sickness has afflicted Lucius. He said all the remedies he tried didn't seem to be helping him, and when he departed, he said, 'I have placed your slave in the healing hands of the god Aesculapius.'"

Quintus said, "Excellency, I could see a small statue of Aesculapius by Lucius' bed from where I stood in the hallway."

Pilate remarked, "You only looked at him from the doorway and didn't go to his bedside?"

"Excellency," said Quintus, earnestly, "I didn't dare go any closer to him lest the demon causing his sickness jump over onto me. Anyway, since Lucius is far too sick to take any dictation today, should I send for his assistant?"

"That won't be necessary, Quintus. I'll write today's report to the Emperor myself; I've done it before."

"Yes, Excellency," Quintus murmured, and began sharpening his razor. "I pray Aesculapius will heal our dear Lucius," he said, anxiously glancing around the room, "and protect all of us here from the evil demons afflicting him."

Pilate replied, "Quintus, I pray the same. Lucius and I have been together since I was a child. Now, let's begin, for when you're finished I must write my daily report."

172

SCENE IV

THE SAME

Later That Day Near Sunset

"Excellency, hurry," said Marcus, as he rushed into the room at sunset, his eyes full of tears. "The physician told me to come get you, for Lucius is dying and may not even live out this night!"

The blood drained out of Pilate's face as he stood and with haste followed Marcus to Lucius' room. Upon entering, Pilate found his physician standing in front of the statue of Aesculapius, praying.

Pilate said, "I received your message that Lucius is dying. Isn't there something you can do? With your training in the medical arts of Hippocrates and your knowledge of healing herbs and tinctures, surely there must be some remedy that can save him from dying."

"Your Excellency," said the physician, after making a deep bow, "I have tried every known medicine in the civilized Roman world, to no avail. Whatever evil spirit or demon has taken up residence in your slave is now swiftly bearing him down to the underworld. Yet there is a flicker of hope of his recovery, so if he is healed and lives, I've promised to sacrifice the customary cock to the god Aesculapius."

Pilate nodded to him and started to walk to Lucius' bedside.

"Excellency, don't get too close or touch him, or the evil spirits possessing him will leap over onto you," warned Marcus, grabbing Pilate's arm.

Pilate nodded. Because of his terror of evil spirits, he was glad Marcus had restrained him and placed a chair for him a safe distance away from Lucius' bed. After seating himself, to hide his great grief at the impending death of his beloved Lucius, he buried his face in his cupped hands. It was now after sunset. Then Pilate abruptly raised his head, saying, "Marcus, send immediately for Petronius, and then go quickly to the dungeon and bring the prisoner Jesus of Galilee here. Don't waste time trying to find guards to escort you; go by yourself, and bring Jesus to this room as quickly as possible. Hurry, Marcus; may the gods put wings on your feet."

As he anxiously waited for Jesus, it felt to Pilate as if the sands of time were clogged in the narrow neck of life's hourglass. His physician, meanwhile, was absorbed in bowing and mumbling prayers to the small statue of Aesculapius, the divine son of Apollo and Hygeia.

My physician is praying, Pilate thought, as he sat with his head slightly lowered and his eyes closed. *I don't know how to pray, yet I yearn to beg, petition, or bargain with something that has the power to heal my Lucius. I remember Jesus speaking of praying to his god; perhaps I should too. Why not add one more god – even a Jewish one – to that pantheon of the countless gods and goddess? But I'm afraid the god of the Jews wouldn't listen to my prayers after all the nasty things I've said about him. Yet Jesus says he is a compassionate and forgiving god. The real problem is how one prays, and does it do any good if you don't believe?*

"Excellency, here is Jesus," Marcus said, as he hurried into the room. "We came as quickly as possible."

Jesus went directly to Pilate, and placing a hand on his shoulder, said, "You sent for me?"

"Yes, I have urgent need of you, Jesus. I recall that Petronius told me you healed his beloved slave, and my dear Lucius has been afflicted by a deadly, mysterious sickness. Please, I beg you, heal him!"

"Your Excellency, stop!" demanded the physician, as he came rushing to stand on the opposite side of Lucius' bed. "Don't let this ignorant peasant near my patient." Then he almost spit out, "This so-called healer is nothing but an illiterate pretender, a village charlatan, who has no knowledge of the ancient healing arts. Do not allow him to interfere with my patient, lest...."

"Silence!" ordered Pilate, just as Petronius came hurrying into the room. "If the Galilean can heal my Lucius, I order you not to interfere with him."

"I do not heal!" Jesus replied quietly. "Only God heals, and healing requires faith. I can see that your slave Lucius is no longer conscious."

"Jesus, I beseech you, pray to your god to heal the sickness that is slowly dragging my beloved Lucius down into Pluto's horrible pit in the underworld, from which none ever return to earth."

Jesus walked over to the bedside, and bowing his head, reverently placed his hands on Lucius' fever-wracked body, causing Marcus to gasp loudly. Then he placed his hands on Lucius' sweat-covered brow and prayed, "O God of life, you who restore the sick to health and heal the sufferings of the afflicted, we who are gathered here pray that you heal your sick son, Lucius." Then, with his eyes closed, he continued praying. His voice grew quieter and quieter until it was only a whisper.

As Jesus quietly prayed, the Roman physician hurried back to the statue of Aesculapius and began praying so loudly that his voice dominated the room. Meanwhile, Pilate felt caught in the middle of this combat of praying healers, and his mind was crowded with conflicted thoughts. *My beloved Lucius is dying, and these two men are each praying to a different god. To what god should I pray? Should I also barter with the gods, as did my physician, who promised a cock to Aesculapius? I wonder in his quiet prayers what Jesus is promising as a gift to his god?*

Petronius also was praying silently, *O God of Jesus, you who restored my sick slave to health, come and do the same for Lucius, who is greatly loved by all of us, and especially by Pilate. I believe this night, as I did that day long ago, that Jesus has the authority to command evil spirits. O God, grant that he may command the evil demon who is possessing Lucius to depart.*

Meanwhile, clustered around the room's open doorway were many of the household slaves. They silently watched the unfolding events at Lucius' bedside as the hours dragged on into the night and the sands of time struggled to force their way through the clogged neck of life's hourglass. At one point Quintus came and knelt beside Pilate and asked if he wanted anything to eat or drink. When Pilate shook his head no, Quintus retreated to the back of the room.

Around midnight, Jesus leaned down until his face was almost touching the sweaty, pale face of Lucius. Pilate, along with those in the room and those gathered in the doorway, watched intently, curious to see what new healing Jesus was about to perform. After a brief moment, Jesus slowly stood upright and reached out and gently closed Lucius' eyelids. Turning to those in the room, he said, "Lucius has returned to God from whom all of us have come, and to whom all of us shall return."

With the realization that his beloved Lucius was dead, Pilate's head slumped down and his body quivered with grief. Jesus stepped back from the bed and went and stood with Petronius behind Pilate to give him the privacy to weep unobserved. Then a low groaning slowly arose from the slaves crowded in the doorway that quickly ascended into loud wailing. One by one they departed, their hands over their noses and mouths to prevent the demons from entering them, for they feared that the demons that had departed from the dead body of Lucius were now roaming about the palace.

SCENE V

THE PALACE TERRACE

The Next Day

Pilate said to Petronius, "I don't understand how Lucius could have died so quickly; he was only sick a couple of days. And why wasn't Jesus able to heal him, as he once healed your slave? Do you think it was because the demon that infested my poor Lucius was more powerful than the one who struck down your slave?"

"I don't know, Sir," Petronius replied.

"Jesus prayed to his god; I heard him. So why weren't his prayers answered? And when Lucius died, whatever did he mean when he said Lucius had returned to god?"

"I don't know that either, Sir. Perhaps you should ask Jesus. Shall I go and get him?"

"Not now! I must write my daily report, and now that Lucius is dead," Pilate said, pausing briefly, "I think perhaps I should begin to use another scribe." Turning to Marcus, he ordered, "Go and get the slave Aristocles, the one who was Lucius' assistant, and tell him to report to me to take dictation."

Marcus bowed and departed, leaving Pilate sitting silently in his grief and depression. The mere mention of his beloved Lucius' name had reopened his grief and stirred memories of their former times together.

"Excuse me, Petronius," Pilate said, "I was lost in thoughts of the past. It seems that like Jesus, I'm also aging quickly, for my thoughts recently seem to be mostly of my younger days. Isn't visiting the past a sign of old age?"

"I don't think so, Sir. After one is past thirty, I believe it's rather common to fondly recall one's younger years."

"I appreciate that, since I don't *feel* old. Now, I noticed when you arrived that you were carrying some scrolls, which I presume are this month's tax reports to Rome?" Then he noticed Marcus with Aristocles standing at the edge of terrace hallway.

"Excellency, as you requested," said Marcus, "here is the scribe Aristocles."

A Greek youth dressed in a slave's tunic stepped forward, carrying a wooden tray with ink, pens, and several blank scrolls. Aristocles was of medium height and average build, with a bronze complexion and a head of curly black hair.

He stopped and bowed in front of Pilate. "Your Excellency," he said, and raising his head, looked directly at Pilate. "I am Aristocles, and I am at your service."

As Marcus placed a stool for Aristocles next to his couch, Pilate thought, *He's a handsome youth; I wonder if Alexander the Great looked like this young man? But I sense in him an air of superiority by the tone of his voice and the way he looked at me. Like most educated Greeks, I suppose he feels intellectually and culturally superior to us Romans, who conquered them. He's likely to be proud to the point of being haughty, so I must be on my guard and keep this youthful Aristocles in his proper place.*

"Excellency, I am ready to begin to take your dictation."

"I'm glad to see you are eager to begin," replied Pilate, in a matter of fact way, "but first, I want to return to my discussion with Centurion Petronius, which was interrupted by your arrival." Aristocles nodded and looked at the floor. "Now, Petronius, as I was saying, Lucius' death was so unexpected."

"I agree, Sir," responded Petronius. "As I've told you, upon our arrival in Jerusalem I asked if he was sickly, and he denied it."

"How easily, Petronius, do we mask what is actually happening within us," replied Pilate, stroking his upper lip as he thought, *Indeed, aren't I now wearing a stoic-faced mask to hide my great grief lest I break into uncontrollable weeping over the loss of my dear Lucius? Since reaching manhood, I've dreaded appearing weak, and crying in public is a sign of weakness. Women are permitted to do so, but not men.*

Then, realizing the day was slipping away, he said, "Petronius, I think it's time we attend to those tax records you brought with you. They'll provide a good opportunity for me to see if my new scribe is able to precisely record the figures as you read them aloud. And when we are finished I want you to go and have Jesus brought up to me."

SCENE VI

THE SAME

Late Afternoon That Same Day

Pilate said, "Marcus, bring a warm cloak for our prisoner; while I find these late November sea winds invigorating, he may not."

"My robe is sufficient, but you're kind to be concerned," Jesus replied.

A feeble, pale winter sun shown dimly down on terrace where Pilate and Petronius were seated on couches and Aristocles was perched on his stool.

"Jesus, come and sit beside me on this couch," Pilate said. As Jesus sat down, Pilate pointed out to the sea. "Today's gray sky appropriately matches the gray sea, which is beautiful in every season, don't you think?"

"Yes, beautiful and also dangerous, like many other beautiful things." After this observation Jesus waited, expecting Pilate to quote some Greek or Roman philosopher, but instead Pilate was silent as he pondered Jesus' words. Then he said, "I've invited you here today so we can talk about the sudden death of my beloved Lucius, which has caused an eruption of questions within me. Why, Jesus, didn't your god answer your prayers and save Lucius from dying? Was Lucius not healed because you prayed to the god of the Jews, and Lucius was a pagan Gentile?"

Jesus responded, "I don't know why my prayers for Lucius were not answered, but I do know it wasn't because Lucius was a Gentile! I've prayed for things before that were not granted, yet that hasn't diminished my belief in the power of prayer. I continue to pray with confidence because God, being compassionate, only grants what is good for us and for those for whom we pray. Like everyone else, I grew up believing in certain things that I now know are not true. For example, I know that sickness is not caused by sin or demons. I also do not believe God uses crippling illness and sickness as a punishment for sins, or that our afflictions are the result of the sins of our parents. The compassionate God I've come to know intimately in my prayer and solitude would never inflict sickness, leprosy, and death as punishment for our sins and our moral mistakes."

"But Jesus," interjected Petronius, "I've seen in reports by our spies that when you heal a crippled or infirm person you say to them, 'Your sins are forgiven; stand up and walk.' Why do you say that, unless you believe their afflictions are caused by their sins?"

"The people believe without any doubt that sickness or being crippled is caused by the sins of those afflicted. Because this is what they believe, as a healer, I treat them according to their religious beliefs. However, I never say to them, 'I heal you,' for only God heals. The same is true about the forgiveness of sins; I never say that *I* forgive their sins, but rather, 'Your sins are forgiven,' announcing to them that God has already forgiven them. I have found that this confirmation has a powerfully healing affect on them."

"You give long and complicated answers, Jesus," said Pilate, frowning. "And while I will have to ponder some of these things you've said, I have another question. You placed your hands on Lucius; weren't you afraid that the evil spirit that was causing his sickness would creep onto you?"

"Pilate, although I don't know what caused Lucius to be sick, I do know his illness wasn't caused by any evil demon or by some moral weakness of his. The world is full of unexplainable mysteries like the source of sickness, or why one person is afflicted and another is not. I try to reverence the mysteries and don't try to explain them."

"I've never met a man like you, Jesus," Pilate replied. "Most people are terrified of death and will not even touch a sick or dying person, and some are afraid even to talk about dying; yet you passionately desire to meet death. As for me, I've learned as a soldier to be ready to greet my own death bravely when the time comes, but I'm in no hurry for that time to arrive. But you, Jesus, are actually in a hurry to die. Is that because you are not afraid of dying?"

"Yes, and no," Jesus said, pausing briefly. "I grew up in Galilee believing, as do a majority of my people, that death ends life. In my youth, I learned that after death the dead go down to Sheol, a dark, gloomy pit deep within the earth that is a place of incessantly burning fires, which we also call *Gehenna*. That name comes from Jerusalem's stinking garbage dump in the ravine south of the city that is a loathsome place crawling with vermin. 'The pit,' by whatever name, is a horrible place of decay and worms from which no one ever returns."

"Your world of the dead sounds much like our Roman netherworld," replied Pilate. "But I also want to ask you about what you said last night when you closed Lucius' eyelids; you didn't say to us that he was dead or that he departed to the netherworld! You said, and your words are carved in my memory, 'Lucius has returned to God, from whom all of us have come, and to whom all of us will return.' Now, what does that mean?"

"My ideas about what happens after death are still emerging, and as they do, they are contradicting my former beliefs. Although not all of my thoughts about death are fully formed yet, as of now I am convinced that those who die do *not* go down to spend eternity in the bleakness of Sheol, Gehenna, or your netherworld."

"If they don't go to the netherworld, then where do they go?" Pilate asked. "It's obvious that the dead clearly depart from this earth, so they must go somewhere. Where did my dear Lucius go?"

"A belief is slowly growing within me, based on my root belief that each of us was created out of divine love. Since divine love is eternal and knows no ending, I believe that we also will live endlessly in the divine love that created us! To love God with all of one's heart, soul, mind, and body isn't a law; it's an invitation to passionately love our creative source, which is also our ultimate destination in life. That is why I said what I did when Lucius died."

Pilate replied, "Your ideas are fascinating and even comforting, and I would like to discuss them further. However, as you can see, Aristocles has been patiently waiting for me to complete my report to the Emperor. I regret that this visit will have to be continued at another time. Petronius, see that the guards escort our guest to his quarters."

SCENE VII

JESUS' CELL IN THE DUNGEON

A Night Near the End of November, 36 C.E.

After hearing the metallic clank of the key turning in its lock as the guards locked his cell door, Jesus went and stood at the window. As he looked at the sea, he soaked up the silence of the solitude that had become his teacher. During these long months, Rabbi Silence had urged him to explore new ideas and sort through his conflicting thoughts.

"Remember, Jesus, your prayer of blessing of the bread and the cup of wine at your final supper with your friends?" asked Rabbi Silence.

Jesus replied, "How could I forget it? Did I not tell my friends to faithfully recall that memory?"

Rabbi Silence continued, "Those words you spoke when blessing the cup—did you consciously mean them to be the fulfillment of Jeremiah's prophecy of a new bloodless covenant with God?"

Jesus responded, "No. I hadn't prepared what I would do or say that fateful night of our last dinner together; I trusted my intuition to guide me. When the time came for the blessing over the cup of wine, I found the Spirit placing the words on my lips, 'This is the cup of the new covenant in my blood; do this in memory of me.'"

Rabbi Silence said, "Your fervent plea to your disciples, whom you now called your friends, to repeat the memory of what you did seems to me to fulfill Jeremiah's words that the New Covenant would be written in human hearts, not in stone. Significant events in life, having been inscribed in the heart, have a greater permanence than those carved in stone."

"I agree," said Jesus, "but until just now I never connected what I said to Jeremiah's promise."

"Think about it, Jesus! That memory of your covenant last supper has serious consequences for you! You look puzzled, so let me explain. Jeremiah promised when the new covenant appeared, it 'would bring forgiveness...and that God would remember their sins no more.' Remember their sins no more!" shouted Rabbi Silence, the words echoing out across the night-shrouded ocean.

As the last echo vanished in the roar of the waves, Jesus recalled hearing about a coming new covenant being read from the scroll of Jeremiah in the synagogue. He said, "If I did create that promised covenant at our last supper, what are its unintended consequences?"

"If God has forgiven and forgotten," Rabbi Silence interjected, "that means the world's sins are gone! By forgetting, the All Holy One has redeemed the world, and there's no need for you, Jesus, or anyone else to die to remove them!"

Jesus clamped both hands over his ears as he violently shook his head, wailing, "Why am I tormented by these voices? Before I began hearing them, my convictions about you, O God, and my mission in life were as strong as these stone walls. O Dear Friend, come quickly to my aid, for doubts are gnawing away at my soul like a pack of hungry rats!"

Jesus listened as wave after wave came crashing ashore against the ageless boulders that had withstood the greatest of storms since time began, and contemplated, *How I wish that my faith was as unchangeable as those giant boulders down there. Once I believed that a great apocalypse was about to appear — a divine holocaust of fire in which all the empires of the world would be consumed. I had adopted this belief from my prophetic cousin, John, and I boldly predicted its coming to my disciples. Now I do not believe in it. The earth and everything in it was created out of love by a Creator who found it all good, so it would be the height of madness for its artistic creator to destroy it in a vicious act of anger.*

"Comrades," he said aloud, patting the hard gray stones of his cell, "not only does my belief in a God of love convince me that the world will not end apocalyptically — so too do you brother stones and you giant boulders down there along the coast. You've inspired me to realize that while kingdoms and kings die, their violence and oppression continues, since they are as enduring as you and the marble up there in the palace! After old King Herod died, did peace and freedom come? No, his oppressive reign was merely replaced by that of the Roman Empire, and the oppression of the poor and weak continued. Even if the Romans are overthrown, another empire will follow them, and then another and another. The exploitation of the weak and poor will go on endlessly, while sadly, just below the horizon, the Kingdom of Heaven yearns to come to completion."

Despondent by that realization, Jesus left the window, went over to his mat, and sat down. Not feeling sleepy, he braced his back against the wall and pondered what he had heard in the silence: "God had forgotten the sins of the world."

"Comrades," he said, gently tapping his head back against the stones, "when Pilate was taunting me about making atonement to God for the sin of Adam, he called the Genesis story a myth. But that's impossible! That Adam and Eve fell into sin is found in the holy writings, which are inspired by God; it has to be...."

Then he began peeling back the layers of that possibility, saying, "If the story of Adam and Eve didn't really happen, then that means that evil, disease, depraved human desires, and even death aren't caused by their sin!"

Jesus almost cried out aloud in pain, for that thought was like a thorn being driven into his forehead. He hesitated, not wanting to go on, and sat silently, trying not to think of anything lest he experience more pain. But Rabbi Silence did what he refused to do and began unpeeling more implications of the story of Adam and Eve.

"Think about it, Jesus; if the holy writings about Adam and Eve did not actually happen, then it would have been impossible for generation after generation to inherit terrible crippling guilt for their sin, and that logically means...."

"There is no need," Jesus said aloud, "for any supreme sacrifice of atonement!"

Again he began vigorously shaking his head as if to dislodge such unthinkable, sacrilegious thoughts. "Like seductive nightmares, I must resist these horrible doubts...or else I will surely lose...no, no!" Then he released a long piercing scream of great inner pain, "I'm already losing my mind!"

His knife-like scream echoed off the walls, then ricocheted up off the floor to the ceiling, multiplying itself over and over until his cell was filled with howling shrieks. Finally those echoes grew weaker and fainter until there was only silence, and he groaned, "Where are you, Beloved Friend? Why have you abandoned me to these soul-shredding thoughts? Why, when I'm most in need of your affectionate embrace, are you never at my side?"

He listened for a reply but heard only a sterile silence, devoid of any sound or voice. Using the wall to steady his unstable legs, he stood up with difficulty from his mat and began slowly pacing in his cell, waiting for God to answer. After waiting a long time and receiving no answer, he cried out, "O God, I've become an orphan of faith."

Tired of pacing, he stopped at the window and gazed up at the night sky scattered with bright stars. "O you ancient sparkling sky creatures, whom God created in the beginning of time, speak to me of your ageless wisdom about death. I am in need of your counsel, for the death of Lucius has forced me to confront my own beliefs about what happens after we die."

Only the familiar sound of the waves crashing on the rocks below answered his question. "Tiny luminous lamps of night, during my first months of imprisonment, I believed firmly that God wanted me to die on a cross. As I considered that death, I found comfort in repeating Psalm 16, 'For you will not abandon me to Sheol, nor let your faithful servant see the pit.' While I felt comfort in those words, they also were troubling, for if I wasn't abandoned to the pit, where was I? I then sought relief in the line from Psalm 86, 'Lord, your love for me is great; you have rescued me from the depths of Sheol.' But that only gave rise to another problem; what did it mean to be rescued from Sheol?"

The stars sparkled, and if they spoke to him, he couldn't hear them. As he listened, however, he did hear in the darkness a soft melodious voice, which murmured, "Yes, Jesus, the thoughts of the pious psalms are reassuring and give great hope, and yet, son of Joseph, do you know of anyone who died, was buried, and returned from Sheol? There's no need to answer, as I'm sure you don't! Your own dear father, the good and devout Joseph, who never did an evil deed in his life—did he ever return to visit you after he died? Be logical both in your thoughts and in your prayers. If you don't know anyone who has died and has returned," the voice said, mockingly, "then why should you, Jesus?"

Jesus recognized the voice, having heard it during his forty days of fasting in the desert as it whispered in the desert wind. He had heard it many times after that in his life as well. Although he knew the sinister source of the voice, he couldn't resist being drawn into conversation with it.

"Enticer, what you say is logical, yet I have faith in the illogical and the impractical. I put my trust in a God for whom all things are possible."

"I'm aware, Jesus of Galilee, that you think this God of yours can do the impossible. I understand it isn't easy to change plain old water into delicious wine, but why was it so impossible to do something as easy as healing Pilate's sick slave?"

Jesus turned his back on the window and the enticing voice and returned to his sleeping mat, where he tried to find peace in sleep. As he tossed and turned, his mind revisited Lucius' sickbed, and he vividly saw himself bending over the dying slave to listen for his breath. He could hear Lucius' soul like a shadow slipping away from him, departing this world, and remembered thinking: *Where is it, or he, going?*

Waiting for the arrival of sleep, he tried to envision Lucius' possible destinations, and saw only gray, shifting mist and fog. He reflected, *I accepted what I had learned in the synagogue, that the body and soul are one and can't be divided; so the dead person goes to Sheol, the Land of No Return. When I began my life as a wandering teacher, I was attracted to the teaching of the Pharisees, based on the writings of the prophet Ezekiel, that after death there is an afterlife. I also knew that this belief of the Pharisees was much debated among their elders, with some saying it was a personal survival, and others saying that Ezekiel's words referred to the restoration of Israel. Lucius' death has pushed me to explore deeper my own uncertain beliefs about where the dead go when they die....* Then sleep concluded his thoughts.

SCENE VIII

THE PALACE TERRACE

Late November, 36 C.E.

"Welcome, Jesus, on this chilly November day," said Pilate. He was seated on a couch with Petronius next to him and Aristocles seated on a stool. "I greet you with good news: today I'm going to resume your trial. Does that please you?"

Jesus replied, "Yes, if you're really serious, since it's dragged on now for almost two years!"

"Here, come sit next to me. Has it been that long? 'Time flies, never to return,' said...uh...," he glanced at Aristocles.

"Virgil, your Excellency."

"Thank you, Aristocles. I learned that quote in my youth from Lucius, but I had forgotten who said it. You see, Jesus, how helpful it is to have a scholarly Greek such as Aristocles as one's secretary! Borrowing from Virgil, time seems to have flown on wings since I came here as Governor, and these years I've now shared with you."

Jesus replied, "I learned in my youth, 'There is a time for everything, a time to kill and a time to heal, a time to be born and a time to die.' So, Pilate, does resuming my trial mean you're ready to set the time for me to die?"

"That's a wise statement—who said it?" asked Pilate, ignoring Jesus' question.

"King Solomon. He also said, 'Why should you die before your time?' I now feel in my bones that it's my time to die."

"All this time you've been feeling that in your bones," noted Pilate. "But enough of exchanging quotations—let's not stray too far from your trial. Aristocles, where were we before Virgil and Solomon interrupted us?"

"Sir, after Jesus quoted Solomon, he asked if you were ready to set the time of his death. When he told you he felt in his bones that now was the time, you replied that he had felt that way for more than two years."

Pilate nodded at Aristocles, impressed by his accurate recording. "Jesus, before responding to your question, I have a question for you connected to your trial. I'm aware that the Law of Moses forbids murder, and I gather you taught that even being angry with another was the equivalent of murder?"

"Yes, because thoughts are simply pregnant deeds that, in due time, give birth." Tapping his chest with his finger, he continued, "Every war begins here in the heart, as does all evil, deeds of violence, lust, greed, and deceit. The thousands murdered in war and the murdering of a single man will only be eliminated by returning to the beginning...our thoughts."

"Eliminate war!" exclaimed Pilate. "That's a mere fantasy, along with the dream that someday men will fly! Let's return to reality; I have a practical question based on your teachings." Pilate paused a moment and then asked, "Jesus, do you love me?"

Inwardly Pilate chuckled as he watched Jesus try to escape the trap of remaining true to his teachings by loving an actual enemy like himself. Jesus, taken aback by Pilate's unexpected question, closed his eyes and tried to compose an answer. Aristocles sat, his black eyes flashing with anticipation of how Jesus would answer Pilate. Petronius also had closed his eyes, for the conversation had carried him back to an old battle in which, blood splattered, he was engaged in a ferocious hand-to-hand combat with the enemies of Rome.

Pilate asked again, "Jesus once of Galilee, and now of Caesarea, do you love me?"

"Yes, Pilate, I love you!" Jesus proclaimed.

Pilate smiled, and in the silence that followed, he allowed those three powerful words to stand as tall as giants. Meanwhile, Aristocles wondered which of the three Greek words for love Jesus meant— agape, eros, or philia?

"Jesus, when you say you love me, do you mean with affectionate feelings?"

"I love you, Pilate, by not judging your motives for endlessly postponing my crucifixion, and by praying for you. The love that God asks us to show to others can sometimes be affectionate; but our loving of strangers, foreigners, and enemies isn't like the love for a spouse or dear friend. God asks that we love our neighbor as we love ourselves; and I don't have any romantic feelings about myself. Does that answer your question?"

"I don't understand—if your emotions aren't involved, how do you love others?"

"I love them by placing their needs and concerns before my own."

"Why would you do that? What good would come from putting the needs of others before your own?"

"It is the will of God, and contrary to all common sense, when you love an enemy or anyone, you are actually loving yourself! We are deceived by what *appears* to be real, for though it may seem that we are each separate, unique, and different, in reality we are all one. As members of one body, every act of kindness or love shown to another is done to oneself, and even more amazing—to God!"

Pilate said, "Now I'm really lost! Whatever do you mean...?"

Marcus came hurrying out onto the terrace and went at once to Pilate. "Pardon me, Excellency, but it is very urgent." Leaning down, he whispered in his ear. As Pilate listened, he slowly nodded his head.

"You were right, Marcus, to interrupt me. Jesus, although I would like to unravel the tangled knots of your recent statement, an urgent issue has arisen that requires my immediate attention." Then, standing up, he said, "Today we've had more than our usual diet of god talk, and as a man who doesn't believe in the gods, I'm surprised how long I lasted! I regret having to postpone your trial yet again, Jesus. Petronius, see that our guest is shown to his quarters."

SCENE IX

JESUS' CELL

The Same Afternoon

After hearing the metallic cling of the key being turned in the lock of his cell door, Jesus went and sat on his mat and spoke to the walls. "Old comrades, when I spoke to Pilate about loving strangers and good friends, I couldn't help but think of John, my young disciple and intimate friend. There are times when I can still feel him affectionately resting his head on my chest as at our last supper, and since I was drawn to him, it was wonderful to know that John was also attracted to me."

That memory caused John's visage to appear before him: his dark brown eyes, his delicate face with its youthfully sparse black beard, and his long, curly black hair. From his treasury of memorized lines of the holy writings came David's funeral poem for his beloved friend Jonathan, 'I grieve for you, Jonathan, most dear; more precious was your love and the love I had for you than for any woman.' After some moments, Jesus thought, *It's been years since I recalled those words I memorized a day long ago when I heard them read aloud from the scroll of Samuel by an elder in the synagogue.*

Then a procession of faces passed before him of his disciples whom he had loved: Andrew, Peter, Mary Magdalene, and the others. As each face appeared, he felt a surge of affection. He said aloud, "I know my love for each of them took nothing away from my love for you, Beloved Friend. But I confess that back then there were times when I was concerned that my love for them was wrong, for I feared it prevented me from loving you with a complete fullness of my heart. So I strove to love you spiritually."

Reaching up, he patted the familiar walls. "O faithful companions of my imprisonment, I confess to you how wrong I was to try to love God spiritually! I now know how ridiculous it was to deny I was made of flesh and blood and could love only physically! How childish, not to realize that only angels can love spiritually." He leaned back against the chiseled stones. "My back feels the chilly bodily touch of this wall as once I felt the warm embrace of young John. I'm grateful for my great love for him and for Mary and the others, for it was the beginning of the path that led me to the great truth that all human love is loving you, my Beloved Friend."

His thoughts then drifted back to the conversation in which Pilate asked if he loved him. *My anger at Pilate for delaying my crucifixion has faded away as I have slowly grown to embrace God's will about my long imprisonment. I've now grown fond of Pilate and even enjoy our spirited debates....* Suddenly he said aloud, "Why didn't I ask Pilate if he loved me?" After pausing, he thought, *Do I even need to ask that question? Is it not the reason he keeps delaying the time when he will pass final judgment on me? If that is true, it explains why each time we begin my trial anew, Pilate keeps asking me questions and involving me in discussions. He wants to use our time together so he can adjourn my trial and send me back down here!*

With difficulty Jesus forced his aching legs to stand up and carry him over to the window, where he stood gazing out at the blue-black night sky with its wide silver river of bright stars flowing across it. "If Pilate has indeed grown fond of me," he said to the night sky, "then I shouldn't be so defensive whenever he asks me those barbed questions that challenge my beliefs. I react that way because his questions force me to choose between something new and what I once was taught and firmly believed. The pull between the two makes me feel like I'm a divided man."

"And stupid, also?" asked a voice out of the night.

"Why am I stupid?" replied Jesus. "Am I not doing what God desires in loving my enemy? You don't sound like the Evil Enticer, yet that's surely who you are."

"Really, Jesus? Doesn't it make sense that if you love someone, they will love you as well, or at least think fondly of you? You dim-witted Galilean, no sane man wants to crucify someone he loves!"

"Then truly I'm a man who is torn asunder. If I don't love Pilate then I'm not obeying God; if I do love him, then I'm only frustrating

191

God's plan. O Spirit, come quickly and show me how to escape from this predicament of loving."

Silently Jesus pondered this new predicament as he listened to wave after wave come crashing ashore. Hearing no answer to his plea to the Spirit, he spoke to the ocean. "I must admit I'm grateful I didn't die before my time, as Solomon said. These long years of solitude have given me time to test my old beliefs and explore new ones. In that time I've found a new intimate relationship with God, and now I can feel in my heart it is time to die, yet that is not in my hands. O cross of my destiny," he said, extending his arms outward as wide as possible with his palms eagerly open, "come quickly."

SCENE X

THE PALACE TERRACE

Early December, 36 C.E.

Pilate stood alone looking out over the harbor now that his report to Rome was completed, deeply inhaling the brisk December air. Aristocles had gone off to make copies and Marcus was away attending to a household matter. Pilate was free to leisurely watch the ships in the harbor being loaded and unloaded. With the rest of his day unburdened of official tasks, he thought perhaps he should send for Jesus so they could continue their recent discussion.

Then, unconsciously, Pilate stroked his upper lip as he thought, *His answer to my question about whether he loved me was fascinating; he actually surprised me by saying yes! I thank the gods he didn't ask me the same question, for I don't how I would have answered, love being a word I seldom use. I could have answered that I am fond of him, which is true, especially since he's stopped pestering me to crucify him. Yes, I'm fond of Jesus in the way a soldier is fond of his comrades in arms...but do I love him? What's the point of exploring such a complex issue? All I know is that I enjoy our discussions about life and what happens after death.*

A quick shudder ran through Pilate's body, and not because of the chilly breeze blowing in off the sea. The mention of death had caused it, awakening his great dislike of even thinking about death, especially his own. What he found so disturbing about death was the thought of no longer existing, of no longer being able to feel the sensual, invigorating joy of being alive as he was doing this December morning.

"I try not to think about death," Pilate said to the boats down in the harbor, "but Jesus does and freely talks about it. I admire a man who isn't afraid, and Jesus doesn't seem to be afraid of anything, including death, which is another reason I'm attracted to him. I find remarkable his ideas that after you die there might just be something other than—well, nothing. Yes, I think I will send someone to bring him up here so we can talk about...."

"Excellency, excuse me." Turning his back on the harbor, Pilate saw Petronius standing at attention, gripping a scroll in his left hand.

"Good morning, Petronius. I must say you look very somber this morning."

"Sir, I regret to inform you that I've just received a report from our spy in Samaria, who says serious trouble is brewing at their holy mountain of Gerizim! It seems the Samaritan prophet agitator named Simon has announced that he will produce the sacred relics left by Moses on Mount Gerizim for all the people to see—Aaron's rod, a jar of the desert manna, and the Ark of the Covenant. Sir, these sacred Jewish relics of the Exodus are extremely dangerous, because there's a Samaritan legendary belief that says when these sacred Exodus relics are revealed in public, the glory of God will shine down at Mount Gerizim to usher in the Messianic Age."

Pilate replied, "I know about manna, but I'm not familiar with any rod of Aaron. At any rate, I thought these things didn't exist anymore."

"They don't, Sir!" replied Petronius. "However, the Samaritans are notorious for being gullible. It seems the Prophet Simon's promise of displaying them is sufficient to draw great throngs who anticipate the Messianic Age, and so are capable of insurrection. This morning's messenger told me that enormous crowds of Samaritans already have begun gathering at the foot of their holy Mount Gerizim."

"Petronius," Pilate snorted, "we have on our hands the birthing of a rebellion. It must be crushed while it's still in its infancy! I warned the Legate Vitellius about just such an impending uprising in Samaria, but his only reply was to lecture me about treating the Samaritans 'diplomatically.'"

"He should have listened to you, Sir. Now it may be too late."

"Not if I act at once, which I intend to do."

"I anticipated that would be your decision, so I've brought with me this map of Samaria." He unrolled the scroll he had been carrying and placed it on the table, and both men leaned over it and studied the map inscribed on it.

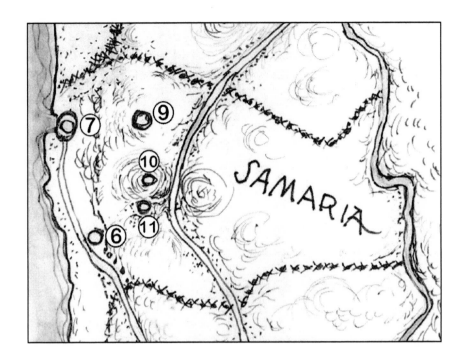

Map of Samaria

6. Lydda

7. Caesarea Maritima

9. City of Samaria

10. Mount Gerizim

11. Tirathana

"Here is Mount Gerizim on the map," pointed Petronius with his finger, "just south and across from Mount Ebal. Between these two mountains is a wide gorge through which runs the main road from Galilee down to Jerusalem. Notice," he said, pointing to the map, "that north of Mount Gerizim is the mountaintop City of Samaria. It was there that King Herod built his temple to the Emperor Augustus, and it is said that if you look west on a clear day from the top of this mountain, you can see the Mediterranean."

Pilate tapped his finger on the map and said, "Petronius, we'll depart here from the main gate of Caesarea, then turn eastward and southward on this highway to Jerusalem, until we reach here." Pointing again at the map, he said, "Just above the village of Lydda we'll leave the highway and travel eastward across the flat plains of Sharon straight for Mt. Gerizim."

Petronius replied, "An excellent route, Sir! This morning's messenger said that massive crowds were already gathering in and around the village of Tirathana, which is here at the base of Mount Gerizim."

"Petronius, we must depart this very afternoon! Make the arrangements for our best cavalry unit and a fully armed detachment of soldiers to be prepared to march at once for Tirathana! And this time, Petronius, it will not be like eighty years ago, when our Roman troops were besieged and slaughtered there by the Jews to the last man!"

SCENE XI

OUTSIDE THE SAMARITAN
VILLAGE OF TIRATHANA

The Next Day

Seated on their horses, Pilate and Petronius were well hidden in a thick grove of trees on a hill that overlooked the village of Tirathana, behind which towered Mount Gerizim. From this excellent vantage point they could look down at the massive crowds gathering in the village without being seen by them. Petronius pointed out that some men in the gathering crowd carried weapons. To the right they could see great crowds of Samaritans coming westward toward Tirathana on the road that led off the main Jerusalem highway in the ravine between the two mountains.

"Petronius," said Pilate, pointing northward, "if we maneuver our cavalry and soldiers off to that grove of trees about halfway up the mountain, that would put us directly above Tirathana. We can reach there without being seen by circling behind that hill over there, and then discreetly climb up the western slope of Mount Gerizim. Halfway up I intend to set an ambush to surprise the Samaritan crowds as they are ascending the mountain."

Later that afternoon, after completing their encirclement tactic, Pilate's cavalry and infantry were hidden in the dense groves of trees on the ridges on both sides of a ravine, through which passed the road up to the top of the mountain and the temple. Although he was well hidden in the dense foliage, Pilate had a clear view of the road leading up to the temple through the ravine. As he studied the road he thought, *It feels magnificent to be back in the saddle in my military uniform, preparing for battle. War gives a sense of purpose and meaning to life; nothing else compares to the intoxication of battle!*

Also concealed in the bushes was Petronius, who reflected, *Because of my assignment as an adviser to Prince Antipas and now to Pilate, I haven't been in armed combat for years. I pray to God that I can keep my*

197

hands clean of another man's blood today. Removing his bronze helmet, he wiped the sweat off his brow as he thought, *I hate war! Yesterday, departing from Caesarea, we rode past the cheering Roman populace of the city. Those poor, ignorant souls think war is glorious and a great heroic adventure because they've never been in battle themselves. They only know the glorified myth of war, while actual war — the brutal slaughtering of other men — isn't glorious, it's ugly and evil.* Patting the hilt of his sword, he thought, *I pray, O sword, that you don't taste blood this day.*

Pilate's choice of a site for an ambush was clever, because it placed his troops facing down the road with the bright afternoon sun behind their backs. The Samaritans, on the other hand, had the sun shining directly in their eyes as they came up the mountain road. The narrow, steep-sided ravine forced the massive hoard of chanting pilgrims to bunch tightly together to funnel through the narrow gorge.

"Petronius, keep a lookout for their leaders," Pilate said in a low voice, "especially for Simon the prophet. I want him taken alive!"

"Sir," replied Petronius quietly, "before you engage are you going to try to negotiate with these Samaritans?"

Pilate answered by loudly shouting the order to attack. Upon hearing the order, his cavalry sprung out of the bushes and came rushing down the sides of the ravine with their swords slashing left and right. The Samaritans who were at the head of the procession instantly stopped and looked up in horror as their holy mountain appeared to split wide open, releasing an avalanche of galloping warhorses. The pilgrims trapped in the narrow valley were terrified by the roaring thunder of the horses' hooves, and behind them the ferocious battle cries of the soldiers who came pouring down the sides of the ravine. Those leading the procession stood petrified, clogging the ascending road, while those in the middle were trapped by the hoards of crazed Samaritan pilgrims pushing against them from behind. From this horrifying chaos many persons attempted to escape by vainly trying to scramble up the steep, rocky sides of the gorge.

The combination of the mounted cavalry and the notoriously brutal foreign auxiliary soldiers sent the terrified pilgrims scattering in all directions like doves before a flock of hawks. Some Samaritans were killed in an attempt to escape, whereas the majority, seeing that escape was impossible, surrendered to Pilate, pleading for mercy. As his cavalry quickly rounded up the stragglers, Petronius pointed out those he thought were the leaders. These men were taken before Pilate and were quickly tried and convicted of rebellion against Rome. It now being late afternoon, there wasn't sufficient time to prepare crosses to crucify the condemned leaders, so Pilate had them executed by the sword. The remainder of the Samaritans he released, telling them to go home. Although his troops rejoiced in their quick and easy victory, Pilate was disappointed that the rabble-rouser prophet Simon had escaped.

For Pilate, the homeward journey to Caesarea was a triumphant march, for he had successfully suppressed an insurrection without losing a single soldier. As he rode homeward he gave thanks to the Goddess Roma who had blessed the Roman army with a glorious victory, which reflected on him as its commander. He thought, *I'm proud not only that I am the victor, but because I handled this entire affair with compassion. I executed only the guilty insurrection leaders, and the others would not have been killed if they had surrendered instead of trying to escape. I graciously allowed countless other Samaritans to go free without any punishment. My victory at Tirathana over the rebels has already sprouted wings and is swiftly flying all across the land. May it teach the Samaritans the folly of insurrection and be a lesson to all Jews who are tempted to follow a Messianic prophet.*

Riding beside the victorious Pilate was Petronius, also deep in thought. *I'm glad to be leaving the bloody battlefield, and I'm grateful that my only duty was to identify those I thought were the insurrection's leaders. I should be happy I didn't have to use my sword, yet my heart is troubled. Pilate ordered me to point out those I thought were the instigators and leaders, and the ones I selected were all beheaded. By identifying them, does that make me just as guilty of their deaths as the soldiers who executed them? The Jews are forbidden to murder, and Jesus forbids even the thinking of angry thoughts; in his eyes, am I guilty of the deaths of the men who died back there? Petronius, Petronius,* he moaned under his breath, *what's happening to you?*

ACT IV

SCENE I

THE PALACE TERRACE

Three Weeks after Pilate's Return from Samaria,
December, 36 C.E.

"Welcome, Jesus!" said Pilate. "It's good to see you now that I'm back from Samaria. My troops and I successfully suppressed an insurrection led by Simon of Samaria, another Messianic prophet. I say 'another,' because this province of Palestine seems to breed a messiah every full moon!"

"It's good to see you as well, Pilate. Did you crucify Simon, as the Jerusalem priests wanted you to crucify me?"

"Unfortunately Jesus, he escaped! Which raises an interesting question: Why didn't you escape from the olive grove the night of your arrest? Ah, but of course, unlike Simon, you wanted to be captured and die on the cross to fulfill some ancient prophesy. At least, that's how you felt a couple of years ago—you may feel differently now. Tell me, do you still wish to be crucified?"

"I desire...well, I desire what God desires!"

"As for myself," Pilate said, "I'm not concerned about what your god does or doesn't desire. I'm only concerned about a certain pledge I made to Caiaphas, and so, Jesus, I suppose we should resume your trial."

"I would like that very much, as long as there are no more interruptions!" asserted Jesus.

Pilate said, "Aristocles, prepare to keep a written record of the trial's proceedings." Then, clearing his throat, he announced, "I, Pontius Pilate, the Roman Governor of Judea, Galilee, and Samaria, now officially call back into session the trial of Jesus the Galilean, who is charged with the subversive crime of claiming kingship. Does the prisoner declare himself innocent or guilty as charged?"

Before Jesus could answer, Petronius came rushing out onto the terrace. "Sir, I apologize for this intrusion, but a Roman centurion has just arrived from Syria along with a cavalry escort. He says he carries a message for you from Legate Vitellius and that he has been ordered to deliver it personally into your hands."

Pilate said, "Well, this is most extraordinary, eh, Petronius? A centurion isn't your usual messenger, even from the illustrious Legate Vitellius."

"No, Sir. Perhaps the Legate has sent his congratulations on your successful victory at Tirathana?"

Pilate retorted, "I doubt that! Vitellius isn't known for giving praise to others for their achievements. Marcus, go at once and instruct the household slaves to make all the necessary arrangements to properly host the centurion and his escort. Then quickly come back here to me."

As Marcus departed, Pilate said, "Petronius, escort the centurion up here to the terrace, where I'll receive him and the message he carries. Then, I want you to remain here with me." Pilate didn't have long to wait; Petronius soon returned with the dust-covered soldier who saluted and then stepped forward and placed a rolled scroll into Pilate's outstretched hand. Marcus by now had returned and stood nearby.

Pilate said to the centurion, "Thank you for making a long and a tiresome journey from Syria to deliver this message. I hope that his Excellency the Legate Vitellius is in good health."

"Yes, Excellency, praise be to the gods, he is in excellent health."

"That is good news; I am pleased to hear it," Pilate replied. "I hope that after your tiring and dusty journey from Syria, you and your men will accept my hospitality. My personal slave Marcus will see that you are given food and wine, and if you need anything else, I command that you ask, and it shall be yours."

"Excellency, on behalf of my men and myself, I thank you for your hospitality."

Pilate continued, "Does the Legate Vitellius want me to send my response with you when you return to Syria?"

The centurion responded, "Yes, Excellency, those were his instructions." Then, saluting, he said, "Again, I thank you for your kindness to me and my men."

As Marcus led the centurion away, Pilate turned to Jesus. "I'm sorry about this unexpected event. Please remain, as I'm sure it won't take long. You stay too, Aristocles, as I will need to write a brief response to the Legate Vitellius."

Pilate then dramatically broke the seal on the scroll and unrolled it. Smiling at Petronius, he said, "Now, I'm eager to see what message Vitellius thinks is so important to have delivered by a Roman centurion." He began reading the scroll, but soon stopped and with a trembling hand dropped it into his lap.

"By Jupiter and all the gods!" exclaimed Pilate. "I've been recalled to Rome by Emperor Tiberius Caesar and am to report directly to him; that's how Vitellius has begun his letter to me!"

Petronius gasped loudly, and both Jesus and Aristocles looked shocked. After taking several deep breaths, Pilate regained his composure. "Vitellius writes that the Emperor has recalled me to Rome to personally respond to accusations made against me by the Samaritans regarding atrocities that occurred at Mount Gerizim!"

"Accusations? Sir," a stunned Petronius interrupted him, "what atrocities?"

"Vitellius writes to inform me that I've been charged with murder!" replied Pilate, his face drained of all color. "I'm accused of recklessly murdering innocent, unarmed Samaritan pilgrims as they processed up to their temple on top of Mount Gerizim!"

"But some were armed...." Petronius pointed out.

Pilate responded, "Yes, I know. I can guess what happened— those damn Samaritans went directly to Vitellius and, in typical Jewish style, wildly embellished the Gerizim incident with acts of reckless, uncontrolled brutality."

"But Sir, you only executed a handful of them, and they were their leaders; the rest you set free," protested Petronius.

Pilate replied, "Vitellius isn't interested in the facts. He's polishing his reputation in Rome as a conscientious legate by sending the Emperor the exaggerated, inflated accusations of the Samaritans. In this letter, Vitellius informs me that the Samaritans are known for their loyalty to Rome and assured him that they were only involved in a peaceful religious procession and did not have the slightest intent of inciting a rebellion. He accepts their accusation that I overreacted when I saw the great crowds marching in the procession, mistaking it for some kind of messianic uprising."

"Nonsense, Sir!" responded Petronius, heatedly. "I was there, and that gathering at their holy mountain was highly volatile, because the prophet Simon had promised to display the Exodus relics. Did the legate make any mention of that?"

"Not as far as I've read in his letter," Pilate said.

"Sir," Petronius replied, "the legate knows you're not guilty of any mass atrocities; he's just ingratiating himself with the Emperor."

"Of that, Petronius, I have no doubts," Pilate said. "I can assume that in his letter to the Emperor, he also listed all my past political mistakes—the riots over the aqueduct and the affair of Emperor's image on the legion standards." Burying his face in his hands, Pilate exclaimed, "My greatest fear has now come about—I've become *friget!*" After a few moments he slowly raised his head and said, "I've told you the consequences to those to whom this happens. They haven't simply fallen from imperial favor; they're dead! Tiberius is notorious for executing people on the flimsiest evidence, and even on a mere rumor from some informer."

Depressed, Petronius slumped on the coach as Pilate picked up the scroll and resumed reading it. As he read the rest of Vitellius' letter, both Jesus and Aristocles sat pondering their personal fates after Pilate departed for Rome. Aristocles questioned what his future would hold, as Pilate wouldn't be sending any more daily reports and would have no need of a secretary. Jesus wondered if Pilate would have him crucified before departing for Rome. Finally, Pilate finished reading the letter, slowly rolled it up, and clutched it tightly in his hand as if it were a viper.

Petronius ventured to ask, "It pains me to ask you, Sir, but when do you have to depart for Rome?"

"Vitellius has given me the traditional three months to put Judea's affairs in order and to pack my personal and household belongings." Then Pilate flung the scroll to the floor. "Vitellius informs me that he has already dispatched Marcellus to Jerusalem to be the new provisional governor of Judea!" He continued, "Marcellus is an old buddy of the legate, and Vitellius has invested him with all the administrative powers as the provisional procurator of Palestine until my case in Rome is officially resolved. Until I've departed from here for Rome, Marcellus is to reside at King Herod's palace in Jerusalem."

Petronius replied, "Sir, you said Vitellius used the term 'provisional.' Does that mean...."

"It's politics, Petronius; read between the lines. Vitellius knows that it's highly unlikely I will ever return from Rome. After the Emperor's verdict is made public, even if it's only imprisonment, the legate will make his pal Marcellus the permanent procurator governor of Judea."

"Sir, you seem to imply that all governors recalled to Rome are found guilty; if you are judged innocent, as surely you will be, what happens then?"

"Very few, if any, are ever acquitted under Tiberius because he considers all accusations, however minor, to be capital offenses. I've heard of some recalled Roman administrators being banished to the most remote barbaric edge of the Empire. Others he sends to prison before their trials, and then endlessly delays their trials so they end up spending years in prison." Pilate paused, and looking out at the sea, spoke in a impassive voice, "It's like drowning in a sea of disgrace to be declared *friget*, so the brave choose the honorable exit—suicide!"

"Pilate, you must order my crucifixion at once!" Jesus exclaimed. "Don't let the sun set today until you've fulfilled my destiny and your pledge to the High Priest!"

"I'm sorry, Jesus," Pilate said, shrugging his shoulders, "but that's impossible! I'm no longer the governor of Judea; didn't you hear what I just read in the legate's letter? I've been stripped of all my authority, and that includes the right to order you or anyone else to be crucified!"

"Oh no, no...no...," Jesus moaned.

"I never wanted to crucify you in the first place, and now," Pilate chuckled mockingly, "I'm impotent to do so! But, Jesus, cheer up; your long-cherished dream of dying on a cross will soon be a reality. The fickle gods of fate have made the Governor Marcellus your judge instead of me, and I assure you he'll nail you to a cross the moment he learns you claim to be a king."

Jesus' eyes brightened as he thought, *Finally...the will of God and the ancient prophecies will be fulfilled. The ways of God are indeed strange.*

"Excellency," said Aristocles, "I encourage you to consider that this tragic news from the legate may actually reveal your true greatness. The poet philosopher Lucretius said, 'It is more useful to watch a man in times of peril and in adversity to discern what kind of man he is; for then the last words of truth are drawn from the depths of his heart, and the mask is torn off, and reality remains.'"

Pilate gave Aristocles a puzzled look, causing Aristocles to quickly stare at the floor, as he regretted he had included the words about a mask in the quote from Lucretius.

"Mask?" demanded Pilate. "I find that implication offensive; do you think I'm hiding behind a mask?" As Aristocles fumbled with some of his scrolls to hide his embarrassment, Pilate reflected, *At least, not now that I'm no longer governor! Now it will be the novice procurator Marcellus' turn to begin to wear a mask to hide his feelings when he's negotiating with Caiaphas and those damn Temple priests.* Inwardly he chuckled, *And Marcellus will need the mask of a stoic face when he attempts to explain to the people his dilemma of how you crucify a man who has already been crucified! That tricky predicament will be a good introduction for him to the future political and religious problems awaiting him as Governor of Judea!*

"So Pilate, you think the new governor will crucify me?" asked Jesus.

"Without a doubt," Pilate replied. "Marcellus will be drunk with his first sweet taste of power, and it will be so tantalizing, it will only make him hungry for more. To show his loyalty to the Emperor Tiberius and his fidelity to his patron Vitellius, he won't hesitate to crucify you."

"When do think he'll...."

"Petronius," Pilate said, with a flip of his hand, "have the guards escort our friend Jesus back to his quarters. I have enough concerns about my own fate to deal with, and have no time to waste chatting with him about his."

As the guards were leading Jesus away, a noticeable change came over the previously morose Pilate. It may have been the sense of being defeated that inspired him to suddenly assume the attitude of a military commander required to attack after a reversal on the field of battle. "Aristocles," he said, in his old commanding voice, "the new governor Marcellus will be itching to explore our archives here in Caesarea for my reports and letters, and may even order that they be sent to Jerusalem. I'm confident that Lucius carefully edited all the archives in Jerusalem, but I want you to purge all my reports and correspondence here. Eliminate all indiscretions and any insulting language about the Jews or Samaritans, and even the slightest implications of any disrespect of the Emperor or the Legate Vitellius. Be ruthless, Aristocles, as you delete everything from the scrolls that might reflect negatively on me. Purge the files with a vengeance, for there's a slim chance that I may be vindicated in Rome."

Pilate stood and began pacing with his hands linked behind his back. "Then, Aristocles, I'll need your help in composing a required final report to the Roman Senate about my administration that must list any occasions of street rioting, serious public disturbances, and the loss of any of my troops as a result of enemy action. Tomorrow I'll dictate a letter to the new Governor Marcellus about the case of the prisoner Jesus of Galilee, whom we have in our custody. The record of his trial, or trials, will have to be edited so that the charge against him of kingship is made as vague and religiously convoluted as possible to challenge our young governor's wits. With your Greek creativity, Aristocles, I'm sure you will be up to the task." Then he stopped and said, "Now, off you go to the archives to begin your scrupulous housecleaning, and while you're doing that, I'll compose a brief response to Vitellius' letter."

Aristocles stood and gathered his writing equipment as Pilate continued, "After I've composed the letter to the legate, I'll be blowing on the glowing ember of hope that I can escape the Emperor's wrath. However, should the gods dictate that this is not to be my good fortune, then, Aristocles, let's bequeath to history the best possible image of Pontius Pilate."

SCENE II

JESUS' CELL

Later That Evening

"O God, forgive me for being so selfish and self-centered," prayed Jesus, after the guards shut his cell door and departed. He walked to the window and stood there pondering, *I realized as I descended the stairs to my cell, that up there on the terrace I was thinking only of myself and my craving to be crucified. I should have shown compassion toward Pilate, who was suffering so intensely upon learning that the Emperor had recalled him to Rome. I've failed not only myself but also you, my God. Forgive me! Aristocles quoted some Roman, who said a man's true nature appears in adversity when his mask is torn off. Those words pierced me like an arrow, since I've taught others to be compassionate and referred to myself as humble, meek, and gentle. I also boldly denounced the Pharisees for being hypocrites – mask wearers. Now adversity has revealed the hypocrite Jesus whose mask has been pulled off, exposing the "real" Jesus: self-centered, uncompassionate, and concerned only with his own needs.*

Majestically the sun had slipped beneath the sea, but Jesus hadn't seen its dying golden splendor, for in his depression he had sunk deep into himself. As he paced in his cell, feeling guilty for his failure to be compassionate to Pilate, he moaned aloud, "I was so absorbed in myself, I failed to even acknowledge the anguish and humiliation so visible on Pilate's face, and neither did I think of poor Claudia. She'll be horrified upon hearing that Pilate has been recalled to Rome." Pausing briefly, he recalled, "And in my self-absorption I also failed to comfort Centurion Petronius, who clearly was sharing in the suffering of his friend Pilate's disgrace and downfall."

Upon reaching his sleeping mat, Jesus laid down on it and stared up at the craggy ceiling for a long time. The sense of guilt that was soaking into his soul, linked to his failure to be a living image of God, wrapped around him like heavy iron chains, causing him to sink ever deeper into an abyss of depression. As sadness often does, it ushered him into sleep.

He awoke sometime later, and still feeling a crushing sense of guilt, cried out, "O Friend, I know you've forgiven me; help me to forgive myself! The past can't be changed, and I mustn't linger there; inspire me rather to think about what lies ahead—my death. I won't know the day and hour I'll die on a cross until I'm brought before the new governor. I couldn't tell if Pilate was serious or jesting with me when he asked if I still desired to be crucified."

Jesus paused with embarrassment as he felt a new guilt added to the others that weighed down his soul. He thought, *I failed to reply to Pilate's question with a firm, unconditional yes; I hesitated and then said I only desire what God desires. Did that vague response come from the Spirit, or do I no longer desire to die on a cross? Yet, I spoke truthfully when I said that I truly desire whatever death God has chosen for me. When Marcellus nails me to the cross, I'll embrace it wholeheartedly.*

He struggled to stand up, feeling the shooting pains in his aching, swollen knees, and as he made his way to his privy bucket, he moaned, "Old privy, it seems that old age has me making more and more frequent visits to you...and each trip seems to require more effort for my aching legs. Governor Marcellus, you'd better nail this old body of mine to a cross quickly, while I'm still able to carry its wooden crossbeam."

A refreshing wind blew in off the sea through the window, and as Jesus paused and inhaled, he heard a slight, metallic creak behind him. Turning around, he could see by the pale moonlight that his large heavy cell door was now standing slightly ajar. Another gust of wind caused the door to slightly move again and creak on its hinges. When Jesus walked over to it and gently pushed on the door, it swung open a bit further.

How strange, he thought, *this cell door is always locked. Yet tonight I don't recall hearing the usual sound of the iron key turning in the lock after the guards closed the door. Were they careless, or is this unlocked door a gift from Pilate? That's certainly a possibility, because he said he never wanted to crucify me in the first place.*

Jesus pushed again on the heavy door, and it temptingly opened even wider, causing him to think, *If I did escape, Pilate could easily blame the guards for their negligence.*

"Jesus," spoke a voice in his right ear, "what difference does it make if this door was left unlocked accidentally or on purpose? What's keeping you from stepping out of your cell and climbing up those steps to your freedom? Even if you're captured, Pilate would have to execute you for attempting to escape!"

Jesus seriously pondered the enticing temptation to escape from his endless, lonely confinement. His initial enthusiasm quickly waned as he thought about the physical effort required to escape, regretting how aging had stolen his strength. Then his urge for freedom conquered his objections and he pushed on the cell door, which swung wide open!

"Your prison door is open, Jesus!" spoke the voice in his right ear. "That's an unmistakable sign that this unlocked door is a gift from God. Go ahead and escape!"

"Jesus, you're an old man," said another voice in his left ear, "and even if you are able to escape from this the palace and flee into the countryside, what then? Where will you go? You can't go back to Galilee; they all think you're dead. How will your disciples explain to the people what they told them about your redemptive death on the cross?"

"You've lived in the desert of the Jordan before," the voice in his right ear said. "Once you're outside Caesarea, you can find your way down to the wilderness of the Jordan and live there with your God; no one will ever find you."

In the midst of his inner debate, like a refreshing breeze on a hot summer's night, Jesus felt the sweet temptation to climb the steps up to the ground level, and he walked out of his cell toward the stairs.

"Escape is a coward's way out, Jesus," said the voice in his left ear.

"Yet didn't you yourself teach your disciples that if they were persecuted in one village they were to flee and escape to another?" said the voice in his right ear. "Sage of Galilee, you should follow the wise advice you gave to others."

As he slowly began to climb the steps, Jesus thought, *It's the dead of night, and the entire household is fast asleep. Keep climbing, Jesus; it's dark, yet you only need to see far enough in front you to find the next step.*

Several times he was forced to stop briefly to regain his strength and rub his swollen ankles. At last he reached the doorway at the top of the stairs that opened onto the hallway by the pool and gave a sigh of relief that no soldiers were on guard there. Cautiously he stepped out into the hallway and looked to his left. By moonlight he could see two sentry soldiers with their backs to him at the front of the palace. To his right, he saw no one, and so he moved along the pool walkway toward the terrace. The recurring crashing of waves grew louder and louder, and the pungent smell of ocean air grew stronger. Upon reaching the end of the hallway, he paused to regain his strength.

"You're tired, Jesus," said the voice in his left ear. "Go back down to your cell; admit that you lack the strength to escape." Disregarding the voice, Jesus walked onto the terrace, now flooded with pale blue moonlight, and proceeded along the northern parapet overlooking the harbor. Finding no place along it from which he could escape, he also searched along the eastern wall, with the same result. It was clear that the tall, sheer walls of the palace, which had been designed to prevent anyone scaling them from below, also prevented anyone from descending them from above. Retracing his steps across the terrace, he went over to the western parapet wall and stood looking out over the ocean. He saw that the moon had created a shimmering silver road leading westward across the middle of the dark blue sea.

"If I could walk on water again, as I once did on the Sea of Galilee" he said softly, "it would be tempting to think of escaping by traveling westward on that rippling silver road." As a brisk wind off the sea caused his robe to flap and cling to his body, he murmured, "But first, I'd have to find a way get down to the ocean from up here."

"But that's easy, Jesus!" said the silky voice in his right ear, "just jump! In the blink of an eye, you'll be down at the sea."

Jesus turned to see who had spoken as he replied, "If I were stupid enough to jump, I'd be dashed to death on the rocks down there!"

"Anyone who can walk on water wouldn't be scratched if he jumped down onto those rocks," reasoned the voice. "If you're not afraid to do it, why don't you climb up on top of the parapet?"

Jesus accepted the challenge and climbed up on top of the wall. The sea breeze felt invigorating, and the view along the coast was breathtaking.

"Now look down; it's an eerie feeling, isn't it?" whispered the voice. "One part of you feels the thrilling urge to just let go and fall, while another part of you keeps your feet firmly planted on the parapet because you're afraid. Yes, fear grips your heart even if you preached to others not to be afraid. Fear not, Jesus; step off the wall and let yourself float like a leaf on the wind."

"It would be suicidal to jump," Jesus said, turning all the way around to see who was speaking. "God wouldn't want me to take my own life."

"Death is death, isn't it?" spoke the voice softly, this time coming from deep within Jesus' chest. "The end result is always the same, whether you choose the time of your death or you sit around waiting for fate to choose it for you. Didn't your great King Saul, who like you was one chosen by God, die by his own hand by falling on his sword? I don't recollect that in your sacred writings Saul was ever condemned by God for trying to find peace from his depression by taking his own life—isn't that so?"

Jesus stuffed his fingers in his ears to silence the voice and prayed he would never hear it again, finding relief for a few moments in his self-created silence.

"Poor King Saul," said the voice, which now spoke inside his head. "He was miserable after being abandoned by his people, his family and friends, and most excruciating, by his God. So it's understandable—and only I know this—that as he fell on his sword, Saul cried out, 'My God, why have you abandoned me!'"

"God has not abandoned me!" exclaimed Jesus. "Go away, whoever you are, and leave me in peace so I can hear God's voice, not yours!"

"Be reasonable, Jesus," replied the seductive voice. "Do you think God has only one voice? Can't all the inner voices you're hearing belong to God? It would only be logical for a God who gives you ultimate freedom to provide a variety of choices from which to choose. Rabbi, you've taught that God is compassionate and loving. If someone, especially one who is beloved of God, was facing a prolonged, painful death, don't you think a compassionate God would offer him the choice of an easy and quick death?"

Jesus tightly closed his eyes, clamped both hands over his ears, and vigorously shook his head. In his pitch-black self-created silence, he recalled that night in the olive garden: *In my prayer in the olive garden I also heard several voices; one told me it was my moral duty to preserve my life and escape back to Galilee.*

"And that full-moon night," whispered the voice from the back of his head, "you also heard another voice, didn't you? Didn't it plead with you not to run away? It told you to stay and allow yourself to be arrested so you would be innocently condemned to death."

"You're right, I heard that voice, and now I'm waiting for it to speak to me again," replied Jesus.

"Why do you need to hear another voice? As I've said before, death is death. Does it make any difference if you die tonight by stepping off this parapet or if you wait who knows how long for the new governor to put you to death on a cross?"

Jesus pleaded, "O God, speak to me, so I'll know you have not abandoned me."

"Don't do anything rash, Jesus," said a new voice from within his chest. "Everyone must die, so what is important is *how* you die. Think beyond the present to the future, when some day far from now disciples will reverence your heroic death on a cross. As insane as it sounds tonight, for your disciples in the future, the hideous Roman cross will be sign of life and hope."

"He's right, Jesus, that really is insane," argued the other voice from the very top of his head. "The Roman cross is now, and forever will be, the most gruesome, hideous sign in the world. Only wildly demented or masochistic disciples would ever use the cross as their symbol!"

"Don't listen to that voice, Jesus," said the new voice, which this time came from within his heart. "It would not be madness for you to convert the cross from a shameful sign of defeat into a sign of life and promise. Such a transformation is consistent with your life, in which you converted what was shameful into what was good. Didn't you transform the repulsive leper into a lovable neighbor, and the sinner into a saint? Be patient just a little longer until Marcellus can crucify you, for then you can perform the final and greatest conversion of your life…the conversion of the cross!"

Jesus looked down below at the billowing clouds of white sprays as the surf smashed against the great gray boulders and thought, *If I fell, or jumped, from here…would anyone catch me?*

So unsettling was that question that he scrambled down from the parapet with his heart pounding and hurried from the terrace with his robe flapping in the wind. He continued down the hallway past the pool until he reached the doorway, where as fast as his aching feet would carry him, he descended in the darkness down the steps to the dungeon.

"Jesus, stop! Don't be stupid!" pleaded the soft voice that was pursuing him. "Don't go back to your cell. Are you absolutely certain that your loving God doesn't want you to escape the agony of the slow death of aging that you're enduring?"

Halfway down, Jesus stopped to catch his breath as he wrestled with the question of whether God did indeed desire that he escape. Then he inhaled deeply and again began his downward journey to his cell.

"Stop, Jesus!" said the voice, now breathing down his neck. "You know that different parts of your body are slowly dying, one by one: your bowels either don't work or work too much, your joints ache and throb day and night, your hearing is failing, and your memory is fading. Turn around, go back up the steps to the terrace, and go home to God tonight, just as the prodigal son did in your parable."

Now only a few steps from the bottom of the stairs, Jesus paused and inwardly struggled to decide whether to go back up to the terrace. The voice continued, "There's nothing down there for you but to slowly waste away in your cell. Why die an inconsequential death of old age? Don't throw away this chance to die a warrior's death, as did King Saul, which will make you a living legend."

Taking a deep breath, Jesus determinedly descended the last few steps, and reaching the bottom exhausted, entered his cell and slammed the heavy door shut.

SCENE III

THE PALACE TERRACE

December, 36 C.E.

"Sir, word just arrived from one of our spies in Jerusalem," said Petronius, as he rushed onto the terrace where Pilate was dictating to Aristocles. "He reports that the Legate Vitellius has removed Joseph Caiaphas as high priest!"

"Really?" Pilate said. "Vitellius didn't say anything about removing Caiaphas in his letter."

"Sir, why has the Legate deposed the High Priest?" Petronius asked.

"Vitellius doesn't need a plausible reason; he could just be wiping the slate clean here in Judea. But by doing so he's also giving a fat plum to his protégé Marcellus, who as procurator has the power of selecting the next high priest. Petronius, be sure that our, uh... *resource* in Jerusalem is rewarded for sending us this fascinating piece of information."

"I already have, Sir, as I anticipated that would be your desire."

"Excellent," Pilate replied. "Your delivery of this news of old Joseph Caiaphas comes at a most auspicious time. I've just finished dictating a letter to Aristocles detailing your excellent service to me as my adviser, and I included a recommendation that you receive a military promotion, or, if you so choose," he added, grinning, "a comfortable retirement from the army."

"I'm overwhelmed, Sir," Petronius said, humbly. "Thank you for your generosity. I regret that I lack the power to ensure a comfortable retirement for you!"

Shrugging his shoulders, Pilate replied, "My friend, my future is in the hands of the Emperor, or in the hands of the gods; and of the two, I prefer that my fate be in the hands of the gods!"

Pilate then nodded to Aristocles, dismissing him to go and make copies of the daily report. Then he walked over to the northern parapet where he stood looking out at the harbor, absorbed in thought. After some time, he turned around.

"Petronius, I've been contemplating my options since the arrival of the Legate's letter." Pilate began counting on his fingers. "First, being recalled under the sinister cloud of misconduct to Rome, I have almost no hope of ever being reinstated here as governor of Judea. Second, I might have to endure being caged up in a cramped underground prison cell for years. Third, if Tiberius banishes me to some grimy Roman outpost on the edge of civilization, I'll die from boredom, and so will poor Claudia. And fourth, my political life having been destroyed and disgraced now that I have been declared *friget*, the most attractive and dignified option is the fifth: a noble death."

Petronius commented, "Sir, I recall Plato once said, 'Man is a prisoner who has no right to open the door of his prison and run away...a man should wait, and not take his own life until god summons him.'"

Pilate replied, "Ah, but Plato was a Greek, and we are Romans! We have a different judgment of opening and walking through that forbidden door, seeing it as a noble, even heroic deed! Over a hundred years ago in an Italian civil war, my paternal ancestor, Marius Pontius, took his own life when he and his dearest friend Marius were captured. Facing a shameful death, the two of them decided to seal their friendship in a death pact. My great ancestor Marius drew his sword and drove it through the chest of his beloved friend, and then he fell on his own sword. Blood and love forever mingled as one: wasn't that a noble and a beautiful death?"

Petronius remained silent, finding it almost unbearable to listen to his close friend Pilate talk about his death, and especially about taking his own life. Pilate seated himself on one of the couches and invited Petronius to be seated as well, as he continued. "More than once as a child I heard that story of their mutual suicide, and each time my father retold the story, it never failed to thrill me. Petronius, I'm sure you find it uncomfortable for me to speak so easily about taking my own life, but remember, I'm a career administrator in the Empire. As such, my fate has always hung by the thinnest of threads on an Emperor notorious for his whims and impulses. So I always kept here in my heart," tapping on his chest, "the realistic option of that honorable exit of my ancestors if I ever was disgraced by falling out of out favor with Tiberius Caesar. Now, Petronius, that option is no longer hypothetical—it's very real, and as to your quote from Plato, my response is that those Greeks are a contradictory bunch."

Petronius said, "You're referring to Socrates' suicide?"

"I am," Pilate replied. "I believe Plato's teacher Socrates did the noble thing by drinking poison. And since we're quoting the ancients, I recall a line that Lucius taught me from Euripides' play *Temenidae*. 'When good men die, their goodness does not perish, but lives though them after they are gone. As for the bad, all that was theirs dies and is buried with them.'"

Pilate sat slowly nodding his head, thinking about what Euripides had said, and Petronius reflected on his own bad deeds, hoping they would be buried with him.

Pilate broke the silence. "As you well know, Petronius, in my life, especially as governor, I've made mistakes, and some rather bad ones. I hope that Euripides was right and they will be buried away inside my stone sarcophagus." Then pausing, he smiled. "As you know, the reason they call a stone tomb a sarcophagus is that it means, 'flesh-eating stone.' If they bury me in a sarcophagus, I hope besides being a flesh-eating stone it is also a bad mistakes–eating stone!" As Petronius smiled in return, Pilate observed, "With all this musing on death, I'm beginning to wonder if I'm becoming a philosopher, and...." Stopping mid sentence, he said, "Petronius, please go get Jesus and bring him here; I'd like him to join us in our conversation about death."

SCENE IV

THE SAME

A Short Time Later

As Jesus and Petronius entered the terrace, Pilate smiled and said, "Jesus, welcome to our gloomy discussion on your favorite subject—death! While speaking with Petronius on the subject, I was inspired to invite you to join us. Please come and be seated next to me."

At that moment, Aristocles and Marcus returned to the terrace. "Aristocles, there is no need for you to record this conversation, but I want you to stay in case I need you later. Now, Jesus, would you share your thoughts on death with us, and more importantly, what happens after one dies?"

"You surprise me, Pilate—I mean, that you are curious about my thoughts on death, as they are likely to be tainted by my Jewish beliefs. But first, I ask you to forgive me for my failure to be concerned about you and your needs when you learned you were being recalled to Rome. I regret that at that moment I was a prisoner of my own needs, so please grant me forgiveness...."

"None is needed, Jesus," replied Pilate. "Now, don't hesitate to share your thoughts with your Roman...ex-governor. I'm a believer that wisdom isn't the sole possession of the Greeks," he said, smiling at Aristocles.

Jesus replied, "Pilate, I question how much wisdom is contained in my thoughts about death, which have been changing in the past two years as I've brooded over my own death in solitude. With the prospect of dying, I've been meditating daily on the psalm verse, 'What mortal can live and not see death? Who can escape Sheol?' As I reflected on those words, I asked myself, since death is inescapable, do the dead have any influence on the living?"

"That's an interesting question," Pilate replied, "and I may have an answer, which I just quoted to Petronius from the playwright Euripides. 'When good men die their goodness does not perish, but lives through them after they are gone.' If Euripides is correct, then after we die the good we do influences the living, which only makes me wish that I had done more good by making better decisions in life."

Jesus said, "It isn't easy to decide if a decision is the right one, because it's only in the future that we find out whether our decision was right or wrong. So we just have to trust that whatever decision we make is the right one, which is what I did a couple of nights ago! I discovered that my cell door had been left unlocked, and I had to decide whether escaping was the right thing for me to do. Obviously, I decided the right thing was not to escape!"

Pilate's eyes reflected shock, and he shot an accusatory glance at an embarrassed Petronius.

"Your face, Pilate, tells me that my unlocked door wasn't a gift from you."

Pilate responded, "Most certainly not! You're not my personal prisoner; you're a prisoner of Rome! As if I weren't already in enough trouble, your escape would have guaranteed my death sentence even before I departed to Rome. You're no ordinary prisoner, Jesus— you're accused of challenging the Emperor by claiming to be a king, and so your escape would have been an Imperial crime. Thank the gods you made the right decision! I haven't yet composed my letter to Marcellus about the charges made against you and your...uh...unusually long imprisonment as you have awaited the completion of your trial. It would have been most awkward and embarrassing to try to explain in that letter how I, Pontius Pilate, had allowed such a notorious prisoner as you to escape."

Petronius interjected, "Sir, I promise you that this breakdown in military discipline will never happen again."

"I'm glad to hear that, Petronius," said Pilate. "Since we're talking about escaping, why don't you repeat to Jesus that quote from Plato that you recited to me?"

Petronius said, "It does seem fitting, Jesus, for Plato says, 'Man is a prisoner who has no right to open the door of his prison and run away. A man should wait, and not take his own life until god summons him.'"

"While I can see the truth in what Plato said," replied Jesus. "I confess it wasn't easy for me not to try to escape from being imprisoned, caged like an animal."

"That's enough discussion of Plato," Pilate interrupted. "Since you're here with us, let's return to our discussion about death. All young people, like our youthful Aristocles here, never think about dying, even if they attend funerals and see dead people. Intellectually, of course, they know that someday they will die...but that day is way, way, out there," he said, pointing toward the western horizon. "For me, that ominous day is now staring me in the face, and I've begun seriously thinking about death. Now, Jesus, I've set the table for our discussion. To begin with, I'd like to return to the issue you raised about the dead influencing the living. Romans, or rather some of them, believe that the dead continue to influence the fortunes of the living and so bring offerings and gifts to the burial places of their dead, and even eat lavish memorial meals at their tombs."

Jesus asked, "Your custom of giving gifts to the dead raises a question; where do Romans think the dead go after they depart from this world?"

"A common belief is that if the dead person has offended the gods, he will be denied entrance to the underworld and be cursed to wander forever across the earth. Those whom the gods favor go down to the underworld, which we call Hades after the Greek god of death, even though we Romans call our god of death Pluto. Hades is a gloomy, unpleasant place, much like your Jewish Sheol."

"Sir, with your permission," interjected Aristocles.

Pilate begrudgingly nodded his consent to speak.

"Socrates taught that instead of being a dark, gloomy, forbidding place, Hades is an enjoyable place, and that is why those who die never return to this earth!"

Pilate said, "Well, Jesus, it seems my secretary has just gifted you with a bit of Greek wisdom, or perhaps Grecian fantasy. Aristocles, you've piqued my curiosity; what possibly could make the netherworld of Hades more appealing than the joys of this world?"

"Excellency, in his *Cratylus*, Socrates says the source of his belief is that of all the gods and goddesses, Hades has the finest intelligence.

Thus to dwell in his witty presence would provide the endless enjoyment of discussing intellectual ideas and so fulfill the greatest of all human desires, to philosophize endlessly."

Pilate responded, "Thank you, Aristocles, for that little gem of Greek insight. However, if eternity in the underworld means engaging in endless philosophical discussions, I would prefer to be cursed by the gods and endlessly wander the earth! But enough of what I think. Petronius, you've been quiet. Tell us, what you think about life after death?"

"I would first like to ask a question of Jesus, Sir. Knowing as I do some of the beliefs of the Jewish people, I'm aware that the Sadducees and the priestly temple scholar scribes, along with the Samaritans, believe that when you die your life simply ends, and that there is nothing after death. The Pharisees, on the other hand, believe that after death there is some kind of resurrection. I'm sure, Jesus, that you're not a Pharisee, because they are among your most outspoken opponents. So why do you yourself believe there is life after death?"

"Good question, Petronius," Pilate said, leaning forward eagerly.

"You're correct," Jesus replied, "I'm not a Pharisee, and yet I too believe in a resurrection after death. My belief in a life after death grew slowly as I united the words of Solomon, 'God did not make death and takes no joy in the destruction of the living,' with those of the psalmist, 'You have snatched me from death, that I may walk before God in the light of the living.' It is my belief that these two verses from our sacred writings were inspired by God, and so they became the stones upon which I built my belief that there is life after death."

"You always quote the words of others," Pilate said, with exasperation. "But what do you yourself believe, and more importantly, why?"

"The source of my belief that there is life after death is that love is stronger than death! The more you love someone, the more you desire never ever to be separated from her or him, even by death. This most human desire never to be separated from those we love must come from God, who is Love, and who created us in the image of love." Pausing, Jesus deeply inhaled. "While there are many things I

224

doubt, I have no doubt that God is love. And since the All Holy One is everlasting, it follows that we who were created to live in love and with love will live on after we die."

Without asking permission to speak, Aristocles broke in, saying, "In his play *Phixus*, Euripides says, 'Who knows, but life be that which men call death, and death what men call life?'"

Pilate frowned, disturbed that Aristocles would take the liberty to speak in their midst as if he were an equal, but ignoring his irritation, he asked, "Jesus, does your belief about life after death exclude me, your Roman ex-governor, since I'm an unbeliever? Your ideas, while appealing, are all based on a belief in that god of yours. I confess there are times when I would like to believe, but I'm simply unable to believe in the gods, and that includes yours!"

"Ah, but God believes in you!" responded Jesus.

Pilate's face revealed that he was stunned by this statement.

Jesus went on, "I've seen how much you love Lady Claudia, and I'm sure you greatly love your two children as well. I've also witnessed how deeply you loved your old teacher Lucius, and I've seen your great fondness for Marcus, Quintus, and even for your advisor Petronius."

Pilate was visibly uncomfortable. "Get to the point, Jesus; where are you going with all this talk about love?"

"I'm not going to ask you, Pilate, if you believe in God. Instead, I simply ask you: Do you believe you love Lady Claudia?"

Pilate said, somewhat irritably, "Of course I believe I love Claudia, and I'm fond of Petronius as a friend and a comrade as well, although I don't know if I could say...."

"Believing doesn't happen up here," said Jesus, leaning over and tapping his finger on Pilate's head, "it begins down here in your heart," now tapping on Pilate's chest. Pilate drew back slightly, embarrassed by the intimacy of Jesus' act of touching him. "As I've said, God is love, and for us humans the closest we can come to experiencing God here on this earth is in loving others. So to believe in your affectionate love of Claudia or of anyone is also to believe in God! It is impossible to separate them."

Pilate said briskly, "As usual, Jesus, your words are thought provoking, and while I would enjoy exploring them further, look up at the sun! This day is quickly ending, and the sun will soon be setting. Claudia and I are expecting guests to join us for dinner tonight, so we must conclude our discussion. Even if I have been stripped of my official powers as Governor," he continued, after pausing briefly, "I officially declare that this conversation is not ended; only postponed until another day."

Standing up, Pilate said, "Petronius, kindly escort Jesus to his quarters, and please make sure that his cell door is securely locked, would you? Marcus and Aristocles, you are dismissed, and to all of you, I wish a pleasant evening."

As the others departed, Pilate strolled over to the western parapet with his hands linked behind his back. Although he was looking out over the sea, his gaze was actually inward. *Jesus has pierced my Achilles' heel — my hidden yearning to believe in something divine. I've always resisted that longing, since I've always thought that only ignorant peasants and slaves believe in the gods. Yet the god that Jesus loves and believes in isn't like all those other gods and goddesses. He trapped me with his question of whether I love Claudia; even though I stumbled in trying to express it, how could I ever doubt it? Now that I've been recalled to appear before Tiberius, my love for her, and for life itself, has increased immensely. The thought of being separated from her by prison or death is unbearable. Jesus says my love for her is God....* Shocked, Pilate stopped, realizing he had just unconsciously pronounced that divine name with the same inflection used by Jesus!

SCENE V

IN THE HALLWAY
BESIDE THE POOL

A Few Minutes Later

Having dismissed the guards, Petronius himself was escorting Jesus down the hallway to his cell. He confided, "Jesus, I've slowly come to accept that I'm not going to find the god I'm seeking in the official state religion or in any of the mystery cults. I've tried a lot of them, such as the religions of Cybele, Isis, and Bacchus, yet none of them satisfied me. Lately, I've become enthralled with your God, whom you say is a God of love and peace, and most important, one who promises life after death. Is there some way that I, an uncircumcised pagan gentile, can become acceptable to your God?"

"Petronius," Jesus said, placing his right hand on the centurion's shoulder, "you're already acceptable just as you are! Neither circumcision nor baptism makes anyone acceptable to God, who loves all persons unconditionally and shows no favoritism toward any people or any religion."

Petronius protested, "But there must be some requirements, some rituals, or...."

Jesus replied, "If you desire to be acceptable, simply reverence God, act justly, feed the poor, and care for the needs of the less fortunate."

"What a relief to hear you say that!" Petronius exclaimed. "I'm trying to do those things. Since coming to Judea I've felt drawn to Judaism, except for...."

"The knife!" smiled Jesus.

"Yes; I don't want to be circumcised!"

"There's no need to be; as I said, Petronius, you're acceptable to God just as you are now."

"You've given me great hope, Jesus, yet as we speak I realize that I desire more than just being acceptable. I want the intimacy with God that you seem to have. How do I achieve that?"

Jesus replied, "It's a gift. But if you pray with great devotion, and passionately long for such deep intimacy, and are patient, I assure you the Spirit will lead you step by step into the close, loving friendship you desire. Meanwhile, as that union is growing, deal fairly with the soldiers under your command. Be kind, even respectful, to lowly peasants and slaves, defend the weak, and be generous to those in need. Most importantly, strive with all your heart, mind, and strength to love God and to love others as you love yourself."

Petronius said, "And there are no secret initiations? It seems too simple, just loving God and others. I listened intently to your conversation with Pilate about love. As a military man on the move, I've been denied the luxury of a home, wife, and children and the pleasures of loving and being loved. I'm now seriously considering accepting Pilate's farewell gift of retirement from the army, with the hope that the luxury of being loved can become a reality in my life."

"That is the divine path for each of us," Jesus responded, "for it is in our loving of others that we love and experience God, as I told Pilate."

They had been standing at the doorway to the steep stairs that led down to the dungeon. Petronius finally said, "Jesus, I wish we could go on talking like this, but you must go down to your cell, and I to my work. Here, take my arm—these steps are steep."

SCENE VI

IN JESUS' PRISON CELL

A Few Moments Later

After hearing the clank of the key turning in the lock as Petronius departed, Jesus walked over to the window that framed the view of a turquoise sky streaked with yellow rays from the sun now just below the horizon.

"Beloved Friend," he said, lifting his arms in prayer, "unlike the sun whose fire is now out, you blaze with an eternal fire. As I grow older, unlike this day when the sun has faded away, the fire of my love for you grows more intense. Beloved; oh, how I long to kiss you...."

He stopped, embarrassed by such an intimate confession, left the window, and walked over to lay on his mat. Looking up at his cell's carved curved stone ceiling, he pondered, *When Governor Marcellus arrives, I wonder if he will crucify me at once right here in the palace courtyard, and if not here, then where?* No answer appeared etched in the ceiling. *I wonder what it feels like to be dead and buried in a tomb?* After a long pause, he thought, *Perhaps no different then I feel being buried under the earth in this dark stone dungeon. Who knows, maybe I'm already dead! This afternoon Aristocles quoted a Greek playwright who asked if what men called death is actually life, and what they call life is really death. I found those words appealing, and they make me wonder: After I'm dead, will I be more alive than I was before I died?*

Each wave seemed to echo over and over, "after I'm dead I'll be more alive," as it came racing to the shore. Because sleep was hiding from him, Jesus listened to that chant of the surf, "more alive...more alive...." Then he asked himself, *After I die, what becomes of that "I" with which I've identified myself all my life?* And then he thought, *You'll soon know, Jesus, for your crucifixion is now near.*

He struggled to stand up, and after getting on his feet, he said aloud, "I feel like I'm ready to die; I've been practicing for some time how to be crucified." Extending his arms outward as far as he could, he said, "Old age, you've shamed me by disrobing me of my youthful flesh, and then scourged me with your razor-sharp ailments. I've borne the burden of a loneliness that's heavier than any wooden cross. And you, old legs and aching joints, you have endured the nails of pain being driven through you, and you, poor head, have felt the anguish of being pierced by the sharp thorns of doubts and uncertainties."

From their extended position he lifted his arms upward in prayer. "O Friend, whom I love, I'm now acquainted with all the implications of what I asked of my disciples when I said, 'Take up your cross and follow me.' Even if they are spared a Roman crucifixion, the time will come when they too shall bear their crosses. When that time comes, O Lord, grant them the strength to bear their cross of aging with all its crippling painful afflictions, as I have tried to bear mine. Send your Spirit to be the companion of those who will taste the dark side of the cross I've borne; the loneliness of being a captive in a place from which they long to escape."

His prayer ended as he entered into the rich silence of lovers who are united without having to speak words. In that silence he heard a voice, which said, "Jesus, why do you speak of your recent sufferings as if they were the same as being crucified? Your destiny was to actually die on a wooden cross, not to suffer some imitation of it. Speak the truth: you secretly never really wanted to die a shameful death on the cross, did you?"

Jesus replied, "Whoever you are, I embraced dying on the cross as fully as I could, since God had chosen it for me. At the same time, in the recesses of my heart, there always lurked a horror of dying on a cross, of which I'm not ashamed; it's only human not to want to suffer. Regardless of my aversion and fears, I am now ready to die however God desires. If Marcellus nails this old body of mine onto a cross, I fully embrace such a death. If he thinks I'm too old to hang on the tree of the cross, I accept that, since I'm confident that my sufferings of aging have been as redemptive as death on a wooden cross. O Beloved Friend, your holy will be done; crucify me whenever and however you please."

SCENE VII

THE PALACE TERRACE

Sunset in Early February, 67 C.E.

"It's just you and me, Jesus," said Pilate, after he dismissed the guards. "Come join me at the parapet so we can watch the sun set over the ocean." As Jesus came and stood by him, Pilate mused, "Way out there, where the sun is just about to disappear into the ocean, is Rome. I find it ironic that while I once sent reports to Rome every day, it is now I, Pontius Pilate, who is being sent there!"

Jesus replied, "It's more sad than ironic, Pilate; my heart aches for you and Lady Claudia."

Pilate looked at Jesus directly and said, "My heart aches too, and that's why I had you come up here, so we could visit in private. I'm sorry to say it will be our last chance to be together. Tomorrow morning Claudia and I, the children, and our personal slaves will depart for Rome."

Jesus drew in his breath and said, "Tomorrow! It seems so soon...." He paused and continued, "I'm sad to see you depart, Pilate. I'll greatly miss our conversations. They've actually been very significant in changing many of my ideas, and even a few beliefs."

"They've had the same effect on me," Pilate said, placing his hand on Jesus' shoulder. "Although some of your ideas threatened my sanity, they certainly altered my thinking on many subjects! But the three months granted me by the Legate are up, and I'm ready to depart. The archives of my years as procurator governor are all in order, I've written my required letter to the Roman Senate, and though I procrastinated as long as I could, I've finally written a report to Marcellus about the imprisonment and unfinished trial of a certain Galilean wandering holy man."

Jesus commented, "I hope you spoke ill of me so he'll waste no time in crucifying me."

Pilate retorted, "I did the very opposite! At any rate, all our possessions are packed and ready to be loaded in the wagons tomorrow when we depart at sunrise, except...," he stopped and inhaled deeply. "While I'm ready, unfortunately, poor Claudia isn't! She's almost in a state of mourning over my fate once I reach Rome. She's heartbroken about having to leave this beautiful marble palace, as are our servants...." He stopped mid sentence. "Did you hear that, Jesus? I referred to them as 'servants,' not slaves! That's just another sign of how you have corrupted me."

Jesus asked, "What do you think will happen when you arrive in Rome?"

Pilate replied, "The *least* likely outcome is that the Emperor will dismiss my case as groundless. To be recalled to Rome means you have fallen from imperial favor, so I most certainly won't be appointed governor of another Roman province. Tiberius could exile me to some distant outpost of the empire, or throw me in prison to await my trial, which might mean being a captive for years. If I even suspect that is to be my fate, like my ancestor Marius Pontius, I shall choose an honorable death."

"Take your own life?" Jesus exclaimed.

Pilate replied, "You respond to the idea with such distaste; what's wrong with such a death? Many great men have chosen it as an honorable way to die: Socrates and Mark Anthony, to name two. Anyway, I'm already a dead man." After a brief pause, Pilate continued, "In fact, Jesus, both of us are dead men!"

"Yes, that's true," Jesus said. "Providence has bonded us together as friends and now is uniting us as blood brothers, only we know not the hour of our deaths."

"You've taught me an important lesson, Jesus—how to die! Since learning I've been recalled to Rome, I've tried to imitate your peaceful acceptance of death. I know that a better word than acceptance is surrender, but as a soldier I never use that word. Yet you peacefully surrendered to my endless delays of your crucifixion, which you so passionately desired. I find your serenity in the face of surrendering quite amazing."

Jesus laughed ruefully. "I deceived you, my friend," he said. "My surrender came at the cost of excruciating pain. I found it agonizing not to be in control of my destiny, for in the past I had always tried to manage events in life to my benefit; thus, bending my will to what God willed was almost unbearable."

Pilate replied thoughtfully, "You're right—I never realized the pain it cost you, and I truly admire you for being able to surrender in the end. Like you, I've always tried to control the events and people in my life—that is, until the Legate's letter arrived! Now I believe I've finally accepted—notice I didn't say *surrendered to*—whatever is to happen.

"Pilate, you're too hard on yourself!" Jesus said, gently patting him on the shoulder. "I've heard you credit your successes to the gods or to good luck, but the gods had nothing to do with them. Your successes were the result of your ability to act on your hunches and to follow those inner voices, even if you didn't know why."

"Like that gut feeling I had in Jerusalem to transfer your trial here to Caesarea?"

Jesus replied, "Yes; and now that you're facing the greatest crisis of your life, it's more important than ever that you follow your hunches and be attentive to what you're thinking."

"To what I'm thinking?" Pilate asked.

"Thoughts lead to actions," Jesus explained. "The kind of thoughts we allow ourselves to think have a profound effect on us. Because my death is now so close, I try to think good thoughts about it, so however I am to die, some good will come from it."

Pilate noted, "Jesus, you just said, 'however'—does that mean you no longer wish to be crucified?"

Jesus replied, "By 'however,' I meant that if Marcellus crucifies me, I've accepted that death wholeheartedly. If for political reasons he decides to keep here as a nameless secret prisoner of Rome to rot to death, I also embrace that more agonizing death."

Pilate responded, "You're no prisoner, Jesus! You're the freest man I've ever known."

"I've always tried to be free, and that's why I desire to die a free man, even if the manner of my death is another's choice. Death is inescapable, so what is truly important and unique is how we die! I realize it's easy for me to say, as I have no family or children, so my heart aches for Claudia, who must be weeping...."

Pilate exclaimed, "I've forbidden her to cry!"

Jesus said, "Why? When those we love are dying or die, tears are as natural as that sunset out there."

Pilate explained, "Romans believe that to cry at someone's death makes the departing soul unhappy to see his or her loved ones so miserable, and thus weeping can cause the spirit not to depart from the body! Weeping over the dead also brings bad luck to the living, or at least that was what we once believed. Today, wealthy persons in Rome are actually staging extravagant funerals in which they hire professional mourners to shriek and wail. They also hire musicians, dancers, and mimes to join with the hired mourners in the funeral procession to escort their dead to the burial or cremation sites outside of the city of Rome. But Jesus, I'm a traditional Roman. I still observe the ancient rule for death: no wailing or weeping!"

"If someone I loved died, it would be impossible for me not to cry," Jesus said, looking into Pilate's eyes. "Tears say what words can't and speak of our love for the one who died."

"When you learn I've died, Jesus, will you cry?" asked Pilate.

Jesus exclaimed, "Yes, if I'm alive! Even now my eyes are almost brimming over simply speaking about it."

"Hold them back, friend!" Pilate said. "While I'm touched that you are so moved, we can't let the dark spirits see you crying over me. Fortunately, I know a way at death to fool the spirits into thinking that no one has died: by dancing joyfully and singing happy songs!"

"Joyful dancing!" exclaimed Jesus. "Your Roman funerals sound more like our Galilean weddings!"

"While I'm not dead yet, Jesus, I likely will be very soon. Since you and I are friends, I'd like to ask a favor of you: Will you help me anticipate my death?"

Jesus asked, "You mean by praying together?"

Pilate replied, "No Jesus, by dancing!"

Pilate wrapped his right arm around Jesus' shoulder as he began humming a lively folk tune, and Jesus promptly put his left arm around Pilate's shoulder. Then Pilate began to gracefully cross his feet left and right in an old Roman shepherd's dance. Jesus said a quick prayer asking God to make him oblivious to the sharp pains in his body as he repeated his dance steps and picked up the melody of the folk song.

Jesus and Pilate, their arms intertwined, were silhouetted against the orange oval of the sun perched on the western horizon dancing to the drumming of the pounding surf. Exhausted, they collapsed onto one of the couches, their arms still intertwined.

"Now...I can go happily...to my death," panted Pilate. "My friend...our joyful dancing fooled the dark spirits...into thinking... no one has died—or will!"

"That...was...marvelous!" replied a winded Jesus, as his old familiar needle-like pains throbbed in his knees and ankles. Then he rested his head on Pilate's shoulder. "Now, friend...I also...can go happily to my cross."

Act V

SCENE I

SUNRISE IN THE COURTYARD
OF THE PALACE AT CAESAREA

A February Morning, 37 C.E.

The rising sun in the east caused the white marble palace to shimmer in yellow brilliance as two guards escorted Jesus out onto the paved courtyard. The enclosed walled courtyard hummed with activity and the sounds of slaves and solders. Slaves busily loaded the last boxes of the family's belongings into three leather-covered carruca wagons. Pilate's personal guard of Roman legionaries stood clustered together as the cavalry escort's horses snorted and pawed the pavement stones. These troops would escort Pilate, his family, and his household on their journey northward to the large Roman garrison at the coastal Phoenician city of Tyre.

In front of the three wagons were two curtained Roman litters now resting on the pavement; one for Claudia and the other for their two children. Beside the litters stood their slave bearers, while another slave at the front of the small convoy stood holding the reins of Pilate's saddled horse. Attired in his full military uniform, helmet, and cloak, Pilate stood with Claudia beside her litter. She was wearing a tunic and stola, over which she wore a long brown *palla*, a traveling cloak she had pulled up on top of her head as a hood.

Glancing over Pilate's shoulder, Claudia saw Jesus come out of the palace, and at once she went to greet him. As she approached, even with her palla draped veil-like over her forehead, he could see that her eyes were red from crying.

"Jesus of Galilee," said Claudia, forcing a smile, "I'm so pleased they allowed you to come out to the courtyard so I could personally bid you farewell. It was truly a gift from the gods to be able to meet you and listen to your teachings. I'll always treasure our brief time together that wonderful night of our dinner. Your words continue to echo in my life; I'll always remember you."

"I also shall remember you, Lady Claudia," Jesus said, with a slight bow. "I have prayed for you and Pilate as you face the road ahead. Try to be brave, for Pilate needs you now more than ever before."

Smiling tremulously, Claudia said, "I'm trying. Thank you for speaking to your god on our behalf. I feel confident that your god hears your prayers."

"Take heart, Lady Claudia; your husband isn't easily defeated. Continue to hope for the best, and for his sake try to hold back your tears, because he fears they bring bad luck."

Claudia responded, "I know he does, and I'm trying." She continued, "I believe, Jesus, that you are a holy man and that your prayers are powerful, so please continue to pray to your god for us. I live in fear of what lies ahead in Rome for Pilate, so pray especially for him."

"I have," Jesus replied, "and I'll continue to do so. Would it be all right if I called the blessings of God down upon you? Such a blessing is an old Jewish custom."

Nodding, she slightly lowered her head, and he extended his hands over her. "Blessed are you, Lord God, creator of heaven and earth, whose love is boundless. Bless Claudia and Pilate and their children, and shield them from every evil. To escort them on their fateful journey to Rome, send your holy angels to guard them and keep them safe. O God of never-ending love, grant to Claudia and Pilate your gift of a long and happy life together. Amen."

Claudia embraced Jesus and said, "Thank you—that was a beautiful blessing, and I'm confident your god heard you. I'm so grateful Pilate was assigned here to Judea, because if he hadn't been, I'd never have met you. I'm also grateful to you for befriending my Pilate as you did." Then she wiped away her tears with the sleeve of her tunic, smiled, and said, "Farewell, Jesus!"

She turned and began walking back to her litter, and as she did so, she moved the top of her traveling cloak lower to conceal her tear-stained cheeks. Halfway to her litter she passed Pilate and nodded to him as he walked over to Jesus.

As the two men stood facing one another, they shared an awkward moment, knowing there was nothing more to say to one another that hadn't already been said. Pilate broke the uncomfortable silence, "Farewell, Jesus. I hope Marcellus treats you justly. I'll leave what 'justly' means to your God, whom you say is compassionate. As you know, I'm not good with words unless I'm giving orders, and I find it difficult to speak of my feelings. So I trust our dance together at sunset yesterday will speak of my great, uh...fondness for you."

Jesus replied, "It shouts it loudly, my friend! And I hope our dancing also tells you, Pilate, how I feel. My heart is overflowing with sorrow at what awaits you in Rome, and the sight of you about to depart...."

Pilate interrupted him, saying firmly, "No tears, Jesus! I can see them welling up in your eyes. Smother them!" Then gripping Jesus' shoulder, he said, "As Tiberius holds my fate, so Marcellus holds yours. If I were a praying man, I'd pray to that God of yours for a miracle to save you from the cross, so you could die gracefully of old age on a bed of straw."

"A bed of straw; that isn't exactly what I've envisioned!" Jesus replied. Placing his hand on Pilate's shoulder, he continued, "I've prayed to God to snatch you out of the Emperor's hands, so you and Lady Claudia can have a long and happy life together."

Each tightly squeezed the other's shoulder and then, unexpectedly, Pilate warmly embraced Jesus with both arms, saying, "Farewell, friend." Then he quickly turned and briskly walked back toward his horse. After he had taken only a few steps, Jesus called out, "Pilate, don't forget, God Almighty is far more powerful than Tiberius Caesar!" Without turning around, Pilate continued walking, humorously shaking his head. As Jesus watched him walk to his horse, he saw Marcus and Quintus waving farewell to him as they stood next to one of the wagons, as he waved back. Petronius, after helping Claudia into her litter, walked to where Pilate stood beside his horse and saluted him.

Pilate said, "Petronius, my old and trusted friend, I shall miss you greatly. You and I had some great adventures together, and regardless of the stupidity of some of the things I did, you always loyally supported me. Take that retirement I arranged for you; you deserve it."

Petronius responded, "Sir, I intend to do just that, and I hope you know how much I appreciate...."

Pilate cut him off. "It's just a small token of gratitude and my...," leaving his sentence unfinished, he warmly embraced Petronius and said, "Farewell, comrade."

Then Pilate turned and quickly mounted his horse. As he did so, the cavalry troopers mounted their horses as well, and the soldiers quickly formed in line as the slave bearers picked up the handles of their litters. Pilate turned around and looked at the palace. He let his eyes slowly move across its beautiful, white marble, now glistening in the bright early morning sunlight. Then he lowered his gaze to Jesus; for a brief moment their eyes remained fixed on one another. Finally, turning around in his saddle, Pilate spurred his horse as he loudly shouted, "Forward!" Slowly the small caravan began moving forward through the courtyard gateway. Petronius walked over to stand beside Jesus.

"My heart goes with Pilate," said Petronius sadly, as he and Jesus watched the cavalry troops follow Pilate out through the gateway. Behind them came the two swaying curtained litters, escorted on either side by double lines of marching soldiers. Finally, one after another, the lumbering horse-drawn wagons disappeared through the gateway.

Jesus said, "I don't understand why Pilate is taking the long coastal road overland north to Tyre, when it would have been easier to just sail to Rome from the harbor here."

Petronius replied, "He's not only going to Tyre; he's going overland from there on to Antioch and then westward to Pamphylia, after that on to Ephesus and beyond! The answer to your question, Jesus, is that Pilate is taking the overland route because it is the longest, slowest possible way to get to Rome!"

"Of course, how stupid of me," Jesus smiled. "After all, he's in no hurry."

"I'd feel more comfortable if I were riding along with Pilate," Petronius said. "To my regret, he ordered me to remain here as his official delegate until the new governor arrives from Jerusalem, which shouldn't take long now. From what we hear, Marcellus is eager to take up residence in this magnificent palace by the sea instead of in Jerusalem."

"And after Marcellus arrives here, Petronius, what will you do?"

Petronius replied, "I'm off to paradise! That is, I will be as soon as I turn over this imperial palace, the harbor, and the city of Caesarea to Governor Marcellus. When that's done I can enjoy the gift of retirement from the army that Pilate arranged for me. I'll be free to go anywhere I wish in the Empire."

"It's no surprise you referred to it as paradise. I'm happy that your future seems so filled with promise. I worry, however, about Claudia if Pilate is imprisoned or...."

"Takes his own life?" Petronius finished Jesus' thought. "I hope he doesn't, but whatever happens, Pilate has secured the future of Claudia and his children."

"How was he able to do that?" Jesus asked.

"Pilate told me he followed the wise advice of his predecessor, Gratus, regarding various clever ways to profit from being governor, such as the annual awarding of the office of high priest to the highest bidder. In such ways he was able to amass a sizeable personal treasury during his years as governor; that's going to Rome with Claudia! Pilate also has taken care to provide for his personal slaves Marcus and Quintus, promising them their freedom after Claudia is finally settled. Claudia carries with her Pilate's handwritten documents which she will present to a Roman magistrate; these documents will legally free them and grant them full Roman citizenship. As you can guess, both Marcus and Quintus are ecstatic about their futures, and Pilate gifted young Aristocles with the enviable position of being the tutor of Gaius, Pilate's son. Like an admirable commanding officer, Pilate meticulously arranged everything in advance so his family and those who faithfully served him will have a good future."

Jesus replied, "I'm glad to hear that. I've grown fond of Claudia, Marcus, and Quintus since being imprisoned here."

"Speaking of which, Jesus, I can't risk you becoming too captivated by all this fresh air out here." Lightly taking his arm, Petronius continued, "As provisional commander of Caesarea, it's my duty to ensure that when Governor Marcellus arrives, he'll find you securely imprisoned here. So as Pilate would say, 'It's time for you to return to your quarters.'"

"I'm glad you told me about how Pilate has seen to the needs of others," Jesus said to Petronius as they walked inside the palace. "He was a good man!"

As they walked down the hallway by the pool, Petronius said, "The longer he was around you, Jesus, the kinder and more considerate he became. And Pilate didn't forget you: until Governor Marcellus arrives, he gave orders that you are to continue to receive your basket of bread and wine every other day."

Jesus replied, "With all he's had to deal with, that was thoughtful of him. You spoke of the arrival of the new Governor; when do you expect Marcellus to arrive?"

"Soon," said Petronius, "yet with Passover being next week, he will have to remain in Jerusalem until that celebration is over. After that it could be any day. Here, let me help you down these uneven steps."

"Petronius, what have you heard about Marcellus?" asked Jesus as they slowly descended the steps. "I mean, have you heard anything about him that might indicate how he'll judge my case?"

"I know nothing about the man other than his name. I do know that no one becomes even the temporary procurator of Judea without being a politician. That being a given, and considering the gravity of your alleged crime of claiming to be a king, Marcellus isn't going to risk his political future by denying or delaying your crucifixion."

They had now reached the bottom of the steps and stood in front of Jesus' cell door. Jesus asked, "What if I'm too old to be nailed to a cross?"

"If you were a hundred years old it wouldn't make any difference," Petronius said as he unlocked the cell door. "An old and decrepit challenger to Caesar's throne is just as dangerous to Tiberius as a young, robust one."

"You've told me what I need to hear, and I'll prepare myself. I appreciate your honesty. God be with you, Petronius," Jesus said, as he stepped inside his cell.

"And God be with you, Jesus," said Petronius. Then he slowly closed and locked the door.

SCENE II

JESUS' PRISON CELL

March, 37 C.E.

"O moon, kindly look down upon Claudia," Jesus prayed, as he stood at his window. "She'll be inconsolable when the Emperor rejects Pilate's explanation of the battle in Samaria and condemns him to languish in prison for years on end," he said, forlornly shaking his head, "or if he ends his life with his own sword! I feel so sorry for Pilate; he dedicated his entire life to serving the Roman Empire, and now it seems likely it will turn against him."

Although moonlight serenely flooded his cell, Jesus felt no tranquility, for he wasn't in his cell! In his thoughts he was far from Caesarea, traveling beside Pilate along some dusty road on his ill-fated journey to Rome. *Even if he and I had conflicting ideas and beliefs,* Jesus thought, *these past months I grew to...to love him. I'm indebted to him for challenging me to rethink many ideas I was firmly convinced were true, including my cherished destiny to die a sacrificial death of redemption on the cross. I'm convinced that although he was unaware of it, Pilate was an instrument of God with his mockery and questioning of my beliefs. Although he created a chaos of disturbing doubts and disbeliefs within me, the Spirit amazingly consecrated that chaos into a more loving, intimate union with God.* Then his thoughts bloomed into a prayer:

> "Beloved Friend, hear this old man's prayer for your son, Pilate. Because he so longs to believe, give him what only you can give; the gift of faith to believe in you. O Holy Worker of wonders, like the parting of the Red Sea, spare Pilate from the Emperor's wrath, and grant him and Claudia a long and happy life together....
>
> "I almost forgot! Shower upon Petronius whatever graces he needs as he searches for you. He hungers for you, so feed his spiritual hunger and give him the gift of belief in

life after death…and find him a good and loving wife. Amen."

Jesus slowly made his way back to his mat, lay down, and closed his eyes. Lingering on the narrow ledge of sleep, ready to drop over its edge, he listened to the pounding surf. As he listened, a scrap of the words of the prophet Isaiah floated before him: "The Lord was pleased to crush him in infirmity." That scrap of prophecy circled around and around in his mind like a leaf in an eddy until he said, "Old Isaiah, your visionary eyesight clearly foresaw my fate. I have indeed been crushed with the infirmities of crippling old age and painful, aching joints. Every day my flesh feels like it is being squeezed under the heavy grinding stone of God's olive press, leaving my skin dry and wrinkled. As I feel that giant stone pulverizing me, seal my lips shut so I'll not grumble."

Just as the soothing night angel of sleep was gently closing his eyes, another scrap of Isaiah's words floated before him: "Because of his affliction, he shall see the light in the fullness of days." Inspired by those words, Jesus whispered, "O God, who created the angels of heaven and the worms of the grave, I implore you, as I close my eyes in sleep, that in the completion of my days I may see the light…the fullness of Light shining in the darkness of my death."

SCENE III

THE SAME

One Week Later

"Jesus, we've just received the news that Governor Marcellus is to arrive here tomorrow or, at the latest, the day after tomorrow," announced Petronius, as he entered Jesus' cell just after sunset. "All the palace slaves are busily preparing for his arrival and that of his guests."

"Thank you for coming all the way down here to tell me that, Petronius. I'm sure that the new governor's guests aren't staying down here, but earlier today I heard several loud voices in the hallway outside my cell."

"What you heard were five Judean rebel bandits who arrived earlier today from Jerusalem, escorted by their guards," Petronius explained. "After he condemned them to be crucified, Governor Marcellus sent them down here to Caesarea under heavy guard. I ordered the guards to put them at the far eastern end of the dungeon so they wouldn't disturb you."

Jesus asked, "If Marcellus condemned them in Jerusalem, why is he crucifying them here in Caesarea?"

"It seems their crucifixions are to be part of his *Magnus Spectaculum,* a grand official reception for him as the new Governor. We only learned about it a couple of days ago when Governor Marcellus sent detailed instructions for his ceremonial reception as the Governor-Procurator of Judea. He wants it to be celebrated inside Herod's magnificent open-air coliseum to entertain and impress the populace of Caesarea. He has ordered a great spectacle that will include chariot races, fights to the death by gladiators, and gory battles between wild animals. Along with these events, Marcellus plans to crucify the five rebel bandits, because gruesome crucifixions are always a great crowd pleaser. And to add luster to the spectacle, we heard today that the Syrian Legate Vitellius is to attend."

"It sounds like it will be quite a Roman spectacle...but I suspect, Petronius, that you're leaving something out."

Petronius said reluctantly, "Well, it's only a suspicion—nothing official—but yes, I suspect...."

Jesus finished his sentence: "...that I'm going to be part of this spectacle! Isn't that right, Petronius?"

"Yes, Jesus, I regret to say that I think you will be. My instincts tell me that as soon as Marcellus arrives, he will condemn you to death, without so much as a trial! Then, unnoticed, he will easily slip you in among the five rebels to be crucified as part of his *Spectaculum.* By making you the anonymous sixth rebel, he can carry out your mandatory death sentence, while at the same time never having to publicly acknowledge that you even exist."

"I don't care if my death is unknown. God will know."

"That's true, and a comforting way to look at it," said Petronius. "I'm sorry, but I have to leave now to administer many details for Marcellus' celebration. I'll try to see you again if I can, but for now, farewell, Jesus."

After Petronius left, Jesus stood at his window. "All that's now left of you, Passover moon, is a silver crescent," he said. "I've just learned that what I've longed and prayed for during the past two years is almost here. Each night, Exodus moon, I've watched you shrink from full to half, then to quarter, and now to just a skinny curved sliver. I wonder if there will be anything left of you when the ancient prophecies are fulfilled."

Jesus tried to imagine what his rapidly approaching crucifixion would be like in the giant Roman coliseum in front of a screaming crowd of thousands. Laying his hands with their palms up on the window ledge, he pictured them pierced by large black nails. Raising his eyes up from his hands, he spoke to the turbulent dark waters, "O ancient sea, you whose waters are fed by the tears of widows and abandoned children, in your dark chaotic depths lurks the ancient Leviathan, the great seven-headed monster of chaos. Tonight, as my impending crucifixion casts its dark shadow over me, I feel like I'm being sucked into your chaotic depths."

SCENE IV

THE SAME

Two Days Later

"His Excellency Governor Marcellus has arrived!" a slave announced with excitement, as he entered Jesus' cell with a basket of food and wine. "The palace is buzzing like a disturbed beehive as everyone prepares for the Syrian Legate's arrival tomorrow and the lavish banquets to accompany the Governor's installation ceremonies. Here's your food; I've got to hurry back to work."

After the slave departed, Jesus ate some bread as he nibbled on this news, thinking, *At the most, Jesus, you have only a day left in your life now, so enjoy each bite of your bread.* Then he heard a key in the lock of his cell door.

"Jesus, Governor Marcellus has arrived," said Petronius, as he hurried into the cell.

Jesus replied, "Yes, I just heard the news from the slave who brought my food. He also said that the palace is in a whirlwind."

"I have more news!" Petronius said. "Marcellus informed me that he condemned six more rebels to be crucified, who are to arrive here later today. It's a good thing King Herod built a large dungeon."

"Petronius, why do you think Marcellus is condemning so many to be crucified at one time?" Jesus asked.

"There are the two possibilities we discussed earlier," Petronius speculated. "He's sending a message to the Jews that their new Governor will rule them with an iron hand and won't tolerate the slightest civil disorder—or he's trying to impress the crowds by adding more bloody crucifixions to his *Spectaculum.*"

"Six more," said Jesus, "along with the other five, plus me, makes twelve. Ah, a notable Hebrew number!"

Petronius continued, "There is a third possibility—that Marcellus is simply trying to impress his patron, the Legate Vitellius."

Jesus said, "Regardless, I rejoice that tomorrow is so close. I look forward to it, because I have longed for this day for years."

Petronius replied, "You may be looking forward to tomorrow, but I can't because of what it will mean for you, Jesus. I'm heartsick that you have to be crucified, even though I know it's what you desire."

"Since my future ends tomorrow I don't have any plans beyond today," said Jesus. "But I rejoice for you, Petronius, that you soon will turn your back on Caesarea and on the army. Do you have any plans for where you will retire?"

"This will surprise you, Jesus, but I'm thinking of staying right here in Judea and living in Galilee. I like the people, and I find Galilee's blend of Roman and Jewish life appealing."

"That is indeed a delightful surprise!" said Jesus.

"From my years there serving Prince Antipas, I know that Galilee has many beautiful women. Once I'm settled, I intend to go looking for a good wife. Who knows, I may even come across some of your old friends, and even though I'm a retired Roman officer and a Gentile, perhaps they'll let me join them."

"That would be wonderful. I hope and pray that all these dreams of yours come true."

"Thank you, Jesus; as do I. Now, I'm afraid I can't stay with you any longer. I have many duties now that the Legate is to arrive." Stopping, he inhaled deeply and said, "I hate to say this, Jesus, but this is most likely...I mean, I'll never see you again...."

"Yes, Petronius, we both knew this sad time was coming, yet it seems to have come more quickly than I imagined. So, we won't see each other again?"

"I regret that this will be last time," he said, pausing, "until I see you entering the coliseum carrying your cross, along with those other condemned men. And when I do, I will close my eyes."

The two men warmly embraced one another and said their farewells. Then, weeping, Petronius turned and quickly departed.

SCENE V

THE SAME

Later that March Friday Night

Jesus lay bone-tired on his sleeping mat, staring up at the chiseled curved stone ceiling. He said, "Ancient stones, long ago you were chiseled out of solid rock by slaves to make this cell. Tonight, I know how you felt, because for some time now an unseen chisel has been eating away at my flesh and bone. Tomorrow I'm to be crucified! Up until half a year ago, I passionately yearned to die on a cross. Now I dread and even fear it; yet I accept it with open arms. Old mat," gently patting it, "you've been my straw cross on which I've endured the excoriating pains of aging—aching knees and shoulders, along with an old bladder that always seems to need to be emptied. While you've taught me, old straw cross, how to be crucified, I'm not eager for the sunrise tomorrow." Then he extended his arms outward as far as he could. "Tonight, as I fall asleep on you for the last time, I lovingly surrender to God's will."

Instantly, a brilliant light filled Jesus' cell. Bewildered, he turned on his right side toward the window to see if it was moonlight, but he saw no moon in his window. Rolling on his back, he said, "What is this extraordinary light filling my...uh, my...." He gasped as intense pain shot through his chest, causing him to claw at it with his right hand, and then the pain surged upward to his neck and jaw, as he began sweating profusely. Feeling as if he were about to vomit, his heart pounding rapidly, and his vision now blurry, he struggled to breathe. Then his entire body jerked violently as another powerful jolt exploded in his chest, then another and another even more powerful.

The pains slowly subsided and he lay panting, gasping for air; his entire body was soaked in sweat as his eyes slowly began to focus. As they did he became aware that the abnormally brilliant light was now gone and his cell was dark. It was then that he began to hear a strange whirling, rumbling, and gurgling sound that grew increasingly louder. Mystified by the strange sounds, he raised his head up off his mat and turned toward where the sound seemed to originate. By the faint, whitish moonlight flowing through his window, he saw something moving on the floor between himself and the window. Squinting, he saw a whirling dark circular hole, out of which came the rumbling, spinning sound. He stared in disbelief as the outer rim of the dark, gurgling hole slowly expanded outward, and the relentless rumbling drowned out the sound of the surf. Curious about this mysterious hole in his cell floor, he said aloud, "Whatever it is, I feel drawn to go over so I can see it more closely."

With difficulty Jesus rolled off his mat and crawled on the cold floor toward the puzzling, expanding hole. Reaching its edge, he peered over the rim into what appeared at first to be a bottomless abyss. Then he saw it was filled with swirling serpentine waves of dark interlacing forces, out of whose spinning center came the terrifying roaring sound. Sheer terror gripped him as tightly as a lion's claws as an almost irresistible force began pulling him closer to the swirling gaping hole. Using all his strength, one knee at a time, he began painfully inching himself backward from its ever-widening rim. As he did so, he couldn't keep from looking down into it. He felt captivated by the multicolored whirlpool of undulating waves interspersed with explosions of fiery sparks, stars, and even the birthing of blazing suns. At that terrifying moment he realized that he was watching the Genesis beginning of creation when the ancient, primordial whirling forces of life first emerged out of the emptiness of the womb of the great abyss.

Even by exerting all his strength he couldn't resist being pulled toward the turbulent, crimson, sparkling energies of the void. He now had the same eerie sensation he felt the night he escaped and stood on the parapet high over the sea, when he wanted to fall and yet was firmly rooted to the floor by fear. In a final attempt to escape Jesus tried to reach behind himself to find any cracks in the floor into which he could dig his fingers, but to no avail. The invisible mystifying force gripping him was relentlessly dragging him over and into the great, gaping pit. As he felt this happening, he thought as he had that night standing on the parapet, "If I let go and fall from here, will anyone catch me?"

Closing his eyes, he surrendered. Instantly he felt himself being pulled over the edge, and as he sank into the thunderous swirling whirlpool, he cried out, "O God, into your hands I commend my spirit." Then he disappeared as he was swallowed by the great abyss, for when the Light comes, the lamp of life is extinguished.

SCENE VI

THE SAME

Early the Next Morning

The next morning at sunrise, when a slave arrived with Jesus' final meal, he was shocked at the scene that greeted him. The cell was empty!

THE END

(or the Beginning?)

HISTORICAL POST LOG

In the spring of 37 C.E., Emperor Tiberius Caesar died, and Pontius Pilate disappeared from the pages of history. After the death of Tiberius, what actually happened to Pilate, who was on his way to Rome, is not recorded, and so it is left to our imaginations. The Emperor's death annulled his recall of Pilate to Rome, so we can envision that he and Claudia lived a long and happy life together and died a peaceful, natural death.

Vitellius, the Syrian Legate, upon learning Pilate had been recalled to Rome by the Emperor, made Marcellus procurator of Judea, but after only one year, he removed him from office. Vitellius, besides removing Joseph Caiaphas as high priest, also returned the vestments of the high priest to the custody of the Temple instead of the guardianship of the Roman procurator.

Even to this day Pontius Pilate enjoys the exceptional distinction of being named in the Apostle's Creed. Both he and Claudia are venerated as saints in the Catholic Ethiopian Church, and in previous ages when baptizing children, it was not uncommon to give them the name of Pilate. In medieval times, the name of Pontius Pilate also was evoked as a blessing.

After the death of Jesus, there were reports of the Risen Jesus being encountered in Galilee. His followers soon spread beyond Palestine throughout the Greek and Roman world, and as they did, they continued to live by his teachings of love and nonviolence while increasing in number. The most powerful appeal of this new religious movement in those early centuries was the strong belief of its members in the resurrection to life after death.

AUTHOR'S POSTSCRIPT

More than a novel, this book was created as a meditative reflection on the contemporary struggles of religious belief in the twenty-first century. It is a meditation on our common struggles with physical and mental suffering, as well as the ultimate mystery of death that we all must face.

This new passion play was written for 21st century Christians living in an era of religious turmoil and who, like Jesus in this novel, can struggle with some of the same religious doubts and questions. Jesus' ancient invitation, "Come follow me," becomes a contemporary challenge to follow him through the ambiguity of believing and religious uncertainties.

In this first century of the third millennium, the cross can take many shapes and forms, regardless of your religious faith or the absence of it. The cross as a global sign of the Cosmic Passion of Christ and the sufferings of all humanity can include the excruciating torture of arthritis and other physical diseases of aging, the loss of memory and mental capabilities, and the anguished loneliness of the incarceration of old age that are experienced by so many persons today.

AUTHOR'S PAGE

"Hos ego versiculous feci, tulit alter honores."

So said the Roman poet Virgil (70-19 B.C.E.): "I wrote these lines, another has taken credit." I choose to rephrase it: "I wrote these lines, but another deserves the credit." While my name appears on the cover of this book as the author, another deserves the credit for the flowing text of this story. That person is my editor, Jennifer Halling, whose sharp eye and creative suggestions for text changes have been critical to *Pilate's Prisoner*. Every author requires the objectivity and insight of an outsider's eye to examine his or her manuscript, and Jennifer provided me with that crucial gift. Authors labor to bring forth a book, but are as blind to its faults as are mothers to the imperfections of their newborn.

Another person who should be credited is Thomas Turkle. As my longtime friend and former publisher, he challenged this work while also encouraging me to publish it. It is fitting then that he — the former publisher of Forest of Peace Publishing who shepherded into print all of my works except eight — should assist in the production of this my thirty-sixth book...and quite possibly my last. I am grateful for his publishing expertise in the complex task of creating the various formats of this self-published work.

Why self-publish?

It is most fortunate that I waited nine years — if not nine centuries — to publish this book. I am grateful that it will be printed in the early years of the 21st century and not the early years of the 13th century when the Inquisition was created. Added to my delight is the fact that this is the year 2012 and not 1254, when Pope Paul III decreed that the Inquisition should scrutinize all books for heresy, and then deal appropriately with their authors!

— *Edward Hays*

Other Books by Edward Hays

www.edwardhays.com

Novels

The Passionate Troubadour
  A Medieval Novel about
  Francis of Assisi
The Gospel of Gabriel

Parables and Stories

St. George and the Dragon
The Magic Lantern
The Ethiopian Tattoo Shop
Twelve and One-Half Keys
The Quest for the Flaming Pearl
Sundancer
Little Orphan Angela
The Christmas Eve Storyteller

Prayers

Prayers for the Domestic Church
Prayers for a Planetary Pilgrim
Psalms for Zero Gravity
Prayers for the Servants of God

Spirituality

A Book of Wonders
Chasing Joy
Letters to Exodus Christians
The Great Escape Manual
The Old Hermit's Almanac
A Pilgrim's Almanac
Pray All Ways
Secular Sanctity
In Pursuit of the
     Great White Rabbit
Feathers on the Wind
Holy Fools & Mad Hatters
The Ladder

Seasonal Spirituality

The Pilgrimage Way of the Cross
A Lenten Hobo Honeymoon
The Lenten Labyrinth
The Ascent of the
     Mountain of God
Stations of the Cross
The Lenten Pharmacy
Make Straight the Crooked Ways
Embrace the Healing Cross
Broadway and Bethlehem

CPSIA information can be obtained at www.ICGtesting.com
Printed in the USA
LVOW130747180113

316095LV00002BB/274/P